Praise for *e-Business Intelligence*

"This book covers one of the most important issues facing today's business manager—how to integrate and maximize your data for business advantage. Filled with relevant case studies and insightful tips, it gives a great roadmap for building your e-business intelligence strategies."—*Bob Sanguedolce, CIO, eBay, Inc.*

"Mr Liautaud's vision for e-business intelligence should be textbook reading for any manager attempting to bridge the worlds of technology and business. We at MasterCard have practiced for some time the strategies outlined in this book, and can attest to the significant benefits we've realized for our customers, business partners, and our company."—*Andrew Clyne, Vice President, Systems Development, MasterCard International*

"Mr. Liautaud gets to the heart of the internet economy with his visionary book on e-business intelligence. Very practical, with great case studies from leading companies, this book demonstrates the power of harnessing and making use of information."—*Rick Sherlund, Managing Director of Goldman Sachs*

"This book takes the important area of business intelligence and puts it in the context of electronic business. The insights and recommendations provided in this book will help both IT and business managers appreciate the central role of leveraging the data in their systems. Turning information into actionable knowledge is the key to electronic business success."— *Judith S. Hurwitz, President & CEO, Hurwitz Group, Inc.*

"How can you gain a leading edge in managing a company today? Read Mr. Liautaud's book and make sure your company understands how to capitalize on data, the currency of the Internet economy."—*Guerrino de Luca, CEO of Logitech International SA*

"The winners in this new global e-economy will be those companies that successfully access, maintain, analyze, and share business-critical information—be it about customers, suppliers, employees, or financial performance. *e-Business Intelligence: Turning Information into Knowledge into Profit* gives executives insight into how they can use this critical information to make strategic, informed business decisions in our new millennium—with an impact that reaches far beyond."—*Mike Schroeck, .Managing Partner, PricewaterhouseCoopers' Global Data Warehousing Practice*

e-Business Intelligence

Turning Information into Knowledge into Profit

Bernard Liautaud
with Mark Hammond

McGraw-Hill

New York   San Francisco   Washington, D.C.   Auckland   Bogotá
Caracas   Lisbon   London   Madrid   Mexico City   Milan
Montreal   New Delhi   San Juan   Singapore
Sydney   Tokyo   Toronto

Library of Congress Cataloging-in-Publication Data

Liautad, Bernard
  e-Business intelligence : turning information into knowledge into profit / Bernard Liautaud with Mark Hammond.
        p. cm.
    Includes bibliographical references.
    ISBN 0-07-136478-1
    1. Business intelligence.   2. Electronic commerce.   I. Title: e-Business intelligence : turning information into knowledge into profit.   II. Hammond, Mark.

    HD38.7 L52 2000
    658.4'7—dc21

                                                                    00-045072

McGraw-Hill

A Division of The McGraw-Hill Companies

1 2 3 4 5 6 7 8 9 0   DOC/DOC   0 6 5 4 3 2 1 0

0-07-136478-1

The sponsoring editor for this book was Michelle Reed, the editing supervisor was Ruth W. Mannino, and the production supervisor was Elizabeth Strange. It was set in Garamond by Patricia Wallenburg.

Printed and bound by R.R. Donnelley & Sons Company.

This publication is designed to provide accurate and authoritative information in regard to the subject matter covered. It is sold with the understanding that neither the author nor the publisher is engaged in rendering legal, accounting, or other professional service. If legal advice or other expert assistance is required, the services of a competent professional person should be sought.

> —From a Declaration of Principles jointly adopted
> by a Committee of the American Bar
> Association and a Committee of Publishers

McGraw-Hill books are available at special quantity discounts to use as premiums and sales promotions, or for use in corporate training programs. For more information, please write to the Director of Special Sales, Professional Publishing, McGraw-Hill, Two Penn Plaza, New York, NY 10121-2298. Or contact your local bookstore.

 This book is printed on recycled, acid-free paper containing a minimum of 50% recycled de-inked fiber.

To my wife, Susan, and my children—
Olivia, Alexa, Parker, and Cristo

and

To the employees and customers of Business Objects who,
everyday, are making the vision of e-business intelligence a reality

Contents

Acknowledgments

This book is the result of the ideas, contributions, and hard work of many people. The concepts of e-business intelligence that we develop throughout the book are not just an interesting theory, they are the result of real world implementations, and collective advances in how to best use business information for competitive advantage. These advances have been developed by a number of "thinkers" in the business intelligence, datawarehouse, and e-business industries, but principally by forward thinking companies who have implemented these kinds of concepts in their business. I would like to thank all of them.

I am especially grateful to those outstanding people who have been working with me on this book. Without them, this project would have never been a reality. I would like to thank all of them:

- Tracy Eiler, for helping to formulate the initial vision of the project, finding a publisher, and for her outstanding work on the overall project management;

- Dave Kellogg, for his strategic input in general, and in particular his help on Chapters Six through Fourteen;

- Alex Moissis, for his great help on Chapters One through Five, and for developing the glossary;

- Randy Cairns, for his tireless work with the numerous companies profiled throughout the book;

- Tracy Beaufort, Jean-Marc Bellot, Ian Clark, Yannick Cras, Marco Cremascoli, Timo Elliott, Jessie Evans, Tom Jevens, Abdel Kander, Nick Kellett, Woodson Martin, Jennifer Meegan, Mark Ritacco, Camino Santa Teresa, Kat Thomas, Wim van Winghe, Chris Warda, Tara Verrek, and Edwin Willems for their help developing some of the concepts of the book, providing ideas, and helping with the final manuscript.

- I would especially like to thank Mark Hammond, who has worked without interruption for several weeks, traveling to meet with many companies around the world, and helping to write the manuscript. He is a great writer.

■ Finally, I would like to thank Michelle Reed, for her editorial input and guidance.

As I mentioned above, the real "creators" of e-business intelligence are those forward thinking business people, CEOs, CIOs, IT managers, marketing, and operations managers who are implementing these concepts. I would like to thank all of the companies who agreed to share their experiences with us: Banca Commerciale Italiana, British Airways, Belgacom Mobile, Eli Lilly, Fiat, French Ministry of Finance, Hertz Lease, Heineken, Ingram Micro, Innovex, Instinet, MasterCard, Penske Logistics, Owens & Minor, Telecom Italia, Transactional Data Systems, VediorBis, Ventro, and Zurich US Insurance.

The Quest
for Intelligence

1

The New e-Business Intelligentsia

Imagine a school with children who can read and write, but with teachers who cannot, and you have a metaphor of the Information Age in which we live.

Peter Cochrane
Chief Technologist
BT Research

What do we mean by *intelligence*? Let us take a close look at how Dictionary.com defines the noun intelligence:

- The capacity to know or understand; readiness of comprehension

- Knowledge imparted or acquired, whether by study, research, or experience

- The act or state of knowing; the exercise of understanding

How intelligent is your business? How fully do you and your employees know and understand the forces driving your profit and shaping your future? How do you acquire that knowledge and understanding? Where do you turn for study, research, and experience? How do you *exercise* the knowledge and understanding acquired to make improvements? Most important, how do you achieve this intelligence in an Internet economy that is turning traditional business practices inside out, and an economy that moves so fast we measure it in months rather than years?

Ten years ago, most seasoned business executives could answer these questions readily. How? They communicated with their employees. They monitored the highlights of sales and profitability. Competitive-intelligence teams tracked the activity of rivals. They relied on raw numbers, instincts, negotiations, and luck. To be sure, those ingredients remain prerequisites for business success. However, the Internet economy demands more in exchange for excellence. The Internet economy demands *intelligence*.

The New Imperative

We all know that the Internet economy is revolutionizing the world—in business, in governments, in society at large. New rules are being written before the ink on yesterday's rules is dry. Small upstarts are capturing market share from giant corporations by leveraging the Internet. Radically new markets—business-to-business electronic marketplaces that broker the sale of goods and services among a network of customers and suppliers—are swiftly reshaping nearly every industry. Competition is intensifying. In some industries, the wolves of the Web are forcing profits to attenuate to scalpel-thin margins or to even turn into large losses. Geographic barriers are dissolving. Faced with an abundance of choices and expectations of instant gratification, customers are becoming more fickle and demanding than ever. Moreover, the speed with which these changes are occurring is overwhelming. Businesses can take nothing for granted—except, of course, the certainty of change. Companies need to be faster, more agile, and, crucially, more *intelligent*.

Why does a company need to be intelligent? An intelligent enterprise—one that makes better decisions faster and outsmarts its rivals—is positioned to excel and satisfy the natural instinct to win. Increasingly, being an intelligent business is a prerequisite not just to win, but to compete in the first place. Amid the hyperkinetic competition of the Internet economy, *intelligence* is fast emerging as a cross-departmental mandate for companies in virtually all industries:

- The customer relationship department needs information on its customers to retain them, to adapt its customer-facing practices and mechanisms, to drive return business, and to win new business.

- The sales department needs information on which products are selling to which demographic population in which markets, by which channel.

- The product planning department needs information on sales rates in order to optimally plan for production and to negotiate the most advantageous contracts with suppliers.

- The marketing department needs information on who is buying which products in order to create intelligent marketing and advertising programs, be they mass-market billboards or promotions targeted at individual consumers.

- The finance department needs information on profitability in order to adapt cost structures for maximum value.

The new cross-departmental imperative for companies in virtually all industries is to empower decision makers to obtain quick answers to their business questions by accessing immediately the information they need. The effective sharing, distillation, and analysis of information among such an array of departments—customer relationship, sales, product planning, marketing, and finance, for example—coalesces into an enterprisewide intelligence that is greater than the sum of its informational parts.

Fundamentals of Intelligence

How does a business achieve the intelligence the Internet economy demands? How does it use intelligence to cultivate customer loyalty and drive profit? How does it outsmart the competition? The answers are in the data. Businesses run on data. They sprint on information. They set Olympic records on intelligence. Data, information, intelligence. What is the difference?

Data is raw and unadorned. It is, let us say, a single record in a transactional database that records the $14.95 purchase of an Elton John compact disk from a Web site by a consumer in Little Rock, Arkansas.

Information is data endowed with some degree of business context and meaning. It is data that has been filtered, synthesized, and aggregated. Businesspeople take raw data and, using their knowledge of the business, filter, sort, prioritize, and present it, thereby transforming it into information. In the instance of our Little Rock CD buyer, it may be a list of that customer's CD purchases over the past year. It may be a list of Elton John CD purchases by consumers of similar characteristics, such as gender, income, and zip code. That information may be analyzed to reveal profitability, purchasing trends over time, and potential lifetime value based on past behavior, age, demographic characteristics, and geographic location.

Intelligence elevates information to a higher level within an organization. Data and information are things. Intelligence is organic; derived from information, it contributes to an organizational state that may be characterized as collective intelligence. Intelligence results from a full appraisal of information, past actions, and options. Once sown, this intelligence tends to propagate itself across an organization. A critical mass of individuals sharing the same insights into a business process becomes a very powerful force. It may be a marketing team that, having examined the month's purchases, finds that a new Elton John greatest hits album was a top seller among European baby boomers. Using this information, the team may implement an intelligent action, such as a reduced-price marketing campaign directed at these buyers that promotes a previous Elton John work that is languishing on warehouse shelves.

Currency of the New Economy

In his latest book, *Living on the Fault Line*, Geoffrey More—the Silicon Valley strategy guru and author of *Crossing the Chasm* and *Inside the Tornado*—starts with the notion that information about an asset is now more valuable than the asset itself: "In this new world, information is king. The more information you have, and the better (and faster) your analysis, the greater the probability that you will make winning investments."

Geoffrey Moore is correct: Businesses thrive on information. Even businesses that do not think of themselves as information businesses *are*, in fact, information businesses. When one thinks of Fiat, for example, one thinks of a company that manufactures and sells cars, such as the eponymous Fiat, as well as the Alfa Romeo, Lancia, and Ferrari. Cars are Fiat's most visible commodity. The element that makes it possible for Fiat to produce those vehicles is, of course, *information*. Fiat needs information in order to make literally thousands of decisions each day on supplier costs, purchase prices, and distribution channels.

Take the lowly lug nut. Seems like a simple, inexpensive part, right? Well, think again. It is a relatively simple and inexpensive part, yes, but the information associated with the lug nut bears directly on Fiat's bottom line.

Let us say that Fiat has been buying lug nuts for a pair of vehicles from different suppliers. Fiat has "data" in separate data stores on the number of lug nuts purchased and the price paid from the two suppliers. The data becomes "information" when Fiat combines the two data stores, thus enabling its managers to examine and analyze that information to make more informed decisions. This information is likely to show that Fiat is paying, say, $0.10 more per lug nut for one vehicle than it is for the other. Understanding that information and forwarding it to the right people in the purchasing department creates a collective "intelligence," which ultimately can be transformed into positive financial value. Indeed, at 1 million vehicles per year, $0.10 per lug nut translates into $100,000. Repeat that exercise with 100 other parts, and you are saving $10 million per year. By transforming its data into information and then into intelligence, Fiat adds a few bits to its bottom line.

Data and information form the bloodline that enables Fiat to be a successful company. However, like blood in the human body, they tend to be taken for granted. The enormous quantity of data that businesses collect has tended to lie fallow, untilled for the intelligence that analysis might yield. Researchers at IBM have arrived at the alarming conclusion that businesses actively use only 7 percent of their data to make strategic business decisions!

Corporations usually do not lack data. On the contrary, they tend to have plenty of it. Through their basic operational business processes, they collect terabytes of information about everything they do: the products they sell, the customers they have, the employees they manage, and the assets they own. This information is generally properly stored in vast corporate databases. However, in most cases, the data stays there, unused and unexploited, collecting dust like old crates in a storage room. Although the information potentially is extremely valuable, it often is hard to find: The businesspeople, the line managers who really need that information, do not know how to get to it, or even that it exists. As a result, simple questions remain unanswered.

Let us take a test: Are you, in your company, able to get a full picture of a given customer? That is, not only the basic information on that company, but the full sales history—how many products they bought over time and at what price, the kind of contract you currently have with them, whether they are satisfied, and what orders are pending? Probably not. Most companies are not able to provide that 360° view of their customers. The information usually exists somewhere in the company records, but it is spread throughout many systems and thus is inaccessible to the people who need it.

Moving to Intelligence Everywhere

This situation is slowly changing as organizations are beginning to realize that information is the currency of the new economy. Increasingly, businesses are tapping into the intelligence latent in their data. We are starting to see pioneering e-businesses turn raw data into intelligence. Vast data stores are now being energized, integrated, and analyzed for insights into key business metrics. Like never before, data is being probed, sliced, skewered, and diced to assess trends and anomalies.

We are seeing companies empowering people at virtually all layers of their corporate hierarchies—from the CEO to the rank and file—allowing them to access, analyze, and share information over the Web. We are seeing companies dramatically improve operations by leveraging the insights, the *intelligence* wrung from purely transactional data. We are seeing them take advantage of newly powerful and user-friendly Web-based analytic tools, using disciplined analytic practices that have matured in only the last several years. This is what we mean by developing enterprisewide business intelligence: turning raw data into usable information and distributing and sharing that information with all of the employees, managers, and executives throughout a company, hence creating a collective intelligence about one's business. In virtually every industry—from retail, to health care, to insurance, to transportation, to financial services—we are seeing companies at the vanguard of e-business exploiting this intelligence to build and fortify relationships with their customers and partners, to drive one-to-one marketing campaigns, and to reduce costs and improve operational efficiencies.

Consider the example of a traditional retailer in the early twenty-first century. A retailer needs to know more than which products are selling and which products are lagging, or it will soon find its sales diminishing. Why? Because a half-dozen dot coms are selling a similar product—tax-free!—on the Internet, and because those dot coms and traditional competitors very likely have e-business intelligence systems and strategies in place or on the drawing board.

The competitive pressures of e-business make it mandatory that retailers go beyond the basics of product sales into the who, what, where, when, why, and how. Who is buying our products? What is their income? Where do they live? What other products do these consumers buy? How can we cross-sell to these customers? How is our e-business channel affecting other channels? What channel is showing the greatest growth? How should we redirect resources? Where are our products selling? What is our profit margin? How do these sales compare to the same time last year? What percentage of these sales is attributable to advertising? How much is driven by direct marketing? What is our sales forecast for the next 12 months? By region? By demographic segment? By product color?

Answering these questions, the retailer will be armed with intelligence and thus able to know quickly and precisely the customer purchasing history, and how it has been evolving over time. On the basis of previous preferences, the intelligent retailer will then launch targeted and personalized marketing campaigns corresponding to the customer state of mind "at the moment." Without this intelligence, the retailer would only be able to send fairly generic marketing campaigns to its customer base, not taking into account personal preferences or most recent purchasing history. Which retailer do you think has the most chance of retaining its customers?

The new imperative for e-business intelligence is not confined to any particular industry, any particular geographic region, or any particular business operation. It applies equally to companies doing business only on the Internet—the so-called pure-play dot coms—as well as to traditional companies bringing their business online—the click and mortars. Similarly, the imperative is not confined to any particular business operation—it applies to customer relationships, financial analysis, human resources, supply chains, marketing campaigns, manufacturing controls, and the clickstream data that records the activity of shoppers and surfers on Web sites. For instance:

- A dot com uses e-business intelligence to assess the strengths and weaknesses of its Internet sales and marketing.

- A financial institution uses e-business intelligence to track and reduce customer churn.

- A manufacturer uses e-business intelligence to assist in quality control of its product.

- A supplies distributor uses e-business intelligence to give its customers a means of analyzing purchasing and delivery patterns.

Regardless of which industry or which business operation e-business intelligence tools and techniques are applied, the key enabler is the Web. We will explore the two principal Web-based means of utilizing e-business intelligence. The first is through an intranet—a Web-based network internal to a company. When a corporation harnesses the power of e-business intelligence through its intranet and hence manages to create a free flow of information throughout its organization, it creates what we will call later a true information democracy. The second is through an extranet—a Web-based network opened to external users. When a corporation uses e-business intelligence to share key information with its customers, suppliers, and business partners, it creates an information embassy, a key agent to deliver better service, and generate new forms of revenue.

The B2B Intelligence Opportunity

The incessant attention lavished on the historic e-business juggernaut over the past few years may make it seem as if e-business is mature. After all, IBM's advertising would lead one to believe that every little old lady in every sleepy Italian village uses IBM e-business solutions to sell olive oil over the Internet. Of course, nothing could be further from the truth. In fact, despite the intensity of the juggernaut, e-business has yet to hit even adolescence. Its first cousin, e-business intelligence, is still a toddler. Technologies that will one day be commonplace—conducting data analysis through a wireless phone, for instance—are little more than a twinkle in an executive's eye.

To take a pulse on where we are in the evolution of e-business, consider the assessment of the Gartner Group, a leading research firm and consultancy in Stamford, Conn., on the two sides of the e-business coin—business-to-consumer transactions and business-to-business transactions. As consumers, we buy airline tickets and books online, for example. We check our stock portfolios and make trades on our cellular phones, and we book dining and entertainment reservations at Web sites that cater to our geographic areas. According to the Gartner Group, worldwide revenue generated by these business-to-consumer (B2C) enterprises totaled $31.2 billion in 1999. Gartner predicts that by 2003, the sum spent online will increase more than tenfold, to $380 billion!

Although that is a pretty robust rate of growth, it is dwarfed by what we are witnessing on the flip side of the ecommerce coin—the economic supernova of business-to-business (B2B) commerce. In Figure 1-1, Gartner predicts that over the next five years, B2B ecommerce will grow at a shocking compound annual growth rate of 119 percent—from $145 billion in nonfinancial goods and services in 1999, to $7.29 trillion in 2004.[1]

Still, that amounts to just 7 percent of all transactions globally, a sum estimated at $105 trillion, which leaves plenty of room for growth beyond what may be discerned from Gartner's crystal ball. Other studies have found similar results. The Yankee Group pegs B2B ecommerce at $740 billion in 2000, rising to $2.78 trillion by 2004. Forrester Research, meanwhile, sizes up the market at $406 billion in 2000, leaping to $2.7 trillion in 2004.

Another strong indication of the nascent state of e-business comes from a study by PricewaterhouseCoopers and the Conference Board. In early 2000,

---

[1] "Gartner Group Forecasts Worldwide Business-to-Business E-Commerce to Reach $7.29 Trillion in 2004," Gartner Group, January 2000.

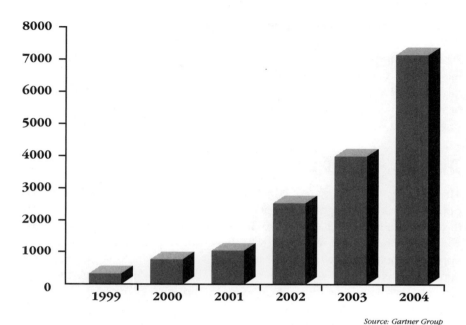

Source: Gartner Group

Figure 1-1   Gartner Group Estimates of Business-to-Business
Ecommerce Growth by 2004.

they reported the results of a survey of approximately 78 large companies.[2] Half of these companies had annual revenues in excess of $5 billion per year, and about 90 percent had annual revenues of $1 billion or more. They said that e-business figures prominently into their plans for the future, but most thought they were a long way from where they need to be. According to the study, only 3.7 percent of the companies surveyed derive more than 10 percent of their revenue from e-business. In three years, however, that figure is projected to grow more than tenfold, to 46.3 percent. In addition, only 28.2 percent of these companies currently have systems in place to take customer orders with online payment over the Web.

Finally, to help gauge our place in the evolution of e-business intelligence, consider the data generated by Survey.com, a market research firm in Mountain View, Calif.[3] In a survey of 472 IT managers published in late 1999, they found that organizations worldwide expect to increase software, hard-

---

[2] "Electronic Business Outlook for the New Millennium," PricewaterhouseCoopers and the Conference Board, March 2000.
[3] "Database Solutions III," Survey.com, December 1999.

ware, and personnel spending on business intelligence and associated technology for data warehousing, from $37.4 billion in 1999 to $148.5 billion by 2003, a compound annual growth rate of 43 percent. They also found that the average volume of data usable for analysis per company is expected to grow from 393 gigabytes in 1999 to 1.1 terabyte by 2003, while the number of users of that data will swell from 626 to 2718 per organization, over the same period.

Do It or Die

The relative immaturity of e-business intelligence presents tremendous opportunities for companies to pioneer the intelligent use of data, to seize the coveted First Mover Advantage. It also creates immediate threats to those companies that will move too slowly. If you have the foresight and will to apply the tools and techniques of e-business intelligence to your company's data, you have a once-in-a-lifetime opportunity to be among the First Movers. You have a window of opportunity that opened yesterday to thrust yourselves into leadership positions in the new economy, and if properly nurtured, they may be sustained for decades.

If you have a traditional business, you will be able to harness the information collected by all the business processes of your company. By allowing intelligent decisions to be made at all levels of the organization, you will become more agile and more competitive. If you already have or are building an e-business—either because your company is a dot com or a bricks and mortar in transformation—you will find that mastering the information generated by your e-business is a key requirement for success. By the time the competition catches up, you will have established a dominance in market position and mindshare that is difficult, if not impossible, to match. What of the competition? Laggards in the new world of e-business and e-business intelligence will find themselves left in the dust, to the detriment of their customers, stockholders, employees, and business partners.

The Ever-Shifting Ground

More than ever, time is of the essence. Leading vendors across all industries are beginning to leverage e-business intelligence to redefine their markets. In this book, we will explore real-world examples of how leading companies in diverse industries are coping with these and other changes at the edge of the e-business frontier. We will learn how companies such as Penske Logistics, Owens & Minor, Zurich U.S. Insurance, Eli Lilly, MasterCard, Fiat,

Outpost.com, Ingram Micro, British Airways, and others are gaining enormous competitive advantage through e-business intelligence.

After looking at organizations making the transition to intelligence, we will examine the successes, the struggles, and the lessons learned from these pioneering endeavors. We will also offer advice as to what your organization's e-business intelligence strategy should be. We will look at case studies, such as Penske Logistics, a provider of transportation services and a Penske Truck Leasing Company. Penske uses e-business intelligence to provide some 750 employees with an instant, Web-based means of analyzing hundreds of variables that affect the cost and speed of delivering its customers' goods throughout North America. As a result, Penske is able to cut costs, drive profit, and build customer loyalty. We will also address the next bold step in Penske's e-business evolution—providing Kmart, Ford, Chrysler, and hundreds of other customers with the ability to tap into Penske data stores through an extranet, while at the same time conducting their own tracking and analysis of their customers.

We will look at how Owens & Minor, a $3.2 billion distributor of medical supplies in Virginia, has built an extranet that empowers its 4000 customers and 1200 suppliers to root through the Owens & Minor data store to identify potential cost savings, analyze purchase patterns, and calculate inventory and delivery times. Owens & Minor was among the first to market extranet capabilities in the medical supplies industry, and that has figured prominently in its capturing and retaining millions of dollars in long-term contracts. We will also examine an extranet at Zurich U.S., a $6.2 billion property and casualty insurer in Illinois, that delivers to its customers Web-based analytic capabilities unimaginable only several years ago. Through a browser, more than 1000 users at 350 of Zurich's corporate clients are able to scrutinize huge datasets in an instant, looking for patterns and anomalies—the very lifeblood of the insurance industry.

We can liken these enlightened enterprises to a rock climber ascending a sheer cliff. The climber examines the wall for the slightest advantage, a foothold or crevice that will enable him to propel himself upward. So too will dominant companies that emerge as leaders in the Internet economy seek out and exploit the slightest advantage for faster, better decision making through e-business intelligence. The Internet not only enables e-business intelligence; it *demands* it, and demands it now. In the rapidly maturing realm of e-business intelligence, speed wins.

2

Information Governance

Information is affected daily, even hourly, in virtually all organizations by power, politics, and economics. This is no secret.

Thomas H. Davenport
"Information Ecology"

As we will discuss throughout the book, managing information for competitive advantage and profit has a lot to do with business and technical issues. However, looking back at how information has been used and shared throughout companies in the past decades, one may be right in looking at it as more of an issue of management philosophy. Information has always carried a lot of power in all aspects of life, but even more so in the business world. In all companies, only a few top executives have access to consolidated financial information, with others in the organization having only partial access. Although not all information about a company can be shared among its employees without restriction, confidentiality and liability issues often are used as excuses for not delivering much relevant information to the vast majority of users within the organization.

When we examine a large panel of companies, their use of information, and how it evolves over time, four models of information governance emerge. (See Figure 2-1.)

- *Information Dictatorship*, where only a few have access to the data

- *Information Anarchy*, where everyone has re-created their own information system, resulting in a state of data chaos

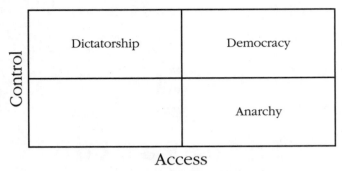

Figure 2-1   The Information Governance Quadrant.

- *Information Democracy*, where information flows in a free but managed way

As we enter the twenty-first century, we will see that a new model is emerging, one that is pushing democratization of information beyond the confines of a single organization. The most advanced companies are establishing *Information Embassies*, which function like beachheads of data outside of their four walls and are built to better communicate with their partners, suppliers, and customers.

Information Dictatorship

Early implementations of business intelligence concentrated the power of information in the hands of a few—an Information Dictatorship. While this model evolved in the 1980s, in some organizations, it still exists even today. This is a direct manifestation of the centralized management culture that prevailed at the time. The model of decentralization that caught on in the late 1980s and was adopted in the 1990s drove information empowerment along with it.

Companies built large mainframe and legacy systems that captured and processed data, but extracting useful information from those systems was difficult and inflexible. Whatever information could be harvested could not be dispersed meaningfully to a majority of employees. Rather, only a handful of top executives had access to this information, often through expensive dashboard-like systems referred to as executive information systems (EIS). (See Figure 2-2.)

The idea was that through a customized dashboard, executives could monitor key areas of the business and make all the decisions based on this

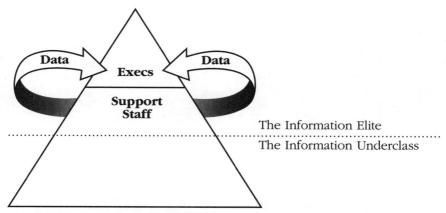

Figure 2-2   Information Dictatorship-Level 1.

information. The CEO was like Captain James Kirk on the bridge of the corporate *Enterprise*, surrounded by screens of information, with his trusted
CFO Spock at his side. Together, they would make all decisions for the
enterprise, thanks to the ultimate information system. "Inventory is building
in warehouse 27." Press a button to cut production in plant 54. "Western
region sales are performing under plan." Press a button on a touch screen
to terminate the regional sales manager. A competitor is launching a new
product. "Put the shields up and lock the phasers on, Scotty."

These executive information systems, however, were complex to program, extremely expensive, and rigid in their use. As it turns out, building
the ultimate information system can be ultimately expensive. Armies of programmers were needed to build these EIS systems, which in most cases
failed because interest and budget wore out before the programmers did.
Moreover, if built, the systems were inflexible. An executive might be able
to run a report—to generate reams of numbers on the old computer paper
of alternating green and white bars—but there was no means for the executive to run an ad hoc query that might satisfy a pressing business question.

In addition, of course, there was a more serious, underlying problem:
Would anyone want to work in that company, where all decisions were
made by just a few and where the brains and talents of the staff were not
utilized? While EIS systems were hard to build, this in fact, was not their
cause of demise. The EIS went away because empowerment came along.
The centralized command-and-control model was simply wrong. It did not
exploit the talent of the huge number of "other employees" outside the
executive wing. (See Figure 2-3.)

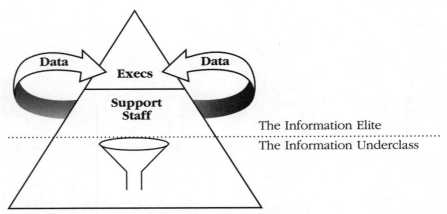

Figure 2-3   Information Dictatorship-Level 2.

In another, more subtle implementation of Information Dictatorship, exec-utives and other business managers would not have an executive informa-tion system. Instead, they would be beholden to number-crunching wizards specially trained with reporting, analytic, and statistical software installed on their computers. The concept was to expand the use of information to many more business users who would call on this "InfoCenter." However, very quickly, this technology-schooled cadre of individuals became, without knowing it, information dictators of another sort.

They held the keys to the corporate data store, and those wishing to see a comparative analysis of, say, sales or distribution figures, needed first to nego-tiate with these information gatekeepers. For the line manager, getting the information would translate most often into frustration. The "data gatekeepers" would invariably have many other reports to build first, usually for higher level executives. Therefore, the reports requested by the line manager would not be ready for weeks. At that time, the information would be of little or no value. As for the executive, the gatekeepers (if they had the time and inclination) would run a static report that provided information the executive would use to make business decisions. The executive was deprived of the ability to manipulate, massage, and query the information. In a sense, executives would make decisions not based on their own independent assessment of information, but rather on whatever information their technology-schooled information dictators deemed fit to provide.

Gianluigi Castelli, the chief information officer of Italian automaker Fiat, chuckles at the irony of such situations. To Castelli, it calls to mind a short story by the science fiction author Robert Silverberg. In the story, an ambitious mid-level manager sets his sights on holding the reins of corporate power. He aims to become company CEO. After years of diligent effort, he succeeds in his goal and is ready to make winning business decisions from the executive suite of his office building.

This newly minted CEO, however, discovers that he is not really making decisions at all. Rather, he is signing off on reports and recommendations provided by his subordinates. After all, as the CEO, he is not to be burdened with the nitty-gritty tasks of information management.

Castelli tells the moral of the story with relish. "The CEO decides to find out who is providing all this business intelligence. He discovers that in the basement, there is a guy with a few computers who does number crunching to produce these reports, and when he does not have enough data to produce, he invents the data. So the CEO realizes he has to do something if he really wants to run the company. He fires the guy in the basement, steps down as CEO and with a change in his personality manages to be rehired as the guy in the basement."

In both sorts of the Information Dictatorship, low- and mid-level employees are disenfranchised from the information that they could use to help drive the business forward. A dichotomy evolves between these informational haves and have-nots. The have-nots may be under increasing pressure to perform, but doing so without the benefit of easy access to sound information is not easy. They instigate an information rebellion, and they begin to construct their own data management systems. The groundwork for data overload is being laid.

Information Anarchy

Information Anarchy results from individuals or entire departments taking their informational needs into their own hands. As businesses grew more competitive in past years, departmental managers realized they needed better information to make good business decisions. They realized that whatever information they could procure from the glass house of the IT department would not be adequate.

With the proliferation of desktop computers in corporations in the 1980s and 1990s, and the availability of desktop databases, spreadsheets, word processors, and other software applications, it became practical for departments to develop their own information systems. This approach swiftly resulted in data fiefdoms, or *data silos*. (See Figure 2-4.)

These data silos were built on heterogeneous hardware and software platforms and applications that could not communicate with each other.

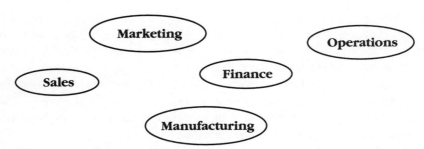

Figure 2-4   The Data Silos of Information Anarchy.

Customer lists and contact information were not stored centrally so that they could be accessed by all members of a sales department, but rather stored on individual PCs. When a salesperson left the company, his or her contact list would sometimes be lost as well. Not integrated, often populated with conflicting and inaccurate data, and utilizing different technologies, the chaos inherent in an Information Anarchy wreaks havoc with communications and profit.

Similar to the brief yet short-lived instances of anarchy in world history, the onset of information anarchy is often followed by a brief period of euphoria. Departments that set up their data silos are briefly enthusiastic about their limited solution, until the point in time when someone in senior management receives two reports with inconsistent data from different departments and questions the validity of the information. The uncoordinated silo approach sooner or later will result in data consistency issues, while little security enforcement on data access is feasible.

Information Democracy

In recent years, enterprising companies have realized the tremendous value of extending information access to all employees throughout their organizations. They realized that in order to become more agile and more efficient, they could not let most of their employees remain uninformed about the company, forced to fly blind and make decisions without facts.

Gut Feel versus Hard Fact

In 1998, Business Objects sponsored a study on decision-making habits in corporations based in the United States and United Kingdom. Researchers found a number of amazing results:

- Among managers, 88 percent admit to using gut feel over and above hard fact up to 75 percent of the time for making business decisions, and 51 percent of sales and marketing managers use gut feel typically 50 to 75 percent of the time.

- Company directors are intolerant of decisions made by managers based on gut feel, insisting that decisions should be made only on hard facts.

- Within management, 93 percent of managers across all disciplines find that they are under pressure to make effective decisions within short timespans.

- Sixty-two percent of management admit that they do not receive the right amount of information to make a decision, yet 99 percent have access to a desktop computer.

- Two thirds of the sample is moving to, or already working within, an open, flat organizational structure, with 35 percent of management encouraged to take risks in an entrepreneurial culture. However, two thirds are encouraged to use hard facts to make decisions in order to reduce the risks.

- A full 100 percent of the sales and marketing managers have to rely on other people for information. Of these managers, only 25 percent believe that the information is up-to-date.

In brief, the lack of data access forces businesspeople to make important decisions without the necessary information. With today's pressure on companies' speed of action, the situation has to change.

New Management Philosophy, New Technology

A new attitude toward information, arising from new theories on decision making, helped pave the way for change.

In his model of empowerment, Peter F. Drucker argues that "a decision must be made at the lowest possible level in the organization and as close as possible to where its outcome will be executed." In order for people to effectively carry out the implementation of a decision, they need to be part of the decision themselves.

In parallel, Internet technology has enabled information access to the masses. Throughout the late 1990s, most vendors of data access software had Web-enabled their products. These packages no longer run on individual desktop computers, but on central servers that can be accessed by a Web browser. Enter e-business intelligence—the powerful convergence of the Internet and traditional business intelligence tools—to open new avenues for corporations to access, analyze, and share information.

User Autonomy and Relief for the IT Department

Progressively, the old model of a handful of specialized analysts crunching numbers is giving ground to an *Information Democracy* model that is providing companies with new speed and agility by delivering accurate information to employees and decentralizing decision-making authority. (See Figure 2-5.)

Take the case of Eli Lilly, the pharmaceutical giant in Indianapolis, Indiana. The user community was dependent on the IT staff to install and maintain their desktop databases and spreadsheet programs. A business user's request for information of any complexity frequently required the involvement of IT to query data stores beyond the realm of the business user's desktop computer.

IT department staffers would frequently be too busy to run a report. The report would take weeks to generate. Often, the answers would not be what the requestor had in mind. This imperfect exercise could be painful and frustrating for IT and businesspeople alike. This misbegotten marriage between business and IT would end frequently in estrangement.

Doug Sharp, a veteran IT staffer at Eli Lilly, has suffered through numerous such frustrations. "You would run a report, and it wouldn't be what the

Figure 2-5   Information Democracy.

business users wanted. You would have to go through numerous attempts to get the report the way they wanted it. They would try to define their business need, and you in IT would try to interpret that and apply it to your data structure, extract the data, and aggregate it so it was exactly the way they wanted it."

Sharp recalls a particular exercise in frustration in 1997. A business user wanted to assess how a prospective realignment of zip codes within Lilly regions in Florida might affect regional sales totals and how the company might maximize the performance of its sales representatives. It involved examining the current alignment by zip code, comparing it to previous zip code alignments, and projecting forward the impact of realignment, a complicated project.

The issue was volleyed back and forth for about three weeks between the business user and the IT department, with the results never quite satisfactory. It was, Sharp says, an ordeal. Ultimately, the business user moved on from her position and was replaced by a person with priorities other than zip code realignment. Therefore dozens of hours of effort went into a black hole.

Things have now changed for Lilly, as they are changing for many companies that are beginning to exploit the convergence of business intelligence and the Internet. Sharp, a technology specialist for the marketing department, is helping to lead an effort that will provide Lilly's marketing business users with Web-based access to the department's 500-gigabyte data warehouse. No longer would the IT department serve as the intermediary between business users and their informational needs.

"We wanted to have a tool that would enable individuals to do their own exploration of data over the Web," Sharp said. "We wanted to come up with an interface for our warehouse that has a Yahoo!-like look and feel—that is very user friendly."

Simultaneously, Lilly's marketing department is growing its warehouse from 500 gigabytes to roughly 1 terabyte, over the coming months, chiefly by adding more historical data for business views that go back further in time and by incorporating data that is more detailed than the warehouse now holds. By enabling the data warehouse to be accessed over the Web, Sharp's department expects that the number of users will explode from about 40 marketing specialists to include 3000 of Lilly's sales representatives.

For Lilly, the Information Democracy is at hand.

At Eli Lilly and other pioneering companies, hundreds or thousands of employees are able to tap into the corporate data store through the familiar interface of their favorite browser. Information that once took weeks for an overworked IT staff to deliver is now available in a matter of minutes.

Information Dictatorships are slowly being supplanted by Information Democracies built around e-business intelligence.

Democratization and Business Value

In a recent study that was conducted by Business Objects among a panel of its customers in Europe, marketing executives established that the value of an organization's business intelligence is highly influenced by three key factors:

1. The level of democratization of business intelligence software within the organization (i.e., the ratio of business intelligence enabled users out of the total number of desktops)

2. The level of empowerment (i.e., the number of users entitled to perform ad hoc requests for data versus the number of total users)

3. The "cultural" propensity to break organizational "stovepipes" (i.e., the number of different departments that are involved in the deployment of the solution times the capacity to get access to other departments' information)

The result was impressive.

The greater the level of democratization and empowerment, the bigger the value. In other words, the larger the proportion of users given access to business data, and the larger the scope of the information given to them, the more intelligent and hence successful the organization. Take Bellini, a small insurance company that had 100 percent of its employees empowered with business intelligence software. Individual contributors as well as entire departments benefited from this policy. For example, with access to information, the sales department was able to better understand on which warranties they were making money versus those on which they were losing money. The sales department renegotiated all the bad contracts in place, while establishing a new type of dialogue with the customers that was based on information sharing. The outcome was a 650 percent return on investment (ROI).

The greater the propensity to break organizational boundaries, the bigger the value. In other words, the greater the number of departments with available data and the greater proportion of users who are allowed to access data from other departments, the more intelligent and successful the organization. The car manufacturer Renault deployed business intelligence technology massively in one of their factories in France. More than 300 people are using business intelligence, 90 percent of them being "blue collar" employees working on the assembly line. By accessing key data regarding all projects in production, and by being so close to the place where the decisions would be implemented, they have been easily able to identify where money could be best used. Thanks to this type of empowerment, the plant became extremely effective in managing project funding and dynamically re-allocating money on the most promising projects.

Information Embassies

The *Information Democracy* need not end at a company's network firewall. Through the Internet, it may be extended via an extranet to customers, suppliers, and business partners. A business intelligence extranet is a secure Web site (or a place in the company's Web site) where external constituencies like customers or other users interacting with the company can access and analyze bits of information. As they represent a virtual beachhead of a corporation outside of its borders to create a better communication with its partners, we call them *Information Embassies*.

Visionary e-businesses are establishing Information Embassies that provide external users with a means of accessing, analyzing, and sharing data relevant to them. By taking advantage of such Information Embassies, these customers, suppliers, and business partners are themselves becoming more intelligent businesses. (See Figure 2-6.)

These companies are providing enormous value to their external parties by giving them instant access to data of crucial importance. The differentiation these extranet-enabled businesses offer is proving time and again to be a key factor in winning business against competitors that lack such data-rich extranets.

Extranet deployments are shaping up across three application areas:

- *Supply chain extranets.* Companies like Owens & Minor are providing customers with supply-chain management extranets to provide a 360° view of the distribution cycle, from supplier to distributor to end user.

- *Customer relationship extranets.* Zurich U.S. and other businesses are cultivating customer loyalty and lock-in by enabling them swift access to data that is critical to fast and intelligent decision making.

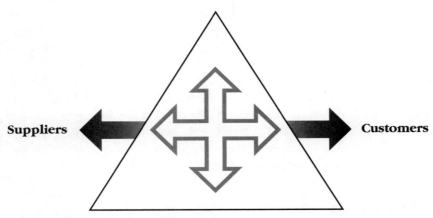

Suppliers   Customers

Figure 2-Ь   Information Embassies.

- *Information brokerage extranets.* Companies in the business of collecting and selling information are finding in the extranet model a fast, secure means of delivering their goods to customers. MasterCard, for instance has accumulated a huge amount of information from credit card transactions over the years. It now sells parts of that information, on an aggregated, privacy-protected basis, to retail companies through a business-intelligent extranet.

These Information Embassies represent the next major differentiator for companies doing business over the Internet. Those who can enhance their product and services with value-added information will be able to provide a better overall value proposition to their customers and eventually ensure stronger customer loyalty.

Take the Test

Pioneering companies that understand the value of information are transforming themselves into Information Democracies and are setting up Information Embassies to improve their relationships with their customers and business partners. How is your company doing with e-business intelligence? Take the e-Business Intelligence Quotient (e-BIQ™) test and find out your score. To obtain more information about this test and how other organizations score, go to www.ebusinessintelligence.com.

Test Your e-Business Intelligence Quotient

This test will help you assess your organization's e-business intelligence quotient—to help you determine the best course of action for increasing your organization's ability to turn data into knowledge and profit.

For each statement, select the answer that most closely matches the use of information in your organization. Focus on the present situation, not future goals.

1. **In my organization, the following types of people have access to corporate data (sales, customer information, financial metrics, human resources, manufacturing, etc.):**
   a. IT/IS staff (programmers, developers, etc.)
   b. Power users and the people they support
   c. All people in the organization
   d. Do not know/does not apply

2. **People in my organization feel that:**
   a. They are empowered to make decisions, but they are not given enough critical corporate information to make them
   b. They can get basic corporate information in order to make the decision they need to make
   c. Have all the corporate information they need to make decisions
   d. Do not know/does not apply

3. **In our organization, information is:**
   a. Rarely, if ever, disseminated
   b. Shared only when necessary
   c. Widely communicated and shared throughout our company
   d. Do not know/does not apply

4. **Users in our company use corporate data (sales, customer, inventory, manufacturing, finance, etc.):**
   a. For limited purposes only
   b. To review performance in the rearview mirror
   c. To forecast the future and drive corporate strategy
   d. Do not know/does not apply

5. We share our information systems:
  a. Only internally
  b. Outside our organization, with our customers or partners
  c. Outside our organization, with our customers and partners
  d. Do not know/does not apply

6. We use corporate data to:
  a. Report on the business
  b. Manage by exception
  c. Transform operational business processes
  d. Do not know/does not apply

7. My view of customers' activities is:
  a. I can see a small part of customers' activities with my company over time
  b. I can see a majority of customers' activities, but not all
  c. 360°—I can see all customers' activities with our company, including their interactions with subsidiaries and strategic business units
  d. Do not know/does not apply

8. In my estimation, people in my organization can access the following percentage of the data they need:
  a. 0–33 percent
  b. 34–66 percent
  c. 67–100 percent
  d. Do not know/does not apply

9. The quality of the data that I can access in our information systems is:
  a. Poor
  b. Adequate
  c. Excellent
  d. Do not know/does not apply

10. We make use of key performance indicators (e.g., sales, inventory, finance, manufacturing, etc.) to manage our business:
   a. Not at all
   b. A little
   c. Extensively
   d. Do not know/does not apply

11. The indicators we track are:
   a. Financial only
   b. Financial and customer only
   c. Financial, customer, business process, and organizational learning
   d. Do not know/does not apply

12. Our information systems:
   a. Present only the information captured internally
   b. Present internal information enriched with market data that has been purchased and integrated
   c. Present enriched internal information for partners and suppliers
   d. Do not know/does not apply

13. Our Web clickstream data:
   a. Is used only by IT staff for server planning purposes
   b. Is presented to business users, but only in canned, stand-alone reports
   c. Is integrated with customer profile, preference, and historical data
   d. Do not know/does not apply

14. Will you have an extranet for self-service customer care (i.e., customers have direct access to account information, orders, etc.)?
   a. Not planning to have one
   b. Planning to have one
   c. Already have one
   d. Do not know/does not apply

15. Will you have an extranet for supply chain management?
   a. Not planning to have one
   b. Planning to have one
   c. Already have one
   d. Do not know/does not apply

16. We sell or barter the information we have with others in our market (partners, suppliers, etc.):
   a. Never
   b. Maybe sometime in the future
   c. Already do
   d. Do not know/does not apply

17. Our information privacy policy is:
   a. Nonexistent
   b. Written, but not well implemented
   c. Written and well implemented
   d. Do not know/does not apply

18. Our view on net markets (online trading exchanges) is:
   a. Wait and see
   b. We are buying from one
   c. We are setting one up
   d. Do not know/does not apply

19. The data in our information systems that I can access is:
   a. Stale: old and out-of-date by the time I get it
   b. Reasonable: not up-to-the-minute but recent enough for what I need
   c. Fresh: up-to-the-minute
   d. Do not know/does not apply

20. I learn about exceptions in the metrics I track:
   a. One month or more later
   b. One week later
   c. One day later
   d. Do not know/does not apply

21. I am automatically notified when exceptions occur in the metrics:

a. No. No such system has been implemented

b. On a regular frequency (weekly, monthly, etc.)

c. Immediately: the event triggers a message to me

d. Do not know/does not apply

22. I can see information:

a. Via static reports only (paper or online)

b. By selecting parameters in static reports (for example, in pull-down menus)

c. With ad hoc, self-service access to data that I can query, build reports, and analyze myself

d. Do not know/does not apply

23. I can get access to corporate information:

a. Only in the office

b. From the office, over the Internet, from my computer, *and* from anywhere in the world

c. From the office, over the Internet, from my computer, from anywhere in the world, *and* from my mobile phone Internet browser

d. Do not know/does not apply

SCORING

To score your test, each "A" answer is worth 1 point, each "B" answer is worth 2 points, each "C" answer is worth 3 points, and each "D" answer is worth zero points. Total up your score, and consult the following to see where you rank.

62–69:

Congratulations. Your organization is among the leaders in e-business intelligence. You are doing the right things to turn your corporate information into knowledge and profit, and you've extended your information enterprise to customers, suppliers, and partners. Keep it up!

54–61:

Your organization is making a successful transition to e-business intelligence. Additional work to make all data accessible to all users at any time will help ensure success; in particular, you should make a plan to extend information to your customers, suppliers, and partners.

46–53:

While you have done some of the right things to make sure you are leveraging corporate data within individual departments, these "islands" of information will not work as a long-term e-business intelligence strategy. To truly leverage your information for competitive advantage, you need to work on extending all information to every knowledge worker across the enterprise.

38–45:

You are doing some of the basics by providing key information to senior management, but without change, your organization will not be able to fully leverage your information assets and increase competitive advantage. Your next step should be to help each department in the company leverage their specific information assets and then extend that information companywide. Redoubling your efforts to achieve e-business intelligence may prevent failure.

37 and below:

Your organization is NOT leveraging your information assets, and this could make you vulnerable in the marketplace. Consider immediate "triage" to create an e-business intelligence strategy.

Summary

Sharing information is key to success in the new economy. More than a technical and a business issue, it starts with a question of management philosophy. Is your company willing to democratize the use of data throughout the entire organization or does it want to do things the old way and control the use of information and limit it to a few executives?

Experience shows that successful companies implement a philosophy of *Information Democracy*, and they are able to reap great returns from it:

- The greater the level of democratization, the greater the value

- The greater the level of empowerment, the greater the value

- The greater the propensity to break organizational boundaries, the greater the value

The road to full information democracy is virtually guaranteed to be a long one. In order to get there, you will need to deal with the overload of information and to define and implement an e-business intelligence strategy that enables you to let any user access any data at any time.

3

The Value of
Information

It is not enough to have a good mind; the main thing is to use it well.

René Descartes

Companies are evolving from *Information Dictatorships* to *Information Democracies*. This change in data philosophy is driven by the realization that each piece of information in a given corporation's information system has value. This value is not related to the data itself, but rather to how the company leverages it to facilitate its day-to-day business. In this chapter, we further explore this value of a piece of information, and we introduce five different organizational stages in the evolution of extracting value out of information.

Most products that are rich in intellectual property see their value increase with the frequency of their usage. The value of a song, for example, lies in how many times it is played. Similarly, the value of a book is in how many times it is read. The same is true of data. Its value is not in possessing it, but in putting it to good use. The value expands with the number of users, as each individual not only gets his or her own personal value, but is now able to share personal insights with others.

Throughout this book, we examine a number of case studies and anecdotes of how specific value can be extracted from data, by generating savings, retaining customers, accelerating decision making processes, or generating new forms of revenue. After dealing with thousands of organizations that use business intelligence, in our experience, the value of a piece of information moves on a continuum. The increases in its usage are propagated throughout the enterprise, and they go beyond the organization's four walls to customers and partners. Modeling a formula for computing the value of information is not an easy task, but we believe it is defined fairly accurately as a function of the number of users who can access and analyze that information and the number of business areas these users belong to:

$$\text{Value (information)} \sim \text{Users}^2 \times \text{Business Areas}$$

That is, the value of a given piece of information increases with the square of the number of users who can access that information, multiplied by the number of business areas in which the users work. We use the square of the number of users as a driver of value inspired by the well-known Metcalfe's law for networks. Bob Metcalfe, also known as the inventor of the Ethernet, came up with a formula for computing the value of a network. He concluded that the value of a network varies with the square of the number of connected units. Indeed, as more units connect to each other, these units can interact with more and more of them, and consequently, the potential value of these interconnected elements grows exponentially. This formula has been widely embraced by the networking and communications industry.

The same "network effect" happens with the value of a given set of data—as more people share the same information, they understand each other better, communicate easier, and make better decisions. In addition to the effect of new users, as soon as a new business area of a company gets online access to that same piece of information, the value of the information jumps abruptly (in step-function form), as substantial new intelligence is immediately created for the organization. If 100 salespeople look at sales information, the formula described above indicates a user contribution of 10,000 (100^2). Adding one extra user from the sales department to look at that same information will increase the value of that information by a modest 2 percent (from 10,000 to 10,201 $=101^2$).

Allowing, however, one user from the marketing department to access that information will add significantly more value. The marketing person will be able to cross the sales data with marketing knowledge and gain completely new insights. That value will be fed back to all the salespeople, allowing them to look at that information with even more understanding. The formula indicates that the value will more than double (10,000 to 20,402 $=101^2*2$). That is, the incremental benefit of adding one more user in sales when 100 are already online is positive, but small, while the incremental benefit of adding the first user outside sales effectively doubles the value of the piece of information. Figure 3-1 illustrates the continuum of value for a piece of information and identifies five different zones through which the data increases progressively in value:

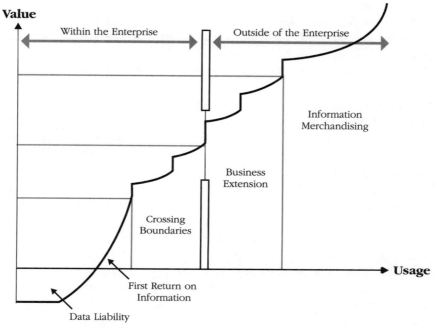

Figure 3-1   The Information Value Curve.

- The Data Liability Zone

- The First Return on Information Zone

- The Enterprise Intelligence Zone

- The Extended Enterprise Zone

- The Information Merchandising Zone

Let us look at each of them in detail.

The Data Liability Zone: When Data Is Just a Cost

Untapped data that just sits in your data store collecting dust can have a negative impact on your bottom line. Instead of being an asset, it becomes a liability. It needs hardware to be stored, software to be managed, and IT staff to look after it, but nobody uses it. In that case, the cost of managing the data is greater than the value of the real or potential information. Until the data is put in the hands of business users and brings real value to these business users, the value obtained from that information does not compensate for the cost of maintaining that data. The data is mostly a cost to the company, and it is not even converted to information, in the sense described in Chapter 1.

In our model, we call this the *data liability zone*. The number of users is limited to the IT staff, whose members interact with the information only for maintenance purposes. In that case, the cost of storing and maintaining the data is higher than the return on that information, which therefore implies a negative business impact. For instance, data about sales prospecting activity is often stored in multiple spreadsheets among the various salespeople, and the data is later consolidated on a large computer, so it is not lost. However, the format does not facilitate sharing or analysis, and therefore the data is not used.

If IBM is right that less than 10 percent of the data stored in companies is actually used, then 90 percent of that data is just a cost to the company. That is a rather frightening statistic, indeed, but also an optimistic one. It means that vast mines of data, which currently represent costs only to the company, do exist, and that their value is waiting to be tapped for the true benefit of the enterprise.

The First Return on Information Zone: Implementing Departmental Business Intelligence

In the first step, information can be transformed from a liability to an asset by enabling business users to access data about their own departmental activity. For example, the human resources staff is given the ability to access and analyze information about payroll, compensation metrics per department, division, country, age range, etc. As another example, salespeople can have ad hoc access to the information from the Sales Force Automation application which they use to track their activity. They can know what interaction they have had with a given client or prospect in the past, and they can know the sales history. However, they do not have access to the information about all the calls the customer has placed to the technical support center, as this is part of another system in another division of the company. In this example, the salespeople do not yet have yet a 360° view of the customer, because that would involve crossing information from many sources of data.

However, the basic sales information is already very useful. As the number of users who can take advantage of this information set increases, the benefits outweigh the costs of managing it, and the value becomes positive. The curve gets steeper as more and more users gain key understanding of the data and discover important patterns that can influence their department, division, or the entire enterprise. Later in the book, we will see how companies achieve these initial results by implementing departmental business intelligence or business intelligence solutions focused on a single business area.

The Enterprise Intelligence Zone: Applying Business Intelligence across Departments

In the second step, companies open a department's business intelligence to other departments or divisions. This brings immediate benefits as the system is open to business users who can look at that data with a different point of view. Let us take the example of a sales force automation system and a customer support center. By opening the customer support center information to the sales force, the salespeople can check the status of a customer's problems, and their satisfaction level, before talking to their customer contacts.

If the customer has had many complaints, it is probably not the right time to discuss additional large scale purchases, however, it may be the right time to ask the customer about the level of service they are receiving and solicit feedback on how it can be improved. Equivalently, by opening the sales force automation system to the customer support engineers, engineers can be informed about the importance of a customer when they handle a call. For instance, the engineer can know how much that customer has purchased in the past year and if there is a significant sales transaction in the pipeline. The initial gain of value for that information is quite high as soon as the data is open to another department, according to the formula we described earlier. As more users get on the system, the benefits grow exponentially with the usage expansion. More people are now more efficient.

This value gain can be repeated many times as the company opens up the system to other departments. Every time a new class of users can interact and share data beyond their own domain, the information value jumps one step forward. As more users of that same class are being used, the value increases exponentially.

As more departments access and share information from other departments, fluidity of knowledge becomes a given. Conventional wisdom is being challenged as users with different perspectives access and analyze the same data. For instance, the same sales information can now be accessible to the finance group, which can have an accurate view of customer profitability by crossing the sales information with expense data. Eventually, we reach a state of Information Democracy where a collective intelligence is being built through open communication and willingness to share data.

In their book *Net Ready*, Amir Hartman and John Sifonis describe how Cisco has become a leader in e-business and indicate that one of the key ingredients of their success was how Cisco cultivated a culture of information sharing: "Today that culture of information sharing contributes to a record of knowledge management that, in turn supports a stupendous level of product achievement." We will see in later chapters how companies that apply business intelligence across departments and eventually throughout the whole organization go on to realize immense benefits from the information they hold in their databases.

The Extended Enterprise Zone: Extending the Value of Existing Relationships through Value-Added Information Sharing

We have seen how companies can get the best return on their information through an intelligent distribution of that information to their employees. Yet the value that these companies can extract from a piece of information does not end here. Companies can generate even more value from the same set of information by sharing it with external constituencies: customers, suppliers, and partners.

As an example, by setting up a customer extranet, a company can provide its customers with historical sales information. This will enable the customers to always have current information on what they purchased, the status of their accounts, etc. As we will see, in many cases it is easier for a supplier to aggregate this information than it is for the customer. The company can also share customer support data, so the customers can have an online status of their support calls, of the technical issues logged, and how close these are to being resolved.

The first extension of data access beyond the organization's four walls to an external constitutent (such as a supplier, customer, or partner) brings an immediate new value to that information. Again, as more customers join the program and access the data, the value of that data increases sharply. Using our formula for the value of information, we equate a new customer with a new business area. Every time a new customer or a supplier is added, the value of the information increases.

As we will see, some companies are starting to leverage that value financially. Provided the data is valuable for customers or suppliers, it can be marketed at a price, transforming a data warehouse into a real profit center. These extranets, however, are primarily designed to enhance the relationship of the company with existing customers or with new customers in the same business. For instance, Cisco enhances the value of its routers to its existing customers by providing them with a "health check" extranet; Owens and Minor provides a customer extranet system to the hospitals they currently service; and Harley Davidson provides information to its existing dealers throughout the United States, through an intelligent extranet.

The Information Merchandising Zone: Selling Data to New Types of Customers via Intelligent Extranets

Using e-business intelligence, companies can look beyond their traditional business models, and identify data that can be marketed and sold to brand new constituencies. As an example, a company's sales information can be marketed to new customers. If the sales information relates to online purchases by consumers, for example, it could be aggregated, anonymized, and then sold to marketing research companies, which need data to target marketing campaigns. (By focusing data aggregated for groups of customers, as opposed to data related to individuals, companies can ensure that the privacy of their customers is not violated.)

In future chapters, we will see how innovative companies have already started to generate brand new forms of revenue and create relationships with completely new classes of customers, by merchandising their existing information. We will see cases of credit card transaction data being sold to retailers, car leasing information being sold to car manufacturers, etc. From the Information Liability Zone to the Information Merchandising Zone, a given piece of information can see its value grow dramatically—from being a negative to becoming not only a positive, but 100 percent return on investment. In the chapters that follow, we will see how applying business intelligence is central to moving along that information value continuum.

4

Data Overload

There's so much damn information.
Bob White
Vice President of
Business Technology Services
eSolutions Group
Ingram Micro

E*Trade, the pioneering online brokerage, notched a hit in the television advertising market when it aired a spot set in a hospital. Doctors and nurses tended urgently to a stricken patient who, as the punch line put it, had "money coming out his wazoo." A business that finds itself prone on a hospital gurney, being hustled into the emergency room, is not apt to be suffering from money coming out its wazoo. The affliction typical of businesses today is *data* out the wazoo. In this chapter, we examine this common problem and offer strategies on how your organization can deal with data overload.

The past decade brought a small revolution in the way companies conducted their business. Packaged applications from SAP, PeopleSoft, Oracle, and more recently Siebel Systems, were embraced as a means of improving operational efficiency. The systems increased the productivity of operations and internal processes which, in some cases, had remained unchanged for decades. However, these packaged applications introduced a major challenge for IT management—managing the distributed data *silos* that emerged. In addition, IT had the additional challenge of handling the increased demands from business users and corporate decision makers for up-to-date performance reports based on the growing operational data.

The emphasis when deploying such software applications was primarily on *automating process*, not on *leveraging information*. IT organizations concentrated their energies on tasks, such as putting in place a new *enterprise resource planning* (ERP) application with SAP, automating the sales force and the call center with Siebel Systems, revamping the order entry system with Lawson, or creating a new system for customers to purchase products online with Broadvision. Little attention was paid to extracting the most value out of the data collected within these systems.

"Using information for competitive advantage" has been the most widely used phrase in the marketing of enterprise software in the past few years, but so far this promise has not been realized. The history of the relational database software industry offers a characteristic example: relational databases like Oracle, Microsoft SQL Server, or IBM DB2 were originally conceived and built with decision support and data analysis in mind.[1] This original design and business goal quickly changed when relational databases began to be used as the foundation for *online transaction processing* (OLTP) systems in the mid-1980s. Only in the late 1990s did the relational database industry return to its original focus of decision support and data analysis.

It certainly made sense for organizations to focus on the operational aspect of their IT infrastructures before turning their attention to data analysis. Without an operational system in place, there is nothing to analyze. The problem is that putting the operational systems in place created a drain of both resources and effort. Companies got sidetracked on an endless quest of seeking to optimize the synergy between operational software and internal business processes. Lost in the meantime was the original goal of maximizing the *return on the information*, by delivering the analytical capabilities for competitive advantage.

Great gains have been made on the operational side of the business. It is now time that businesses look at exploiting these vast amounts of collected data. To take control of its information system, a company needs to address the complexities associated with data overload:

- The inexorable rise of data volumes

- A multiplicity of information sources, resulting in isolated data silos that cannot communicate

---

[1] Reflecting this early priority is the name of the industry standard language used to interact with a relational database: Structured Query Language. Had the early emphasis been on operations, the name would have referred to transactional processing or data updates, not queries.

- The challenges of globalization

- Issues with data quality

Let us now examine each of these four symptoms of data overload in more detail.

The Inexorable Rise of Data Volumes

The volume of data that companies capture and store is rapidly increasing, as is the complexity of that data and the number of unconnected data stores in which it is situated. Companies find themselves buffeted by a data deluge of Biblical proportions. Only a decade or two ago, a company's information assets consisted chiefly of data in transactional databases. The quantities of data involved tended to be fairly modest—a gigabyte was considered a lot, and it was expensive to store that data, given the high prices for hardware and memory at the time.

Now, concurrent with falling prices for both hardware and memory, the data equivalent of Moore's Law is manifesting itself. Much like the observation of Intel Chairman Gordon Moore in 1965 that computer chip performance tends to double every 18 months, so are we now witnessing exponential growth in volumes of data at similar rates. Researchers at IBM's Almaden Research Laboratory in San Jose, California have tracked this phenomenon. IBM estimates that the world has one exabyte of data online today—in databases, file systems, and PCs. (See Figure 4-1.) This one exabyte (1000 petabytes or 1,000,000 terabytes) is equivalent in size to telephone books stacked to the moon and back again.[2] In contrast, these IBM researchers estimate that 20 times as much digital data (20 exabytes) exists in offline media, such as audio CDs, DVDs, and digital tape. As for analog data—such as data on paper and film—IBM estimates the total at 300 exabytes.

The Internet is contributing to this rapid swelling of digital content. IBM estimates the Internet holds 100 terabytes of information today. By 2006, that sum is projected to grow to one exabyte. That contributes heavily to the increase in the world's digital data, which is expected to eclipse analog

---

[2] Terabytes, petabytes, exabytes, just like the more familiar gigabytes, megabytes, and kilobytes are all measures of computer memory storage. A kilobyte is 1,000 bytes, a megabyte 1,000,000 bytes or 1,000 kilobytes. Equivalently a gigabyte is 1,000 megabytes, a terabyte is 1,000 gigabytes, a petabyte is 1,000 terabytes, and an exabyte is 1,000 petabytes.

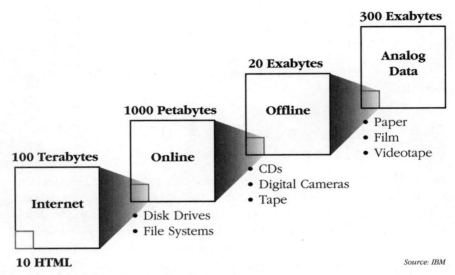

Figure 4-1 How Much Data Exists.

data by 2006. (See Figure 4-2.) "Data is growing exponentially," says Armando Garcia, IBM's vice president of content management solutions. "The amount of digital data is going to cross analog data in about 2006, and then exceed it."

This rise in digital data is not just an ivory tower proclamation from the data gurus at IBM. It is taking hold in practically every company on Earth, with very real implications for business success. "Every corporation that touches its customers or supply chain with what used to be paper forms, telephone conversations, and faxes," Garcia says, "is now capturing that data digitally, online, because that's what they need to be more responsive and improve customer service and lower their costs." The issue is not only how businesses cope with this data overload, because merely coping is quite like chasing one's digital tail, while a smarter competitor races ahead.

The issue is how businesses can learn to master this data overload and turn data into information, intelligence, and profit. The issue is how businesses describe data, integrate it, manipulate it, analyze it, archive it, and find it at the snap of a finger (or click of a mouse). The issue is how businesses avoid the dreaded trap—being data rich and information poor. In later chapters, we will explore strategies for how companies can and are mastering their data and deriving intelligence from it. But first, let us look at how this data deluge occurred.

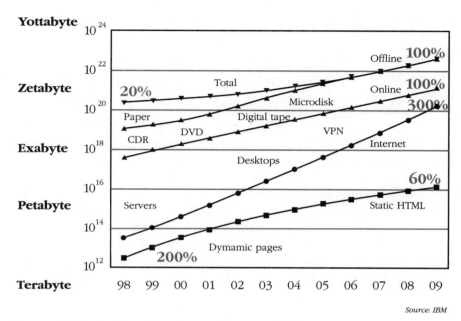

Figure 4-2   Information Grows Exponentially.

The Data Silo Problem

Over the last decade or two, companies have undertaken many worthy initiatives to automate their business processes. More recently, they have launched aggressive bids to thrust themselves into e-business. The typical Fortune 1000 company will now have in place hundreds of databases and applications running back-office functions, customer-facing systems, and Web servers and data engines that serve as the hub of e-business. A reconnaissance mission through the enterprise of a sizable company will likely turn up multiple iterations of the following kinds of systems:

- Legacy systems, often on a mainframe

- Transactional databases

- Back-office enterprise resource planning applications (order entry, billing, manufacturing, human resources, logistics, inventory, and asset management)

- Front-office applications (call centers, customer support, customer relationship management, and marketing campaign management)

- Ecommerce engines (online stores, personalization, and content management)

- Desktop applications (word processors, spreadsheets, email, presentations, HTML files, and business intelligence tools)

The principal problem is that for the most part, the data stored and processed in those systems is simply that, data. Few companies have thus far succeeded in turning that data into information, and then turning that information into intelligence.

A second problem is that these hundreds of databases and applications tend to exist as archipelagos—sets of unintegrated data islands. Worse yet, those data islands are very likely contaminated with inconsistent data. That is, the data on a customer in a billing system—even basics such as name, address, and phone number—may differ substantially from data on that same customer in a separate order-entry system. As business managers familiar with customer-centered operations know all too well, that sort of conflicting data can have profound and unhappy consequences for the company's bottom line.

The Back- and Front-Office Data Silos

The acceptance and proliferation of packaged application software in the last decade has been a chief contributor to the data silos for two reasons. First, vendors of *enterprise resource planning* (ERP) and other business software designed their systems with only analysis of their own data in mind. Hence, each application installed came with its own set of data and its own set of business reports. Second, many companies have not had the time, money, and personnel necessary to build a parallel analytic system—the data warehouse—which is designed explicitly for e-business intelligence and brings together data from a company's multiple back- and front-office systems.

Certainly, thousands of data warehouses and associated analytic data stores have been built and are delivering tremendous value. Practitioners recognize that much work remains to be done to enhance the information in data warehouses and extend it to the masses for better, faster decision making.

The New e-Business Data Silos

The rush to e-business has added a number of new data sources while following a pattern similar to the deployment of ERP systems when it comes to data analysis. Much as back- and front-office systems were built first to run operations, with data analysis a secondary consideration, so have we seen the same pattern in the rush to e-business. Companies have rushed to plant a stake in the virtual marketplace as quickly as possible.

Early efforts at establishing a Web presence consisted largely of mere brochureware—assemblies of product and company information that were good for little more than informational browsing. Next came Herculean efforts to build Web-enabled transactional systems with a decided emphasis on the customer, using software engines that served up personalized content and catered to individual whims. Amazon, the online general retailer that began as an online bookseller, helped to pave the way with targeted email marketing campaigns and by serving up to the customer at its Web site content particular to his or her past preferences.

With their Web-enabled transactional systems now functional and scalable, the dot coms that will make it to the second phase of the evolution of Internet retailing are now wringing e-business intelligence from the reams of data they collect through data analysis. It is not an easy chore. For one thing, Web-begotten datasets tend, like their sister ERP systems, to be islands unto themselves, just begging to be integrated with other data. That is a key mission for many companies at the forefront of e-business. Through data integration, a company is able to track its sales to the same customer via multiple channels—store sales, telephone sales, and Web sales. The result is a more holistic view of the customer for more precise and profitable marketing, which enables a company to easily size up its sales by channel.

These e-businesses have at their disposal three distinct sets of data that they collect on their Web sites: the clickstream Web log files, transaction records generated, and customers' electronic feedback. Let's look at each one of these data silos in more detail.

The electronic trail that surfers, shoppers, and business partners leave as they traipse through the electronic marketplace is recorded on Web servers as log files. This clickstream data can provide a means of monitoring the success of your e-business endeavors. It leaves a trail that may be examined for weaknesses in your Web site, to track the links and banner ads most frequently followed, and to assess where these visitors came from. It can, if properly harnessed, provide a more precise and profitable view of customers and suppliers.

Secondly, business transactions that these visitors conduct will be recorded in a transactional database, apart from the clickstream. This sales data will create its own data silo that includes valuable information on customers. The challenge for e-businesses is to integrate this e-business data channel with data from other channels (such as telephone sales and store sales) to provide a broader view of the customer. One of the many e-business intelligence initiatives under way at Ingram Micro accomplishes that exactly. The $29 billion distributor of computing products in Santa Ana, California has rolled out a system it calls WIP, or *Web Insight platform*. WIP tracks user activity at Ingram Micro's e-business Web site, an increasingly visible sales channel as it broadens beyond traditional telephone sales into Web transactions. Only several weeks into the rollout, Bob White, the vice president of business technology services at Ingram Micro's eSolutions group, was delighted by the results.

One thing Ingram Micro quickly learned was that activity on its Web site varied substantially by day of the week. Monday and Tuesday tend to be heavy days for resellers to check price and availability of computing products, and on Wednesdays, Ingram Micro sees a spike in orders. Thursday and Friday bring some orders, but more price, availability, and order-status inquiries.

"You do not see that unless you combine the Web logs [the clickstream] with the transactions actually executed," White says. Such is the beauty of data integration. As a result of its insight, Ingram Micro has structured its systems maintenance to ensure high availability of its Web site on Wednesdays. We will take a look at more insights that Ingram Micro is gleaning from WIP and other e-business intelligence systems in a later chapter.

The Web also provides a means of gathering feedback and complaints from customers via email. The successful e-business will have in place not only a means of promptly responding to a customer comment, but for storing it, integrating it with other customer comments, and then applying an analytical tool to that dataset of customer comments. That analysis should examine the aggregated data for a pattern:

- Are many customers complaining that our Web sites' graphic product illustrations are too small?

- Are they spending very little time on a content-rich page?

- Might the font be unreadable or the layout intrusive?

The influx of data from e-business is enormous, and only now is it beginning to be tapped. The challenges in making intelligent use of this new form of data are not small. Clickstream records can swiftly grow into multiple terabytes, data quantities that it took brick-and-mortar retailers and financial institutions years to amass in the years before e-business. Online companies are wrestling with questions such as how many years' worth of this data to store and whether to store it in its most detailed form or as summarizations. Here, Internet-only e-businesses have something of an advantage over their click-and-mortar competitors, because as freshly minted merchants, they do not have legacy data stores to contend with. Nevertheless, this new data source promises to put the best of business intelligence and data warehousing technology and practice to the test, with certainly some new lessons learned added to the mix.

Data Silos Purchased from Third Parties

Businesses are increasingly complementing their own data with information from external providers. These companies make available massive lists of consumer and business information, with detailed data on tens of millions of individuals, households, and businesses. While such third-party data can provide a business with a fuller picture of its consumer and business customers, the data poses a challenge to business and IT teams in that it must be cleansed, integrated, and blended with internal data and analyzed to pay full dividends.

The Internet as a Giant Data Silo

With the emergence of the Internet, there is now an immense reservoir of information immediately open to businesses. Companies can find data on their competitors (revenue information, product prices), on their suppliers, or on their industry (market share, size, growth). This information however, is stored in many different systems and is made available only through static pages of text on Web sites. Because of this limitation, Internet data is rarely well integrated into a corporation's information systems. At best, a business manager may refer to the Web to get information that she will enter into her own spreadsheet.

Another issue limiting the use of Internet information is the reliability of the source.

In the future, though, standards like XML (eXtended Markup Language) will be adopted throughout the Web. Web site data sources will receive stamps of approval from independent quality bodies, and the data will add a significant new dimension to business intelligence. XML will help in tapping into another very important data silo—the set of unstructured information available to a corporation.

Unstructured Data Silos

Outside of transactional databases and number-centric applications, other realms of corporate data exist that remain largely untapped. This is unstructured data, in the sense that it is not compartmentalized into the rows and columns of a relational database. However, getting at this data for the purposes of e-business intelligence can in many ways be more problematic than leveraging traditional datasets.

Text documents in Microsoft Word or other word processing programs contain a wealth of information, as do files in Microsoft Excel or other spreadsheet programs, and in Microsoft PowerPoint and similar presentation programs. The problem with the data in these applications, however, is that they tend to be isolated on individual PCs and inaccessible to anyone other than the PC's user.

Email is another valuable source of data that tends to exist as its own island, although correspondence among employees and managers contains information that could and should be tapped. One example: a sales rep for a software manufacturer is close to sealing a multimillion dollar deal when she is suddenly snatched up by a competitor. She has not bothered to log details of her sales bid with this prospective customer into a centralized database. As a result, key information about the opportunity exists in only one place—email. Her replacement is forced to start from scratch.

Few companies have implemented the capability that provides access to such unstructured data to its knowledge workers. However, the power for employees to search centrally accessible text to find information is powerful indeed. The sales representative's ability to locate relevant documents that relate to the prospect and combine the information with structured data on the customer can mean crucial hours that could make or break the deal. By providing easy access and a reference structure to these documents, XML promises to help facilitate the extraction of useful information out of this important data silo.

Multiple Versions of the Truth

The problem is not necessarily that corporations maintain too large a volume of data. Data is fairly easy to store. The problem is that a legion of disparate applications, legacy systems, and databases leaves a company's informational terrain fractured. The multiplication of data stores results in multiple versions of the truth. Information that business managers want and need cannot easily be found. Depending on the gravity of the information fracture, a manager's view of the business can be as distorted as a reflection in a carnival funhouse mirror.

Which database contains our revenue figures for Europe? Why do we have different customer lists for each region? Why do we have two separate systems to track shipping and delivery? Where are the numbers on how our new peach peeler is selling in Georgia? Finding the truth amid the contradictory information in disparate data stores is like letting loose the 101 Dalmatians and trying to pick out which one is Pongo as the hounds race past.

Let us consider an account manager and the pickle in which he finds himself. He is new to his company and this account, and has to prepare in a matter of hours for a meeting the next morning. He needs data on the client's history of ordering, payment, delivery, support, and marketing. At his last employer, all of this information was centrally located and accessible through a Web browser. At his new employer, though, he is baffled. He has several applications on his desktop computer, but none seem to deliver all that he needs to know.

It is no wonder. The client's ordering and payment records are kept in the accounting system. Installation and support information is in the customer service database. A separate contact management application tracks the proposals and sales call history. These systems do not speak the same language, and there is no simple way for this nontechnical business user to get the answers that he needs quickly.

Without a centralized e-business intelligence system, the manager's only means of acquiring the desired information would be to prevail upon the IT department to run a query against these disparate data stores, aggregate the data, and produce an informational report. This would take days, weeks, or months, depending on the alignment between business and IT, and it would waste valuable IT resources better spent elsewhere. Regardless of the turnaround time, the results would seldom be to the manager's satisfaction. Answers invariably trigger new questions, and a vicious circle arises between business managers and the IT department. As a later example at Belgacom will show, it is quite likely that these disparate applications contain multiple versions of the truth.

The Globalization Challenge

The globalization of business, extended and accentuated by the Internet, adds another dimension to the data silo challenge. Data is not only dispersed in silos across departments within an organization, but also across different time zones, currency regimes, legislation umbrellas, and disparate languages and customs. Companies face vexing obstacles in generating e-business intelligence from data that is geographically dispersed and differs in language, format, and definition. Two operational subsidiaries, one in France, the other in the Netherlands, may each have built a very efficient information system for its local customers, but the systems may be based on completely different software applications, allowing no communication between the two.

Well, then, is intelligent global business an oxymoron? Definitely not. More companies are taking the plunge into the substantial undertaking of building and maintaining a global data warehouse. In fact, a very pragmatic way of being global is letting the regional organizations have some freedom in building systems and running their operations at a local level. But have them operate under one rule: everybody needs to report data centrally at defined intervals, in defined formats, and corporate will integrate it all into one large warehouse, where they can analyze their business globally using current information.

The dissolution of boundaries brought about by the Internet and e-business is forcing this centralized approach to business data analysis. So is the uptick in acquisitions and mergers of companies based on foreign soil. In Europe, companies have to move rapidly as the borders have disappeared and the currency has been unified. It is no longer possible to do business differently in Belgium than in Italy. Prices need to be aligned, commercial practices need to be similar, and customers need to be treated the same way. Customer information therefore cannot be stored and managed differently from one country to the next.

Most companies recognize that in several years, it will not be sufficient to maintain isolated, unintegrated datasets on sales, finance, human resources, and other key areas in individual countries. The global company's customers want data relevant to them across borders, a service that many multinationals have yet to deliver. European companies are taking the lead in this area, as their business is, by definition, based on multiple countries, with different languages and different business cultures.

Zurich Financial Services Group is one such company. Headquartered in Switzerland, it is building a global warehouse of data from its commercial insurance operations in 60 countries. It will expand on an early effort that has approximately 5 percent of the global insurance business' data warehoused, says Frank Colletti, director of e-business solutions at Zurich U.S. Insurance, located outside Chicago. Not only will this global insurance warehouse, called Global Financial Intelligence, deliver a single globalized view of transnational operations to Zurich's own managers, it will also be extended to customers. A company with Zurich-insured operations in the United States, the United Kingdom, and Peru will have access through a Zurich extranet to claims and policy data in all three countries. To start, Zurich has in mind about 200 clients. "Each country can provide the information, but what our customers are looking for is a consolidated report of all their risk around the world and what it is costing them," Colletti says. "They want one report worldwide that tells them what the risks are."

Later, we will take a look at how Zurich's success with a customer extranet called *RiskIntelligence* has helped paved the way for the global warehouse deployment.

The Data Quality Issue

Data overload spawns a multitude of problems. Data quality is one—the overload of data can be so overwhelming that businesses necessarily forsake the details of accurate record keeping and data management. Such data quality details will eventually metastasize into a problem that can reach epic proportions, with implications for efficiency, customer relationships, and profit.

Koen Vermeulen was a 24-year-old IT consultant in 1994 when he found it necessary to approach his supervisor at Belgacom, the Belgium telephone company, with a bit of disturbing news concerning the quality of the company's data. Belgacom's IT team had begun preparing to build a customer-centric data warehouse, and one of the first steps was examining the customer data that Belgacom held in an array of disparate databases (customer billing, customer orders, inventory controls, and technical networks information). The team's job was to move the data from those systems into a data warehouse that would serve as a centralized analytic repository of everything Belgacom knew on each of its millions of customers. That would enable Belgacom to make better, faster decisions, extend intelligence across to its line-of-business employees, cut costs, and mount targeted marketing campaigns. As it was, Belgacom's data offered little in the way of intelligence. Why? The disturbing news: Some 60 percent of the data was wrong.

The different databases held conflicting information on the customers. A record in one database had one telephone number assigned to one customer; another database had that same telephone number assigned to someone else. The data had different file formats and different definitions. In short, it was a mess. Belgacom had a bad case of data overload.

During a meeting on the seventh floor of the Belgacom Tower in downtown Brussels, Vermeulen laid out the grim facts. The supervisor's reaction was one of disbelief and denial: "That can't be right," Vermeulen was told. "Go back to your programmers. Have them double-check their programs." So, Vermeulen went back, double-checked the programs, and in fact whittled a few percentage points off the 60 percent inconsistency figure. Now it was down to around 55 percent.

In short order, Belgacom managers listened. "They knew we had data quality issues, but they were astonished to see how bad they were," Vermeulen says. "It escalated. Once they realized there was a revenue loss and it was impacting our revenue cycle, that made them very nervous." Belgacom launched a data-cleansing jihad. Roughly 100 business and IT employees scrubbed the data in some 2.5 million records and rendered it in a consistent format suitable for the data warehouse. Some customers were contacted for marketing campaigns, and Belgacom took the opportunity to double-check the customer's information. After more than a year of hard work and perspiration, the task was done. Not only was the data ready for the warehouse, but it was also cleaned up on the operational side, as well, and primed for better business.

Through the exercise, Belgacom business executives learned the unsavory truth about data and information. To paraphrase Geoffrey Moore's comment on market research, information is like sausage—it may taste good, but you would not want to know what is in it. Belgacom's experience is, of course, not unique. Thousands of companies that have launched data warehousing and e-business intelligence projects have encountered similar data quality problems. "A data warehouse triggers these kind of realizations," Vermeulen notes. The thousand of companies without data warehouses and e-business intelligence systems have data quality problems, too; they just do not know it. Their business processes are choking on data overload.

MasterCard Masters Its Data Volumes

MasterCard International's data warehouse is a little like the Energizer bunny: It keeps growing and growing and growing. In fact, it has grown so much since its first iteration in 1995 that Andrew Clyne, MasterCard's vice president of systems development, decided to adopt a new technology to keep up with the demand. In order to keep appropriate quantities of data online to satisfy the demands of MasterCard's thousands of users in risk management, finance, sales, marketing, and franchise management, Clyne implemented an innovative compression technology that saved millions of dollars. "We've been growing our data very quickly," says Clyne, at MasterCard's technology center in St. Louis, Missouri. "Since 1995, we've had over 400 percent growth. We started with just over a terabyte of disk in 1995 and are now at 15 terabytes capacity with an order in for three more terabytes of EMC disk." With such data warehouse growth rates not uncommon in today's business world, "You are going to need ware-houses to warehouse your data warehouse, unless you adopt new effi-cient methods for online storage," Clyne says, tongue in cheek.

MasterCard's original strategy was to maintain 13 months' worth of both summarized and detailed data in an Oracle-based data ware-house, which by mid-1999 amounted to about 5 terabytes of raw data. Data more than 13 months old was then transferred to tapes to be pre-served off-site for many years. The problem, according to Clyne, was that MasterCard's financial institutions began to request access to data more than 13 months old. They wanted to take longer, historical views and analyze the data for trends over a period of years, rather than months. That data was no longer in the warehouse and had to be retrieved from tape.

In late 1999, MasterCard built a second data warehouse that would house five years' worth of data. The key to this system, Clyne says, is a software tool that compresses data so that volumes are reduced by about 80 percent. No more trips to the tape farm! "We have statisticians going directly off that data store and there's no more need for them to mount tapes on a mainframe. They are the ones with an insatiable need for this data," Clyne says. Users in franchise management have a need to access data that is 24 months old or older and had asked for access beyond even that.

The compressed data warehouse is saving MasterCard valuable resource time and money. "Without it, we'd have to spend significant resources going back to process the data that was offline. The costs were not necessarily in the hardware and systems; it was in the people and the time spent. You'd have to create a special project to meet some of these needs, and it could take six months."

The complementary compression system leaves Clyne and staff a lit-tle more time to build out the principal data warehouse and roll out Web-enabled e-business intelligence tools to a MasterCard user com-munity that numbers nearly 7,000 users at nearly 2,000 member finan-cial institutions in 10 countries. For the thousands of staff hours and millions of dollars (Clyne will not say exactly how much) that MasterCard has invested in data warehousing, it still has 30 percent of its transactional data left to load into the warehouse.

MasterCard has learned that while it's important to capture the data and make it accessible across the organization, the real value to an organization comes when it leverages data into a revenue engine.

MasterCard has mastered the two skills required: technical ingenuity and close collaboration with nontechnical business unit sponsors.

As MasterCard's expertise in managing the data warehouse has grown, so has internal user demand for new applications that use the data warehouse. Initially Clyne had one project to support; now there are over 50. Few data warehouses achieve the benefits that drove the project. MasterCard not only reached the goals that initially drove the project, but also makes money on its investment. Clyne calls that "priceless."

Using the best e-business intelligence practices, MasterCard is reaping significant benefits for the company and its customers.

Strategies to Deal with Data Overload

So, can your organization cope with this ever-increasing amount of information? Yes. Many companies do and do it well. Careful consideration needs to be given in order to derive maximum value from this massive amount of data. The following five strategic recommendations should be kept in mind by business managers as their company builds a business intelligence system to cope with data overload:

1. Start with the business.

2. Define the data architecture in a joint effort between business and IT.

3. Develop a business intelligence strategy with the user in mind.

4. Build it to grow.

5. Think beyond your borders.

Let us examine each of them in detail.

Start with the Business

Define Your Business Requirements. The business case for an e-business intelligence system should be clear-cut. Gaps and fuzzy areas in strategic and tactical implementation often signal a weakness in the plan that may render it unproductive. The business case includes an identification of the business need, the data sources to be tapped, and the business benefits that a business intelligence system can be expected to deliver. It approximates the cost of the system versus the revenues it may be expected to drive and the costs that it may help cut—not an exact science, as business intelligence will frequently help identify hidden cost-cutting opportunities or unacknowledged revenue sources.

Business Managers Drive e-Business Iintelligence.   The most successful e-business intelligence systems begin with a business user's business need.

Occasionally, an IT staffer will propose using technology in a way that he or she believes will improve a business process. However, in the vast majority of cases, it is a business-side individual who will provide the business impetus for a successful data warehousing implementation.

Never Let Technology Take Over the Business Goal.   The real root cause of data warehousing failures is often an overly ambitious goal driven by a desire to do what engineers often do by default: solve the problem in the most general sense possible. Engineers are trained to solve the most general problem—the equivalent here would be an attempt to build a data warehouse that can answer any question. Left to their own devices, a technical team may be tempted to take the "build it and they will come" approach, saying, "we do not know why they want it, but let's build it so it can answer anything." By losing sight of the business requirements and by defining a project too large in scope, they may doom the data warehouse to failure. The data warehouse becomes a sinkhole of time and resources, and it is eventually shut down by a businessperson who sees a huge, behind-schedule project that is not specifically linked to the solution of any particular business problem.

Ensure High-Level Sponsorship.   As practitioners know, building a data warehouse and e-business intelligence network can cost millions of dollars and take well over a year. Far more frequently, a data warehousing failure is the result of insufficient sponsorship and inadequate political will. A business-side project champion able to marshal the project through both technological and organizational land mines significantly improves the chances for a warehousing project's success.

Define the Data Architecture in a Joint Effort between the Business Users and IT

Once the business goals have been defined, it is critical to define a robust data architecture for the purpose of information access and analysis. This is an exercise that needs to be done as a joint project between IT and the business users. As it takes data from the large and complex production databases, it needs to be orchestrated by IT; however, the data required needs to be identified by the business users. Traditionally, a business intelligence system will consist of at least three key components (see Figure 4-3):

- An *extraction, transformation, and loading* (ETL) utility. This is the tool to transform data and transport it from transactional systems (like ERP or front-office applications) to a data warehouse.

- A *data warehouse*. This is the place where the data to be accessed, analyzed, and shared by business users will be stored. In short, this is a database for decision support. It is derived from the production or transactional databases used to automate the business processes.

- An *e-business intelligence tool or platform*. This is the tool that the businesspeople will use to access, analyze, and share information stored in the warehouse. It can either be used out of the box as a tool, or used as the basis for application development (i.e., as a platform) for customization into a specific analytic application.

Size Up the Enterprise.   Business managers who want to ensure that their company's data assets are turned into intelligence for competitive advantage need first to understand the enterprise computing landscape of their business. Some key questions to ask include:

- What data do we have and in which databases and applications?

- How can we make that data clean and consistent?

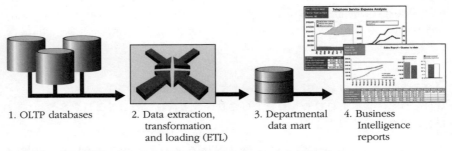

1. OLTP databases   2. Data extraction,   3. Departmental   4. Business
                            transformation   data mart   Intelligence
                            and loading (ETL)   reports

Figure 4-3   Standard Data Architecture for Business Intelligence.

- What should we do to make it easily accessible as information to managers and subordinates?

- What sort of analysis can we conduct?

- How does that analysis add value?

- How can we further extend the value of our data analysis?

Once the landscape is inventoried, the company is ready to implement a business intelligence system or further build out and improve the systems already in place.

Inventory Your Data Assets.   Cardinal rule: You have more data than you realize. Inventory your data assets with an eye to providing as complete a picture as possible of the given subject area, by feeding the warehouse from a variety of sources. Look beneath your corporate rocks to empower your e-business intelligence system for maximum return on investment.

Polish Your Data.   As experiences with messy and inconsistent data illustrate, data quality is of paramount importance. Make sure it is as clean as possible, with inconsistencies and redundancies eliminated. Then double-check it. Try to standardize your information on a corporate data model that uses standard definitions across multiple departments and lines of business. Be sure that the sales department defines "customer" the same way as the product management department does, or you may have two customers and no one paying their bills because their records have been lost.

Develop a Business Intelligence Strategy with the User in Mind

Map the Right User Requirements.   In mapping requirements, interview the user community. Be clear on what information they need, and in what format. Ensure their satisfaction with the system, particularly their interface tool. Training the users obviously is essential, but the tool should be simple enough to use that minimal training is required.

Pick the Right User Solution.   For all the time, money, and sweat invested in the building of a data warehouse, the acid test of value frequently boils down to the front-end e-business intelligence software tool that hundreds or thousands of users will utilize every day. It is not important to your business users that the CEO, CIO, data warehousing project manager, and a team of a half-dozen intrepid data warehouse architects have just spent 11 months and a few million dollars on a spectacular technological behemoth; nor is it important to them that your genius programmer finally mastered that nettlesome database design problem, consisting of fouled-up Cartesian products caused by inconsistent concatenations of multiple tuples. Your business users do not care about tuples.

No, your hard work and visionary thinking may be squandered for want of a mouse click. If the users' front-end tool requires them to spend five days in training in order to understand the esoteric terms used in the database to name tables and columns, they are not going to be happy. They will grumble. Worse, they will not run the query. If the users have to call the IT department every time they need to create a report, rather than generating it with a single click, productivity slips a notch. The key to driving maximum value from an e-business system often comes down to these kinds of details.

Hence, when selecting and customizing a front-end e-business intelligence tool for use by nontechnical business users, make every effort to ensure that the tool:

- Has an inviting graphical user interface

- Is easy to use

- Provides flexibility to tailor reports and ask questions

- Insulates the user from the complexity of the back-end systems

Use the Internet as the Foundation.   The Internet changes everything, including business intelligence. Web-based e-business intelligence platforms that enable users to access, analyze, and share information through a browser offer substantial advantages over traditional business intelligence software installed on a user's desktop computer (a so-called fat client). These Web-based platforms:

- Enable employees to access the system while traveling or at home

- Use a browser interface familiar to the majority of users

- Broaden availability from power users to casual business users

- Save the IT department the installation, maintenance, and support costs of desktop applications

Give the Business Context to the Business User. An overarching objective of e-business intelligence is to empower your business users with the information they need to make decisions. The majority of companies are finding it desirable and competitively necessary to flatten their decision-making hierarchies to accelerate processes and time to market. This compression of decision-making cycle times requires endowing more employees with decision-making authority. In doing so, consider the business environment in which your users perceive themselves to be working. Consider, for example, how a stone mason regards his work.

- Is he placing stones side by side and cementing them together?
- Is he building a wall?
- Is he building a cathedral?

All three job descriptions are correct. But if the mason regards his work in the context of the third definition—the noble endeavor of building a cathedral—this strategic information will help nourish his motivation and will to excel. He will be better able to make decisions and respond to a changing work environment if he understands how the rest of the building is progressing, how many stones he has at his disposal, and how other masons accomplished his task in the past.

Knighting your knowledge workers with the autonomy to follow their own curiosity is a powerful business proposition. It is supported by a tenet of knowledge management theory that holds that human intelligence is a key factor in business success and competitiveness.

Build It to Grow

When formulating a business intelligence strategy, do not underestimate the power of the word of mouth within your user community. In most organizations, users are starved for consistent, accurate, and easily accessible information. Once you begin to roll out business intelligence to a group of users within your company, other users will quickly find out and will request to be included. More often than not, companies witness a rapid embrace of e-business intelligence by the user community—be that community internal to the company, or external with its business partners. Make the investment up front in systems that will deliver the high performance and scalability required to support hundreds or thousands of users, and that will ably accommodate high volumes of complex data. Plan for a surge in use.

Think beyond Your Borders

Business users internal to your company need easy, analytic access to your data. Chances are your customers would like access to it as well, especially if it affects their bottom line. Much like banks are providing customers with online access to their accounts, so too are businesses in practically all industries gaining competitive advantage by opening their data stores to their external customers, suppliers, and business partners.

Peter Blundell's Top Lessons Learned

Through the broad windows of his corner office, Peter Blundell, the knowledge strategy manager for British Airways, has a fine view of Heathrow Airport. He sees his shares of ups and downs every day, the mesmerizing ascent and descent of aircraft. In many ways, Blundell's 28-year career at British Airways has been like a pilot's—getting data warehousing and business intelligence projects off the ground, navigating through turbulence, dealing with the occasional unruly passenger, and bringing the complex piece of machinery in for a graceful landing.

Given his long experience with business intelligence, Blundell is at no loss to tick off a few of his favorite dos and don'ts:

1. *It is about business, not technology.* "You have to have the right people skills, the right management culture, and the right behaviors. That is much more important than picking exactly the right tool, or making sure you have your data model exactly spot-on right."

2. *Expect the unexpected.* "You learn that value will come from being prepared for the unexpected. Long before we had any business intelligence stuff, in response to a fuel crisis, we had to analyze in a very short time frame fuel costs, fuel usage, and so forth—it was costing the airline a small fortune. Now, with a good business intelligence strategy, we are not caught short by the dynamic, changing airline environment."

3. *Data grows like a weed.* "You never stop needing more hardware. I have got as much disk storage on my PC at home now as I had on our first data warehouse."

4. *Return on investment (ROI) is up to you.* "Your return on investment is zero unless you start making some decisions off the information. If your organization suffers from large organization decision-making syndrome—you cannot possibly do anything unless you write 15 business cases, get approval from 17 business managers, and issue it in triplicate with copies to every country manager—then data warehousing will not help."

5. *Do not tool-hop.* "Do not change your mind too often regarding business intelligence tools. No one tool can be the feature leader across the board all the time. You need to design your architecture and build your applications for the long term."

Summary

It is easy for any company to become consumed in data. Most companies have much more than they can actually use. If not used properly, data is more a liability than an asset. However, if you follow the five key principles outlined above in dealing with data overload, your chances of success will be greatly enhanced:

1. Start with the business

2. Define the data architecture in a joint effort between the business users and IT

3. Develop a business intelligence strategy with the user in mind

4. Build it to grow

5. Think beyond your borders

In addition, do not try to solve everything at first. Proceed with little steps, get quick wins, and create enthusiasm for the solution in the early phases. In short, your motto should be "manage data, deliver information."

5

e-Business
Intelligence at Work

Know thyself.
Ancient Greek saying

How does one identify and deploy the technologies needed to attain business intelligence? In this chapter we introduce the key components. While focusing on the business questions that decision makers ask in their day-to-day roles, we navigate through widely quoted technical terms and demystify common buzzwords and acronyms, such as OLAP, RDBMS, data warehouses and data marts, query, reporting, data mining, and portals.

Buzzwords may come and go and technologies evolve. However, the key process remains the same: employees need to access, analyze, and share data on their business, in order to support their decisions using factual information. The data may come from within the corporation, from external sources such as data purchased from information brokers, or data collected from the vast and rapidly expanding domain of the Internet.

Study after study demonstrates that human beings make decisions based on incomplete information and are prone to biases and *decision traps*, as discussed by Russo and Shoemaker in their best-selling book of the same name.[1] Better information, available exactly when needed, can help decision makers avoid these traps and lead them to smarter decisions and thus to a higher degree of intelligence.

---

[1] Russo and Shoemaker, Decision Traps.

Questions People Ask

Let us look at three case studies of types of questions that people would ask in the course of their workday and examine what it takes to empower them with business intelligence. What is often striking is that the business questions people ask are simple, straightforward, and easy to understand. Not so simple is the technical infrastructure required to deliver instant answers to their questions. We will look at three examples of people using business intelligence, one involving a national sales manager, another involving a marketing analyst, and a third involving a purchasing manager. We will examine both their interaction with the data as well as the database infrastructure needed to enable their data access.

The National Sales Manager

It is Friday morning at the U.S. sales headquarters of a $1 billion widget-producing company. Four weeks remain before the end of the fiscal quarter. The vice president of U.S. sales is preparing to report on the status of sales to her boss, the head of worldwide sales. She knows that the Friday afternoon discussion will start as usual with the same simple question:

How's the quarter going?

Empowered by business intelligence, the vice president can prepare for her meeting by viewing her weekly national sales *status report*. (See Figure 5-1.) The report displays bookings to date for the quarter, along with her national sales quota for the quarter and sales forecasts for the remainder of the quarter. Also visible on the report are the budgeted and actual operating expense levels for the division and the projected operating margin. Note that the quantitative information is presented in various formats, including tables and charts. It may also incorporate maps and animation.

Since she meets with her manager regularly every Friday afternoon, the vice president has set up the report to be refreshed or updated automatically on Friday morning, and she has it sent to her inbox. It encompasses the latest information available to the company collected automatically from various parts of the organization.

A review of the U.S. sales forecast for the quarter quickly reveals that the forecast is low relative to her quarterly quota, while operational expenses also appear to be lower than budgetary projections. Bookings appear to be in line with the forecast. To understand more closely the status of her division to date, the vice president decides to look in more detail at each region

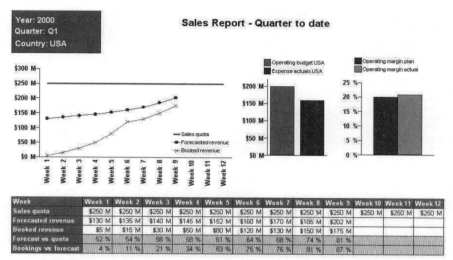

Figure 5-1   Sample Countrywide Sales Report. Report shows bookings (quarter to date) forecasted revenue for quarter, sales quota, budgeted and actual operating expenses and operating margin (plan versus actual).

in the United States (Eastern, Central, Western). She can do so easily with a simple click of the mouse button on the report. Instantly, a new display appears with a breakdown of bookings, forecasts, and expenses by region. (See Figure 5-2.)

The simple step of shifting from a more general (country level) view to more detailed (regional level) view is commonly referred to as *drill down*, since the user reveals a *deeper* or more granular level of detail. Equivalently, moving in the opposite direction, from more detailed (for example, regional level) to more general (for example, country level) information, is often referred to as *drilling up*.

Next, the vice president decides to view the key performance indicators (bookings, forecasted revenue, quarterly sales quota, projected operating expenses) by sales channel (direct sales versus indirect sales through partners). The step of switching the perspective of the report from one point of view (geographic breakdown) to another (breakdown by sales channel) is often referred to as *taking a slice*. Slicing reveals that the drop in forecasted revenue originates from the direct sales side.

This terminology, drill down and drill up, along with *slice and dice*, is usually encountered in the context of OLAP, or *online analytical processing*. Ignore the fancy acronym for now, and let us focus on the origin of these

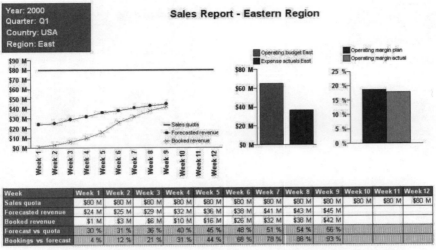

Week	Week 1	Week 2	Week 3	Week 4	Week 5	Week 6	Week 7	Week 8	Week 9	Week 10	Week 11	Week 12
Sales quota	$80 M	$80 M	$80 M	$80 M	$80 M	$80 M	$80 M	$80 M	$80 M	$80 M	$80 M	$80 M
Forecasted revenue	$24 M	$25 M	$29 M	$32 M	$36 M	$38 M	$41 M	$43 M	$45 M			
Booked revenue	$1 M	$3 M	$6 M	$10 M	$16 M	$26 M	$32 M	$38 M	$42 M			
Forecast vs quota	30 %	31 %	36 %	40 %	45 %	48 %	51 %	54 %	56 %			
Bookings vs forecast	4 %	12 %	21 %	31 %	44 %	68 %	78 %	88 %	93 %			

Figure 5-2   Sample Regional Sales Report after Drilling Down from Country to Region. In this case data for the Eastern region is displayed.

terms. As it turns out, they originate from the notion of representing graphically the information that the sales VP analyzes as a cube. (See Figure 5-3.)

Think of each axis of the cube as a major perspective for the analysis, viewing the data, say, by geographical region (Eastern, Central, Western), or by sales channel (direct, indirect), or by time.[2] Each cell of the cube includes information on the key indicators that we track (bookings, forecast, expenses) for a specific geography, sales channel, and time period. By slicing and dicing the cube (Figure 5-4), we can view the data from different perspectives. Examples may include viewing bookings for all geographies and sales channels for a specific fiscal quarter, or viewing bookings for only a single region, for all sales channels and all recent fiscal quarters, and so on.

The end result is the ability of the decision maker to view corporate information from different perspectives and thus to get a better sense of what is going on in the business. This very natural notion of examining key business indicators (in this case, bookings, forecast, expenses, and margin) from different points of view or dimensions (in this case, by region, sales channel, or period) also has a technical name: *multidimensional analysis.*

---

[2] In OLAP-speak the axes are typically referred to as "dimensions," while the indicators tracked as "measures."

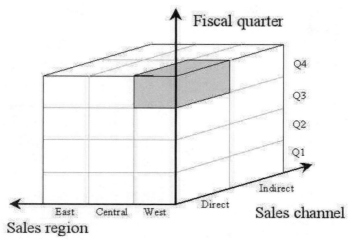

Figure 5-3 Cube with Region, Channel, Quarter as Axes. Each
cell of the cube, such as the shaded one shown, contains values
for the indicators being tracked. The shaded cell contains
values for the performance (for our example, sales quota,
forecasted revenue, booked revenue, operating budget, expense
actuals) of the western region's direct sales team in the
fourth quarter of the fiscal year.

Let us see how the national sales VP continues her analysis. As she looks
at regional data for the recent quarter, she realizes that the forecasted sales
for the Eastern region are low. (See Figure 5-2.) The report lets her drill
down farther to view bookings and forecast for each individual sales representative in the East. (See Figure 5-5.)

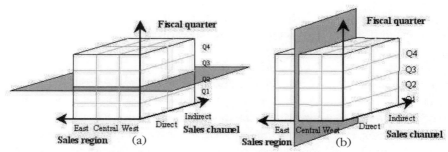

Figure 5-4 Slicing the Cube. (a) The slice projects data for a
specific quarter; (b) the slice encompasses data for an
individual region.

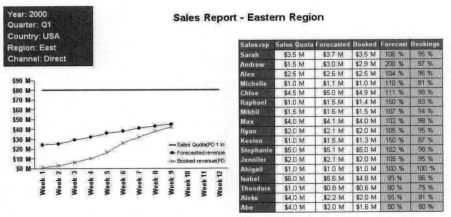

Figure 5-5 Report Displaying the Sales Forecast by Individual
Direct Sales Reps for the Eastern Region.

However, this step does not seem to help: All sales representatives appear to be at or near their sales quota. Hence, their performance does not explain the low forecast. The operating expenses in the East offer a clue as to the potential source of the problem: they too are relatively low. The manager knows that the key contributor to a sales region's expense base is related to salaries for the sales team. Hence, she suspects that the region may be behind in hiring and thus behind in expenses and forecasted revenue. To confirm her suspicion, she quickly creates a report that shows budgeted versus actual staff numbers for the Eastern region by month for the past two quarters. The report illustrates clearly the problem: A slowdown in hiring in the East has contributed to the drop in the forecast. (See Figure 5-6.)

Drilling down to view the same indicators by state reveals that three states are at the origin of the open headcount problem. The analysis is confirmed by a quick call to the Eastern region's sales manager. Since the report that she created from scratch was not one that already existed, it is referred to as an *ad hoc report*.

One often sees the terms *ad hoc* versus *canned* used to distinguish the prior availability of a certain report, and in some cases the freshness of the data. As the terms suggest, following the canned food analogy, a canned report is often associated with more stale data. This need not always be the case, however, as a user may have the ability to *refresh* or update the contents of a predefined report, thereby making only the structure and not the actual data within the report canned. A more technical term to describe the request for new data is *database query*.

HR Report–Eastern Region

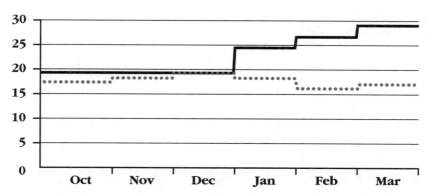

Figure 5-6   Ad Hoc Report of Staff Numbers Info by Region.
Solid line = total head count; dotted line = actual staff.

State of the art business intelligence technology makes such ad hoc queries or ad hoc reports easy for any businessperson to put together. Figure 5-7 illustrates one such user interface for creating queries. The users simply select the business indicators that they wish to view and, without any additional technical knowledge on their part, they are presented with a fully formatted report that displays the selected indicators. The figure also illustrates the indicators selected by the VP of sales for her ad hoc query. By selecting region, month, total headcount, and actual staff she was able to identify quickly the hiring shortcoming in the Eastern region.

What distinguishes state of the art business intelligence technology is that the user is completely insulated from the technical intricacies of the design of the database (table or column names, database access language commands required to retrieve the data, etc.).[3]

---

[3] Users familiar with database technology will note that, depending on the choice of business indicators, the actual database query and source tables may vary. For example, choosing the indicators revenue, region, product will return product revenue by region, while a query which includes revenue, salesperson, quarter will return quarterly revenue by salesperson. While the indicator selected by the user, revenue, is the same from the user's perspective, the actual meaning of the term differs depending on the dimensions which appear on the query. The indicator "revenue" can thus be described as "semantically dynamic" since its meaning (semantics) varies depending on the query. Semantically dynamic query technology, which was invented and patented by Business Objects, is what makes it possible to insulate users from the intricacies of database design. The user simply does not need to know where the data came from as long as it answers his or her question.

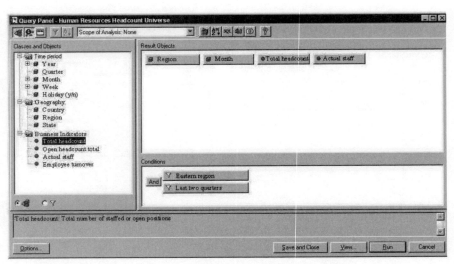

Figure 5-7 Screenshot of Query Panel That Allows a
Businessperson to Easily Formulate an Ad Hoc Database Query
Using Familiar Business Terms. The businessperson simply drags
business terms from the list on the left-hand side of the
screen, drops them inside the boxes on the right, and then
presses the run button. What appears shortly thereafter on
the screen is a fully formatted report (optionally as a table
or a chart) that encompasses this information.

The Marketing Analyst

Next we examine how business intelligence can empower a marketing analyst in the credit card department of a bank who seeks to identify target
prospects for a marketing promotion. His objective is to identify prospects
likely to bring a good return to the promotion. The analyst suspects that
some existing customers may benefit and may be interested in the promotion. He also knows that the cost of acquiring new customers is significantly higher than the cost of selling to the existing customer base. Hence, he
sets out to identify the ideal customer segment for the promotion.

His examination starts with a simple question:

Are my frequent customers also profitable customers?

For his analysis he defines *frequent* customers as those who use their
credit cards at least once a month. Profitable customers are the ones who
bring the best return to the bank, typically the customers who do not pay

their credit card bill instantly, but only after a delay of 30 to 60 days. The reason that customers who pay after a delay of 30 to 60 days are the most *profitable* for the company is that they incur interest and late payment fees. Customers who delay payment beyond 60 days are less profitable because the company then has to incur charges in its effort to collect their overdue payments. Customers who pay their credit card bills immediately are also not the most profitable for the bank, since they do not incur substantial interest or penalty fees. Once again, the business question may be very simple; enabling the analyst to answer it instantaneously, however, requires a sophisticated business intelligence infrastructure.

With specific business criteria on what constitutes a frequent customer and what constitutes a profitable customer, identifying the list of members of each group is simple. In business intelligence technospeak, one refers to *setting a condition* on a parameter (in this case, customer), or introducing a *filter* to a query.

To answer the business question introduced above, the marketing analyst creates a report that displays the overlap between the list of frequent customers and the list of profitable customers. (See Figure 5-8.) This type of analysis, where membership of two or more different groups is examined and compared, is actually very easy to undertake given the right tool, and it is a subset of what is referred to as *set-based analysis*. Sets are the membership lists or groups being analyzed—in this case, the set of frequent customers and the set of profitable customers. In marketing terms, the notion of sets corresponds to the notion of market segments.

The marketing analyst observes that the overlap between frequent and profitable customers is actually small. This indicates that the bank's preferred customers are, in general, not frequent users of their credit cards. For the marketing analyst, this suggests that a promotion to profitable customers in an effort to increase the frequency of their credit card usage would make good sense. One idea for a promotion would be to offer double frequent flyer miles for charges in a given month.

In theory, the analyst could proceed by using the entire list of profitable customers as the target list for a promotion. The problem is, this list is a very large one (over 72,000 customers), and his marketing budget will only allow him to target about 36,000 customers. (He wants to mail the target customers a promotional package that costs $1.25 and his total budget is $45,000.) His next question is thus

Which segment of my profitable customer list
should I focus my marketing promotion on?

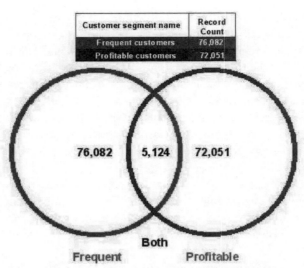

Customer segment name	Record Count
Frequent customers	76,082
Profitable customers	72,051

76,082   5,124   72,051

Both
Frequent   **Profitable**

Figure 5-8   Report Comparing Total Number of Profitable and Frequent Customers. Note the low overlap between profitable and frequent customers.

In other words, which of my profitable customers are most likely to become frequent customers? To answer this question, the analyst decides to examine more closely the customer list to determine what the likely characteristics of a profitable customer are. Do not worry, doing so does not require him to manually go through each and every customer name listed in the customer database. Tools are available that can quickly give him a clear description of the characteristics of the customer list. The tools are also able to identify the factors that distinguish the profitable customer list from the rest of the customer population. Figure 5-9 illustrates the breakdown that the marketing analyst sees.

The technique used here, where patterns within a data set are identified automatically, is referred to as *data mining*.[4] People often think of data mining in the context of *black box* applications that use sophisticated algorithms invisible to the user to make predictions and deliver a recommended approach without explaining why. However, data mining also encompasses extremely useful *descriptive* technology that can enhance an analyst's understanding of his data. It is this descriptive part of data mining that we use here. Figure 5-9 simply describes clearly the properties of the company's customer list, while at the same time identifying (from left to right) the factors

---

[4] In fact, the data mining technique used here is called *decision tree technology*.

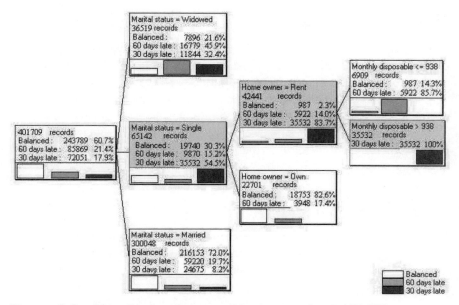

Figure 5-9 Data Mining Report. Of the total of 401,709 customers of the fictitious company in our example, single individuals who rent a home and who have a monthly disposable income over $938 are most likely to pay their credit card bills late.[5]

most important in determining whether a person belongs in the profitable customer list. Visualizing the properties of the customer list in this way can enhance the analyst's understanding of his customer base.

By looking at Figure 5-9, the analyst observes that single customers who rent their homes and have relatively large amounts of disposable income are most likely to belong in the profitable customer category. In an effort to make profitable customers out of those who are less than profitable, the analyst decides to target the marketing promotion to the 35,532 frequent customers

---

[5] To read the chart, start from the "root node" box on the left-hand side: It tells us that there are a total of 401,709 customer records, of which 60.7 percent pay their credit card bills on time and therefore have a balanced account, 21.4 percent are more than 60 days overdue on their bill, and 17.9 percent are 30 days late. Moving to the next set of boxes, we see a breakdown of the customers by marital status (36,519 widowed, 65,142 single, 300,048 married). Since the single customer list had the highest proportion of "30 days late" (profitable) customers, we focused on this list, moving on to look at how that group is subdivided. Repeating this step ultimately lets us traverse the tree-like graph from the left-hand root to the right-hand branches and leaves. The bar charts at the bottom of each box provide a quick visual display of the relative shares of the number of customers with balanced, 30 days', and 60 days' overdue credit card accounts.

who happen to be single, rent their homes, and have high levels of disposable income.[6]

The marketing campaign ends up being a huge success. By targeting his promotional mail package to a very specific portion of 35,000 profitable customers, instead of sending it to 35,000 random profitable customers, he was able to bring in an excellent return on the marketing investment. Past campaigns that focused on random lists of profitable customers, or worse yet, on random lists of customers profitable or not, had failed consistently to achieve a similar incremental increase in the bank's revenue and as high a return on the marketing investment.

The Purchasing Manager

Our third example of questions people ask involves a purchasing manager responsible for negotiating nationwide contracts and rates with his company's suppliers. His question is also simple:

How can I reduce purchasing costs for my company?

One area where he hopes to reduce costs relates to the cost of indirect supplies or services. Indirect supplies are items that do not contribute directly to his company's end product. Examples of indirect supply costs include office supply expenses, telecommunication and computer equipment costs, and facilities costs. Direct supply costs, on the other hand, consist of the costs associated directly with the production of the goods and services that the company sells: automobile parts for a car manufacturer, health care supplies for a hospital, paper supplies for a publisher, and so on.

In their quest to minimize costs, companies have historically focused primarily on direct costs. It is in the context of direct costs that companies have managed their purchases diligently, establishing strategic relationships and securing explicit service agreements and volume discounts with their key suppliers. When it comes to indirect costs, however, companies typically have a weaker record. Few companies have sought to leverage volume discounts for pencil supplies across dozens of offices. It is these indirect costs that the purchasing manager decides to investigate. He believes that the advent of the Internet gives him a unique opportunity, unavailable to past generations of purchasing managers, to reduce indirect supply costs for his company.

---

[6] He obviously limits his marketing campaign to those customers who have expressed interest in and have given his company their permission to contact them with new promotions.

He starts his analysis by looking at the consolidated telephone bill that his company just received via the Internet from its telecommunication service provider. (See Figure 5-10.) The telecom provider offers online billing via a business intelligence *extranet* service. The telecom provider's customers have the option to *subscribe*, at no extra charge, to receive their consolidated and itemized bill online. The telecom provider distributes or *broadcasts* the consolidated reports to its customers once a month.[7] For an extra nominal fee, the telecom provider allows its customers direct access to its data warehouse, thereby enabling them to interactively analyze their telephone charges.

By looking at the October bill, the purchasing manager suspects that the relative share of cellular phone charges seems higher than in past months. To identify opportunities for reducing costs, the purchasing manager creates a report aggregating telephone costs across all of the company's four production facilities in Nashua, New Hampshire; Toledo, Ohio; Austin, Texas; and Reno, Nevada. (See Figure 5-11.) The report shows that telephone costs have been increasing steadily in the course of the current year (January to October). A quick comparison of the rate of increase of telecommunications costs to the rate of increase in personnel indicates that per capita telecom costs have also increased in the past year.

Consolidated monthly telephone service bill - October 2000

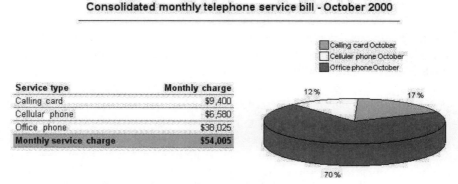

Service type	Monthly charge
Calling card	$9,400
Cellular phone	$6,580
Office phone	$38,025
Monthly service charge	**$54,005**

Calling card October
Cellular phone October
Office phone October

12%   17%

70%

Figure 5-10   Consolidated Monthly Telephone Service Bill Broadcast by a Telecom Provider to Its Customers via a Business Intelligence Extranet.

---

[7] While the term *broadcasting* is typically associated with twentieth century one-way communication technologies such as radio, television, or "push" technology and the Internet, the word was actually first used to describe an ancient agricultural method for planting seeds by spreading them. The technique was deemed to be inefficient during the middle ages as agricultural techniques progressed. (See Mokyr, *Lever of Riches*.)

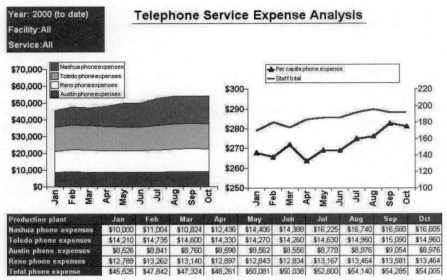

Production plant	Jan	Feb	Mar	Apr	May	Jun	Jul	Aug	Sep	Oct
Nashua phone expenses	$10,000	$11,004	$10,824	$12,436	$14,406	$14,388	$16,225	$16,740	$16,560	$16,605
Toledo phone expenses	$14,210	$14,735	$14,600	$14,330	$14,270	$14,260	$14,630	$14,960	$15,090	$14,960
Austin phone expenses	$8,526	$8,841	$8,760	$8,598	$8,562	$8,556	$8,778	$8,976	$9,054	$8,976
Reno phone expenses	$12,789	$13,262	$13,140	$12,897	$12,843	$12,834	$13,167	$13,464	$13,581	$13,464
Total phone expense	$45,525	$47,842	$47,324	$48,261	$50,081	$50,038	$52,800	$54,140	$54,285	$54,005

Figure 5-11 Report Showing Total Nationwide Telecom Expense by Month and by Division, Side by Side with Staffing Levels and with Calculated per Capita Telecom Expense by Month. The report combines data from the telecom provider's extranet system and from the company's internal HR system.

He then drills down to view the same key indicators (telephone costs, staff levels, per capita telephone costs) by month and by business division. He notices that per capita costs have remained fairly steady for most divisions, but have posted a significant increase month by month in the Nashua production facility. Focusing now on the Nashua plant, he drills down further to break down the phone bill by service type. He quickly notices that the relative mix of services has changed over the past year, with cellular phone charges accounting for an increasingly larger share of the bill. (See Figure 5-12.)

The analyst remembers that the Nashua plant manager recently approved cellular phones for her entire management staff. The report clearly reflects the impact of the new cellular phone policy. Presumably, however, access to cellular phones also contributes to the productivity of the staff, which is why they were approved. The problem is, when the cellular phones were distributed to employees the estimated billing cost was expected to be lower. Other divisions do not show as dramatic an increase. Drilling further to see a breakdown of the cellular phone bill items, he notices a significant contribution from international calls, particularly to the United Kingdom. (See Figure 5-13.)

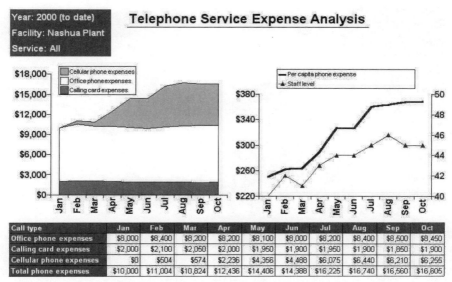

Call type	Jan	Feb	Mar	Apr	May	Jun	Jul	Aug	Sep	Oct
Office phone expenses	$8,000	$8,400	$8,200	$8,200	$8,100	$8,000	$8,200	$8,400	$8,500	$8,450
Calling card expenses	$2,000	$2,100	$2,050	$2,000	$1,950	$1,900	$1,950	$1,900	$1,850	$1,900
Cellular phone expenses	$0	$504	$574	$2,236	$4,356	$4,488	$6,075	$6,440	$6,210	$6,255
Total phone expenses	$10,000	$11,004	$10,824	$12,436	$14,406	$14,388	$16,225	$16,740	$16,560	$16,605

Figure 5-12 Nashua Production Facility Phone Bill by Type of Service and by Month. The report shows the sharp increase in the division's cellular phone bill beginning with the introduction of the service in April. Also visible is the steady increase in the division's per capita phone bill, which is also probably due to the introduction of the cellular phone service.

A call to the regional manager reveals that the production facility recently forged an alliance with key suppliers in the United Kingdom. The calls to the United Kingdom were thus requests for updates on delivery schedules. The alliance with U.K. suppliers is expected to expand to other production divisions. Armed with this important information, the purchasing manager calls his telecom supplier and signs up the company for a special plan that offers discounts for calls to the United Kingdom. By subscribing to this plan the manager expects to save his company several millions of dollars per year. Not only does he save money for the company, he also earns the gratitude of the Nashua plant manager who expects to see savings immediately.

What is interesting about this example is that the telephone billing data that the purchasing manager analyzed was actually data provided by the telecom supplier. One would think that companies can easily aggregate and view divisional costs across the country or even across the world. In many cases, however, as in the case of telephone bills, the supplier may actually be in a much better position to aggregate and report on the customer's service usage.

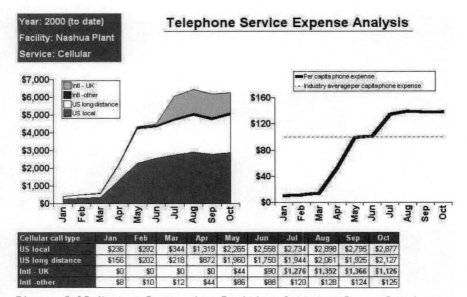

Cellular call type	Jan	Feb	Mar	Apr	May	Jun	Jul	Aug	Sep	Oct
US local	$236	$292	$344	$1,319	$2,265	$2,558	$2,734	$2,898	$2,795	$2,877
US long distance	$156	$202	$218	$872	$1,960	$1,750	$1,944	$2,061	$1,925	$2,127
Intl - UK	$0	$0	$0	$0	$44	$90	$1,276	$1,352	$1,366	$1,126
Intl -other	$8	$10	$12	$44	$86	$88	$120	$128	$124	$125

Figure 5-13 Nashua Production Facility Cellular Phone Service
Bill by Month. The report shows the sharp increase in the
division's cellular phone bill beginning with the introduction
of the service in April. The introduction in itself, however,
does not justify the increase in per capita expense beyond the
industry average (chart at right). As the chart at the left and
the table clearly illustrate, this jump can be attributed to the
sharp increase in calls to the United Kingdom, beginning in
July.[8]

After all, the service provider needs to aggregate the information on a regular basis in order to bill the customer.

The purchasing manager was thus able to access the telecom provider's *extranet* system.[9] The Internet makes delivery of such information much more cost effective than it had been in the past. All the purchasing manager needs is an Internet browser and a login account which ensures *secure* access to his company's information. Using e-business intelligence technology, he can access via the Internet data hosted by the telecom provider. He can then easily combine the external data with internal company data, such total employ-

---

[8] Note that the report also identified automatically the sharp increase in calls to the U.K. and highlighted them, thereby alerting proactively the purchasing manager.

[9] Some suppliers, in fact, hire a third party to host and manage their extranet application. This external hosting service provider is referred to as an ASP (application service provider) or in this case ESP (extranet service provider).

ee numbers, from the internal HR system. Even though he may be accessing data via the Internet, sophisticated *data encryption* and *user authentication* technology available with the business intelligence system ensures that his company's sensitive data is secure and protected as it crosses the Internet.

Companies, such as the telecommunications service provider of our example, who set up extranets for their customers often start with a simple setup where reports (for example, telecom service bills) are distributed or *pushed* to their customers. A fancier term for this automatic distribution of reports is *broadcasting*. Similar in concept to the one-way transmission of radio or television signals, report broadcasting refers to the one-way distribution of reports to a large number of recipients, for example, telecom service customers. This distribution may be based on a predefined schedule (e.g., monthly), or may follow the occurrence of a specific event (e.g., phone charges for an individual exceed a certain threshold amount). In some cases the users themselves specify the reports they wish to receive by *subscribing* to receive these reports. While one-way transmission of reports may suffice as a first step in a customer extranet, sooner or later customers are likely to request interactive access to data similar to the scenario described above, in which billing information was combined with internal HR data.

Data broadcasting is often associated these days with *wireless devices*, such as cellular telephones or personal digital assistants. Following the introduction of formats[10] that enable the incorporation of Internet browsers on these wireless devices, they are expected to play a key role in the proliferation of business intelligence in the coming years. Following the experience with intranets and extranets, however, it is fair to expect that wireless application users will, in turn, also opt for interactive access to data as opposed to one-way broadcasting and receipt of information.

Sources of Data

We have explained how the decision maker can use available data to support decisions, but where does all this data come from? Typically, data is collected and stored in databases. What do the databases look like? The concept of a database plays an essential role in powering the recent massive changes in corporate processes and operations. Behind every software application—in finance, logistics, order entry, manufacturing, design, or engineering—lies a mechanism that, in one shape or another, is for storing data.

---

[10] One such format is the Wireless Application Protocol or WAP supported by many cellular telephone vendors.

Take a typical day (say, Friday) of a businessperson. The day may start with the person finishing up a business trip. As she prepares to leave for the airport, she quickly connects from her hotel room to her company's email system to check for new messages. She then calls for a taxi service to take her to the airport and checks out from the hotel using the automatic checkout service available via the room's TV set. At the airport she checks in for her flight, requests a seat change for her flight, and secures her desired aisle seat 16B (lots of leg room). As she awaits her flight, she notices an Internet kiosk in the airport departure gate area. She quickly connects to the network and checks the status of the market and of her investment portfolio and also the weather forecast for the weekend. She boards the plane and uses her headset to listen in on the conversation between the pilot and ground control (channel 9 on her audio selection). As her plane takes off, her eight-year-old son, who anxiously awaits her at home, monitors in real time the progress of her flight via the Internet. While on board the airplane, she is thinking of her son; on the shopping catalog available in front of her seat she notices a new electronic gadget that she knows her son will love. Using the airplane's phone and her credit card, she orders the item and requests next-day delivery. She is now ready for what promises to be a fun and sunny weekend.

Nothing unusual about the story above; what may not be obvious at first glance, however, is that each and every step described above involves a database. Behind the email system sits a database that manages all the messages. Behind the taxi reservation service sits a database that manages the taxi schedules. Behind the hotel checkout system sits another database. The airport check-in process, Internet stock and weather reports, air traffic control and monitoring systems, catalog shopping, and credit card transaction management system also involve powerful databases.

A database is essentially a place to store data. A database management system is the sophisticated mechanism that manages the update, storage, retrieval, and archiving of the data. The storage mechanism ultimately determines the accessibility of the information, and hence the choice of database technology is a critical component of a business intelligence strategy. Most of us maintain some kind of database. Examples may range from a paper-based address book (it boots instantly and does not require a battery) to a *personal digital assistant* (PDA) such as a Palm Pilot, or a spreadsheet.

While adequate for personal use, spreadsheet technology cannot adequately address the information storage needs of large corporations, which need to collect and store massive quantities of information. Moreover, modern companies need to enable their employees, customers, and partners to update and access this information concurrently. On a typical day, a company's set of databases may need to incorporate instantly millions of trans-actions and thousands of requests for updated information. While the users modify the data in real time, the database needs to maintain at any point in time an accurate snapshot of the state of the company.

Let us look at the example of our interaction with our bank via automated teller machines, or ATM (also known as cash dispensers in some countries). Every hour thousands of the bank's customers withdraw, deposit, or simply transfer funds between their accounts. With every transaction an individual makes, his or her credit balance changes. The ATMs and behind them the bank's database system can at any instant update each and every customer on the exact status of their account balances. The database that processes the transactions behind an ATM system and behind every operational system is often referred to as an *online transaction processing* or OLTP system. OLTP systems are set up to concurrently process large numbers of short transactions: an update to a bank account, a change in inventory status, a customer order or shipment, an update in a monitored patient's health condition. The systems are designed to protect the integrity (or atomicity) of concurrent transactions so that a bank account's exact balance, a product's inventory level, and the status of a customer's order are recorded accurately.[11]

An OLTP system thus records transactions. It is ideal for answering questions such as:

What is my account balance right now?

How many units of this SKU are currently in stock in my warehouse?

What is the status of the shipment I am expecting?

An OLTP system is typically not designed to answer quickly questions such as:

How much did I spend with my credit card on airline tickets this year versus the same period last year?

What was the average inventory level for this SKU each month last year?

---

[11] OLTP database textbooks often summarize the characteristics of transactions with the acronym ACID (for atomicity, consistency, isolation, and durability). Atomicity refers to the fact that a transaction has to complete in its integrity and cannot be broken up into smaller components. Consistency means that all parties who participate in a transaction have a consistent view. Isolation means that one transaction does not interfere with another. Durability means that a transaction can only be undone when all parties involved accept such a change.

*Will my current inventory suffice to meet
forecasted demand for this item?*

Who are my frequent customers?

The reason a database designed for OLTP has trouble addressing quickly these questions is because each answer requires scanning thousands if not millions of historical transactions, aggregating data, and making comparisons between different sets of aggregated information.[12] In many cases the information required resides in several separate operational databases and needs to be consolidated. In fact, studies show that a significant share of corporate information technology (IT) budgets is dedicated to this consolidation or integration of data from different parts of a company.

The most popular OLTP database systems in the market today employ what is known as *relational database management system* (RDBMS) technology. RDBMS systems were popularized in the 1980s as an alternative to prior OLTP database technologies, such as hierarchical and network database systems that typically ran on legacy systems. The key innovation behind RDBMS systems was their ability, at least in theory,[13] to separate OLTP database design from the design of the applications that ultimately accessed the database. RDBMS systems could be accessed via an industry standard query language, known by its acronym SQL (which stands for *structured query language* and is pronounced like "sequel"). This gave organizations more flexibility vis-a-vis the potential use of the database system. RDBMS systems also came with a rigorous and formal mathematical model that facilitated database design. Oracle, IBM, Microsoft, Sybase, and Informix are the leading OLTP relational database vendors today.

A Separate Database for Business Intelligence

The best way for an organization and database system to respond to inquiries such as those discussed earlier is by setting up in advance a database environment dedicated to business intelligence. This type of environment delivers quick answers to questions that relate to historical information and to data consolidated across multiple company divisions. Such systems

---

[12] For a comparison between OLTP and decision support systems, see introductory chapters in Inmon or Kimball.

[13] In practice, the applications accessing the RDBMS do indeed influence the design of the database and in particular the physical distribution of the data and the design of indexes which speed up data access.

have indeed been available in legacy environments for over 30 years, yet they were popularized in the 1990s under the old term of *data warehouse* and under the newer buzzword *data mart*.[14]

If you recall the three examples discussed previously, you will notice that answering the business questions posed by the sales VP, the marketing analyst, and the purchasing manager each required the consolidation and aggregation of information from different parts of the company or from outside the company.

The sales VP, for example, was looking at sales forecasts, bookings, operational expenses, staffing, and open headcount status, for each of the company's operating divisions. Each of these indicators may need to be retrieved from a different system: forecasts from the spreadsheets submitted by the regional sales managers each week,[15] bookings from the company's order-entry system, operational expenses from the company's finance application, and open headcount from the company's human resources management software. In larger organizations, particularly those born of mergers and acquisitions of previously independent entities, each business division may employ different operational systems, so data may need to be consolidated from an even larger number of distributed, disparate, heterogeneous, and incompatible systems.

If you are still unclear as to why business intelligence data should be separated from transactional data, consider the following analogy: one could think of an OLTP system as a large water reservoir that is replenished by rainwater. (See Figure 5-14.) The reservoir refills thanks to millions of raindrops falling on the surface of the reservoir. The larger the reservoir surface, the more water collected. In our analogy, each raindrop corresponds to a transaction, such as the ATM transaction for a bank. While the large surface area is ideal for the accumulation of water, it is not necessarily handy or relevant for the consumption of the water.

For well over two millennia, societies have constructed entire distribution systems to transfer water from the reservoir to our glass (or cup). This is done via aqueducts or more recently pipes connected to the reservoir, via water processing and treatment plans, intermediate storage tanks in our neighborhood, and potentially via storage tanks in our own home. Finally, before reaching our glass, the water may also be stored temporarily in the refrigerator in our home.

---

[14] Inmon describes data warehouse content as "subject oriented, integrated, nonvolatile, and time variant."

[15] In the presence of a sales force automation system from vendors such as Siebel Systems and PeopleSoft, this information may already be consolidated.

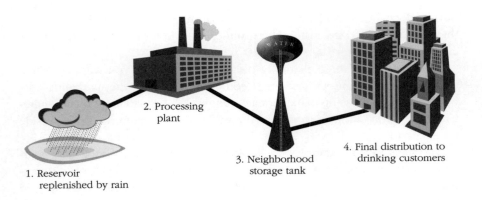

2. Processing
   plant

3. Neighborhood
   storage tank

4. Final distribution to
   drinking customers

1. Reservoir
   replenished by rain

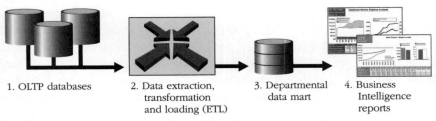

1. OLTP databases   2. Data extraction,   3. Departmental   4. Business
                            transformation   data mart   Intelligence
                            and loading (ETL)   reports

Figure 5-14   Analogy between Data and Water Distribution
Systems. One can think of the raindrops as transactions, the
reservoir as the OLTP system, and the water distribution
system with intermediate storage tanks as the business
intelligence system.

If we think of the reservoir as the OLTP system (and the raindrops as the transactions), the system of pipes, local storage tanks, and the water tap in our kitchen corresponds to the components of the business intelligence system. To fill a glass of water, we would simply run water from the tap; we would not seek to accumulate droplets off the surface of a reservoir. Equivalently, an OLTP system is designed to manage short bursts of transactional activity (the raindrops); it is not designed to respond to complex queries (the glass or pitcher of water).

In our analogy, the water reservoir corresponds to the OLTP system, the water distribution and processing plant corresponds to the *data extraction, transformation, and loading* (ETL) process that needs to take place before the data is consolidated in the data warehouse or data mart, and the neighborhood water storage tank corresponds to the data warehouse or data mart. The glass of water corresponds to a user's database query, while a pitcher of water corresponds to the concept of running several queries as a *batch process*—say, on a regular schedule after hours, to offload interaction with the database.

Different schools of thought exist in the technical community regarding the best way to make data available for business intelligence. One school of thought advocates the design of a single large decision support database, which consolidates data across an entire enterprise. Such a system is known as an *enterprise data warehouse*. Another school of thought proposes the modular design of departmental databases or *data marts*. Whatever the school of thought and design, all experts seem to agree on one thing: the "build it and they will come" philosophy does not apply to decision support databases. The scope of the warehouse or data mart—in other words, the types of questions it will be designed to address—needs to be considered before the database system is put together. End user interviews play a critical role in this process.

Business Intelligence Database Technologies

When introducing online transaction processing (OLTP) databases, we noted that relational database management systems (RDBMS) have been the dominant choice in recent years for such applications. RDBMS systems (and SQL) have also made great strides in the 1990s, becoming the database technology of choice for decision support systems. Many of the same companies—Oracle, IBM, Microsoft, Sybase, Informix—are the protagonist vendors in this space, with NCR also a prominent player.

In parallel with the growth of RDBMS systems geared for decision support, another type of database technology has also emerged in decision support systems. These databases are known as *multidimensional databases* (MDDBs) or *OLAP databases*. OLAP databases were designed from the ground up to facilitate highly interactive multidimensional analysis. Given its emphasis on data analysis, this technology has been popular with highly skilled financial analysts. Unlike relational databases, which store data in tables and rows (much like a collection of multiple spreadsheets), OLAP databases store data in terms of cubes (or, more precisely, *hypercubes* for cases where more than three dimensions are involved). Storing data as cubes makes it easier for an analyst to navigate through data and view information from different perspectives (as previously described in our examples).

As the decision support features and performance of relational databases steadily improved in the 1990s, the difference in analytical speed offered by OLAP databases diminished. As we enter the third millennium a happy balance seems to have been established between relational and OLAP databases: all major relational database vendors offer in one way or another OLAP database extensions. Consequently, a head-on confrontation between RDBMS and OLAP technology was avoided with the relational vendors embracing and, to some extent subsuming OLAP databases. For users, all this means is that one way or another, a multidimensional view of their data will be available to them, regardless of the choice of underlying database technology, relational or OLAP.

Business Intelligence Portals: Entry Point to the Business Intelligence System

We close the discussion on business intelligence technology with a quick mention of a relatively newer member of the business intelligence (BI) buzzword family: *BI portals*.

In the examples discussed previously, we illustrated different views of corporate information, typically in the context of reports. In addition to reports, however, analyzed data may also appear in spreadsheets or word processing files. The accumulation of such reports, spreadsheets, and text files has led to the need to store, categorize, search, and quickly retrieve such files. The report itself has become as critical an element of the business intelligence system as the raw data stored in the company's databases. One could, in fact, argue that reports are even more valuable than the raw data, because they encompass the business intelligence of the individual who created the report. Much as a newspaper editor can give a different emphasis and context to a news item by selecting its placement on a page, a report creator can highlight the business value of a data set by selecting the position and format of the data on the report.

The Internet technology that has emerged to facilitate the presentation, navigation, and searching of business reports is known as *business intelligence portals*. As their name suggests, BI portals focus on a company's BI resources and can be integrated with *enterprise information portals*. Many companies are creating such enterprise information portals to give their employees a common and consistent entry point to corporate resources and the Internet.

Information
Democracies

6

Enterprise Business Intelligence

Technology is not the biggest challenge anymore.
The challenge is to use the information in an intelligent way.
Koen Vermeulen
Director, IT Business Analysis
Belgacom

Think globally, act locally. This bumper-sticker phrase popular with environmentalists argues that the actions people take at the local level to improve environmental quality have a cumulative effect on the environment as a whole. It supposes that while it is worthwhile to be concerned with pollution in Russia, if you happen to live in St. Louis, your hand wringing over the degradation of the Russian environment has little effect. Your efforts are better spent agitating against state and local governments and businesses for tighter controls on industrial discharges into the Mississippi River.

This principle applies to enterprise business intelligence, as well. Attention to data and information problems at local departmental levels of a company is the first step to enhancing the intelligence quotient of the company as a whole. Incremental deployments of systems in individual departments provide a sound roadmap and a checklist of do's and don'ts, as an organization proceeds toward a broader goal of building business intelligence for the entire enterprise. For global companies, the challenge is twofold—deploy not only among different departments, but also among offices around the world. Successful incremental deployments provide a critical mass from which broader, interconnected, enterprisewide deployments may be launched.

- *The challenge:* bringing together a network of data and information silos and technologies in multiple departments and geographic locations into an overarching system for data access, sharing, and analysis, as well as smarter, faster decision making—among hundreds or thousands of employees in a company over the Web.

- *The solution:* Escalating business intelligence to the enterprise level. Enterprise business intelligence may be likened to a seamless informational fabric that builds on the successes of departmental deployments. The linking of these smaller systems into a greater whole then builds new degrees of value for every department, at many levels of seniority and authority, and the organization itself.

Andrew Clyne, vice president of systems development at MasterCard International in St. Louis, Missouri, phrases it well: "The approach in the past has been to go business area by business area to meet everyone's needs. Then you take a step back and, yes, you've met everyone's needs, but now you need to do it in a way that brings synergies to business processes, and new efficiencies across business areas."

In Chapter 3, we built a model to examine the *Value of Information.* (See Figure 3-1.) The model shows that the value of information increases exponentially with the level of its use throughout the enterprise. Once it is mastered within a department, information increases dramatically in value as other departments discover synergies by cross-sharing the data. As more and more departments come online and share more information with each other, the value increases. Once everyone is empowered with the right information at the right time, then the corporation reaches an optimal agility.

In this chapter, we will first examine how companies can make better and faster decisions by having better intelligence on their business at all levels of the organization. We will then look at the direct bottom-line impact of business intelligence, as companies are able to use their information better, navigating upward on the *information value curve.* We will then develop strategies and recommendations on how to implement business intelligence throughout the enterprise.

Making Better Faster Decisions

One Big Decision versus a Thousand Little Ones

Companies make basically two kinds of decisions: the big strategic decisions made by the very few executives and the myriad of little decisions made by all the employees on a daily basis. When corporations look at their own decision-making processes, they tend to examine how the big decisions are being made: How did we go about deciding to acquire that company, or to invest in that brand new activity, or to divest that business? Although many mistakes are made in these large decisions, they usually are made carefully: a lot of information is gathered, deep analysis is conducted, and options are carefully reviewed. Because of the strategic nature of these decisions and the fact that they are made by the executives with a great many resources at their disposal, the companies usually invest what is needed to gather the intelligence needed. Surveys are outsourced and research is done by a staff of analysts.

A company's performance, however, is heavily determined by all the smaller decisions being made every day by all the other members of the company. A salesperson deciding whether to give a marginally profitable customer a discount, a manufacturing manager deciding whether to start producing a higher-quality part at a greater cost that might better satisfy customers, a marketing specialist deciding to launch another direct mail campaign, or a purchasing manager deciding whether to order additional materials: all these decisions bear directly on business success. These decisions are not made by executives; each of them in and of itself is somewhat tactical and does not fundamentally affect the course of the business. As a whole, though, they are highly strategic as they result in the actual execution of the company's strategy. However, these operational decisions made by line managers and the staff are the ones that tend to suffer the most. The people making them usually do not have the resources to demand the information needed; they have little time, no staff analysts, and a long list of quarterly objectives to attain. As a consequence, these decisions are rarely based on facts, but mostly on experience, accumulated knowledge, and rules of thumb.

It takes years to develop experience, knowledge, and rules of thumb. Some workers never acquire them. Those who do may still fall prey to decision traps or biases in judgment. Improving the quality of everyday business decisions has a direct impact on costs and revenue. For instance, giving a customer a discount may or may not help the bottom line, depending on the profitability of the client over the duration of the relationship. To improve the quality of decisions, a manager can:

Option: Do all the critical tasks him- or herself
Result: This would lead to burnout, bottlenecks, and opportunity costs of not doing more strategic work

Option: Hire additional skilled staff
Result: This would result in an unrealistically large cost increase

Option: Attempt to define a single policy that would cover for all possible decisions

Result: This leads to decisions that do not meet with the rapidly changing needs of the business

Option: Give existing staff the means to make better decisions

Result: This option creates an agile enterprise and is the most cost-effective solution

Better Decisions

What is a good decision? It is one that helps the corporation move closer to its goal, be it greater profitability, lower costs, shortening distribution times, increasing shareholder value, or having a certain percentage of customers respond positively to a direct mail campaign. A good decision is also one that is made on time. Making the right decision too late is like making the wrong decision. How does an employee know if the decision he or she is about to make will help the enterprise meet its objectives? The employee needs data pertaining to the decision to be made and strategic information to have the full business context, and the employee needs to have those virtually instantly.

The Vision.   An account manager, on the way to visiting a client, looks up past proposals, as well as the client's complete history: ordering, payments, delivery, support, and marketing through her company's enterprise business intelligence system. She has at her fingertips mission-critical information that has been made available through her company's vision and initiative to deploy an enterprise business intelligence system to expand knowledge access among its employees.

At a glance, the account manager can tell that the client's ordering volumes have dropped lately. A few queries later, she discerns that the client has a support issue with a given product. The account manager places a call to the support department, and learns that a defective part will be replaced within 24 hours. In addition, the marketing records show that the client recently attended a user conference and expressed interest in the new product line. The account manager is now fully prepared for a constructive sales call. She masters all aspects of her client's relationship with her firm, understands the client's issues, and can confidently address new sales opportunities.

The Problem
Vast Quantities of Data...   As businesses increase their reliance on enterprise systems, they are rapidly accumulating vast amounts of data in organizations. Every interaction between departments or with the outside world is entered into an information system of some sort. Historical information on past transactions is archived for future access. External information on markets is also supplied digitally.

...Yet Very Few Answers.   With all this data available, it may seem surprising how difficult it is for managers to get a clear picture of business fundamentals, such as inventory levels, orders in the pipeline, or client history. In most companies, it takes the account manager hours or days to get answers to questions.

- The client's ordering and payment records are kept in the accounting system.

- The installation and support information is stored in the customer service database. Contact management software tracks the proposals and sales call history.

- The marketing contact history is kept by marketing.

These systems constitute a multitude of data silos that are unintegrated. They usually do not speak the same language, and there is no simple way for a nontechnical user to get answers quickly.

As a result, the information has to be requested from different departments, which then have to dedicate staff to pulling together reports. Alternatively, a special request has to be made to the IT department to run a complex query on the company's databases. Responses can take weeks, by which time the information may already be outdated.

The Solution.   To improve decision making within the user base, five steps need to be taken:

1. Give employees the big picture.

2. Close the loop.

3. Unlock the information.

4. Give people the tools they need.

5. Encourage users to find root causes of trends.

Give Employees the Big Picture.   Employees are held accountable for making the right decisions. However, in many cases, they miss the big picture, lacking the strategic goals or not understanding the overall business context in which operational decisions need to be made. To use the example in Chapter 4, too often the employee feels like that mason placing stones side by side and not understanding that he or she is in fact part of a team building a cathedral. Directions—like gaining market share versus optimizing profitability or ensuring total quality versus time to market—will make an important difference in how the employee sees a particular choice he or she has to make. It is essential that management reinforce communication on corporate goals of the company, so that the everyday decisions are made in the right business context.

Let us take an example of a bad decision made because of the lack of high-level business context. A company is trying to increase profits through an intelligent segmentation of its customer base. The segmentation will allow it to identify the key loyal customers, so that the company can focus on and invest in this select list of clients. The full picture developed by the executive team has not been fully explained to the lower ranks. The only thing the staff knows is that the company is trying to improve customer satisfaction. In one of the branches, a customer has recently complained about a service charge. It happens that this customer has not been a particularly profitable one, but the branch does not have that information either. In response to these complaints, and because he is under the impression that customer satisfaction is the number one goal, the branch manager establishes a rule of thumb to wave service charges under $25 when someone complains. As a result, an unprofitable customer got a $20 charge waved. A little later, a top profit customer complained about a $30 charge, but her charge was not waved, having exceeded the $25 rule. Unhappy with the service, the customer closed her account and moved on, taking $1,250 in annual profit with her. In the context of the information he had, the branch manager did not make a bad decision, but in the high-level context which was not shared with him, the decision resulted in a poor outcome.

It is therefore fundamental to constantly communicate the high-level goals of an organization, be it a department, a division, or the whole enterprise. CEO speeches, kick-off meetings (where goals are explained), intranets with clear reminders of the company strategy and the ways to implement it—these are all important communication vehicles. The goals must have tangible targets, and metrics must be developed and tracked. The key performance indicators serve as metricized communicators of what the goals mean. For instance, a car dealership had as a goal to "delight our customers." This goal became meaningful to the employees when it was translated into tangible targets:

- To increase average satisfaction rating from 4.2 to 4.4 for people who buy cars in our dealership

- To provide one-day service for minor repairs in at least 85 percent of all cases

Close the Loop.   Increasingly, managers' incentive plans are based on quantifiable objectives, such as profitability, percentage of on-time deliveries, and proportion of satisfied customers.. However, managers often have limited ways of knowing whether they are progressing toward their objectives. At the end of the year, they receive their bonus, and they are told how well they did. They may be pleased or disappointed, but they have little way of predicting the impact of their actions on corporate welfare.

Management by objective only works if the employee has a way to monitor his own progress in reaching his objectives. Business intelligence gives each user the means to see how well they are doing vis-à-vis these objectives and how a given action will impact the attainment of a given goal. Complex incentive plans may not be as necessary if workers can see which of their actions improve or hurt their performance.

At Penske Logistics, drivers have incentives attached to improving their driving performance and their cost-effectiveness in such things as miles per gallon or wear and tear. Penske's e-business intelligence system tracks these metrics, which are tabulated for drivers after they finish a shift. At first the drivers were not supportive of an automated system that tracked their driving performance. However, they soon became enthusiastic supporters of the system, as great incentives and reward were tied to meeting performance goals. Now, the drivers view it as a core system that can be used to win great incentives, as well as to help improve their skills and value as operators of large trucks.

Unlock the Information.   A company's various information systems may be successful at accomplishing their specific tasks and streamlining automating processes, but they are generally not designed to provide information to end users. With enterprise business intelligence systems, companies can unlock the information by giving authorized users a single point of access to data in diverse systems. Wherever the data resides—whether it is stored in operational systems, data warehouses, data marts, and/or packaged applications—users must be able to get answers to questions quickly and drill deep down into the information to understand what will help them achieve their goals without having to master a technical knowledge of the underlying data structures.

Eli Lilly

In only a few years, pharmaceutical manufacturer Eli Lilly has grown its enterprise business intelligence system to some 6000 end users in multiple departments, unlocking information and accelerating decision making in the process. "We use business intelligence in just about every aspect—human resources, legal, regulatory, sales, marketing, finance, project management, IT, manufacturing, and medical research," says Brent Houk, senior systems analyst. "It helps us in our goal to reduce the cycle time in bringing products to market. Anytime we can speed up the process, that is money in the bank. It makes our processes more efficient and makes our users more empowered. They can access the data without having to go through the IT department to get it."

Lilly has found the flexibility in enterprise business intelligence to go beyond sales, marketing, and financial analysis into a less conventional application: analyzing variables in its pharmaceuticals manufacturing processes for quality control and more efficient production. Lilly's Tippecanoe Laboratories in Lafayette, Indiana, uses enterprise business intelligence atop a data warehouse to analyze factors that contribute to drug manufacturing, such as temperature, airflow, pH, back pressure, and oxygen uptake. Chemical engineers are able to perform analysis on such variables, generate reports, and distribute them over an intranet.

Managers and colleagues then have an easy means of tracking quality control and are able to spot problem areas practically as soon as they arise, rather than examining a paper report several weeks later. They are able to spot areas of misdirected or wasted resources to improve process efficiency and overall yield. The time savings and enhanced product quality amount to significant cost savings and higher revenues for Lilly.

Lessons Learned

1. Get immediate benefits by starting to build business intelligence in the most data-driven divisions (sales, marketing, finance).

2. In a second step, unlock the information in additional business areas.

Ben & Jerry's

Ben & Jerry's enterprise business intelligence system allows the ice cream maker's sales, finance, purchasing, and quality assurance people to access, analyze, and share information on consumer response to products, promotional activities, diverse supplier usage, and much more. The Vermont company tracks more than 12,500 consumer contacts with an enterprise business intelligence system on such issues as which type of milk consumers prefer and what is the ideal number of chunks in Chunky Monkey or cherries in Cherry Garcia. By using business intelligence to track and analyze consumers' stated preferences, Ben & Jerry's is able to modify its products to suit consumer demand. The real benefit comes from the fact that questions do not have to be determined in advance: Users can come up with new requests everyday and get answers right away by easily interacting with the data.

An example of an initially unplanned activity is the company's use of the business intelligence for analysis of customer feedback on which charities should benefit from Ben & Jerry's policy of donating a portion of revenues to socially conscious causes. The system also helps monitor compliance of its suppliers with the company's code of social ethics. The company uses business intelligence to support its supplier diversity program, designed to ensure that the supplier base reflects the overall population mix. Indeed, Ben & Jerry's is now able to track spending by plant sites and by its 80 suppliers to gauge compliance with the social diversity goal.

Another application enables the sales department to track 2000 annual promotional events. "My department now creates custom reports with several fields that help us track distributors and chains that sell our ice cream," says Susan Bittermann, Ben & Jerry's sales budget analyst. "With this information, we can determine if we are staying within budget, view how well the products are selling in different regions and how a certain chain or supermarket is performing." Unlocking the information to users who previously had limited access to it made the ice cream company much more agile than it was before.

Lessons Learned

1. Unlocking the data enables users to answer any kind of question from customers fast and easily, enhancing customer service.

2. Unlocking the data across the organization enables unplanned uses of information.

Give People the Tools They Need.   One key to better decision making is to give users the tools that they will feel comfortable using. Not everyone has the same needs nor the same ability to deal with information. Some users will be satisfied with standard reports, updated on a regular basis, such as current inventory reports, sales per channel, or customer status reports. Of Lilly's 6000 users, Houk estimates that two-thirds rely mostly on reusable, prepackaged reports that the IT department has developed and deployed.

However, answers can lead to new questions. Some users will want dynamic access to information. The information that a user finds in a report will trigger more questions, some of which will not be answered in any prepackaged report.

While users may spend 80 percent of their time accessing standard or personalized reports, you will find that for 20 percent of their tasks they need to go "off road" and obtain additional information not available in the original report. An enterprise business intelligence system that lets users autonomously make ad hoc requests for information to corporate data sources addresses this need and avoids frustration and related report backlog for the IT team.

In addition, experience shows that the needs of business users tend to evolve over time, as in a "conveyor belt" effect. As soon as a user experiments with one set of features and feels comfortable with it, he or she wants to achieve even more functionality. As they move to the next step, the same happens and they want to move up again. For instance, users who can only retrieve static reports may want to be able to refresh these reports with new data. Once they are familiar with that, they may want to perform basic analysis functions on the data they retrieve. At a later stage, they may want to create brand new queries and build their own reports.

Encourage Users to Find Root Causes of Trends.   If one division is doing better or worse than others, you want to identify the root cause and either generalize a best practice or fix the problem. Was it better/worse management? A regional market trend? A different sales strategy? Finding root causes requires in-depth analysis of the many factors that contribute to success or failure. Quite often, managers ask a question and then do not go beyond the first answer. It may be because the managers do not exercise enough investigative skills, but it is also often because getting to the next level is not easy to do. Actions taken based on a first level of answer may not be the right ones, because they do not affect the root cause.

With enterprise business intelligence, you can find root causes both to problems and to best practices, by repeatedly asking the question, "Why? Why? Why?" The process is initiated by analyzing first a global report, say of sales per quarter. Every answer is followed by a new question, and users can drill deep down into a report to get to fundamental causes.

Once users have a clear understanding of root causes, they can take effective action. (See Figure 6-1.) For example, a clothing chain discovered, through the use of enterprise business intelligence, that its pricing policy during sales promotions was not optimal. By analyzing its data, the company was able to readjust its prices dynamically based on demand price elasticity. As a result, it has reduced its stock-out periods, optimized the management of inventory, and improved its key performance indicators: working capital requirement, sales, and margin.

Faster Decisions

In a changing economy that places a premium on speed of execution, it is critical to reduce the decision-making times. More generally, the time needs to be reduced between a question and the action that needs to be taken. Decision cycles are an important concept, because in the end an organization's agility is a direct function of how fast that organization can make decisions in response to changing market conditions. In that context, the right information is valuable only if it reaches the user at the right time. Experience shows that decisions have to be made in a time window: making an investment, selling off an asset, or launching a marketing campaign are only possible at certain times. After that, the decision has been made by default as the opportunity no longer exists. Consequently, the value of

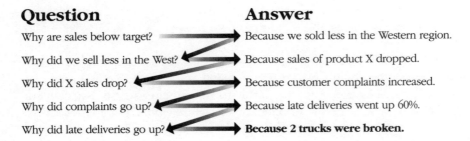

Question	Answer
Why are sales below target?	Because we sold less in the Western region.
Why did we sell less in the West?	Because sales of product X dropped.
Why did X sales drop?	Because customer complaints increased.
Why did complaints go up?	Because late deliveries went up 60%.
Why did late deliveries go up?	**Because 2 trucks were broken.**

Intelligence: Increase in late deliveries due to broken trucks is the root cause of below target sales.

Action: Fix the truck maintenance issue.

Figure 6-1   Root Cause Analysis.

information is highly correlated to the time when the related decision has to be made or the action has to be taken. When we consider all the poor business decisions we make, most of the time, it comes down to "I did not have all the information, or I got it too late." See Figure 6-2, which shows the correlation between the value of information and the time of decision. It does not mean that the underlying data is no longer valuable and should be trashed. It means that in the context of a particular issue, the information related to that issue is no longer of any value after the decision point.

Strategies for reducing decision time include:

- Spending less time on information gathering and more on decision making

- Using push technologies to be immediately alerted to events.

Changing the Time Mix of Information Gathering versus Decision Making

You can break the time required to make a decision into two distinct phases: an information-gathering phase and a decision-making phase. Because we are so accustomed to poor information access, people have started to blur these two distinct phases. They might think they are working on making a decision on the correct level of investment in a new product line, when in fact, what they are spending their time and energy on is gathering informa-

Value

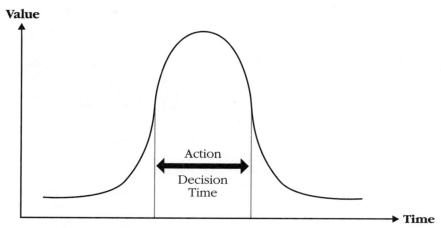

Action

Decision
Time

Time

Figure 6-2   The Value of Information Is Correlated to the Time
of Decision.

tion: calling people in IT for different reports on historical sales, churning through spreadsheets to analyze forecasts, and perhaps going through some old paper reports as well. In fact, we think that about 80 percent of the time people spend on making a decision is actually spent on gathering information.

What is especially dangerous about this situation is that organizations have deadlines for decisions that people do not like to change. As a result, what happens is that people spend most of their time gathering information, with the result that the time and effort actually put into making the decision (e.g., analyzing alternatives, weighing pros and cons) is relatively low. Businesspeople end up burning their available time on information gathering, and then making hasty decisions at the end of the cycle in order to meet the deadline.

What is desired, of course, is to not just to make decisions faster, but to make better decisions faster. In Figure 6-3, this means we wish to compress the overall time required to make the decision, but in doing so, increase as much as possible the time spent on truly making the decision instead of on information gathering. Using e-business intelligence, you can benefit from a massive decrease in the time it takes to gather information. Building a data warehouse, for example, can result in a huge economy of scale in information-gathering time, and allows businesspeople to spend time working on what adds the most value—making the best possible decision.

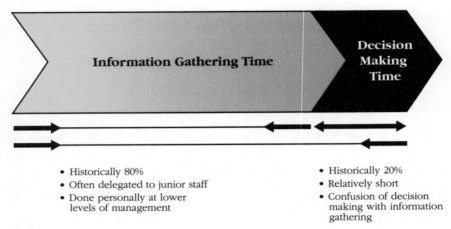

- Historically 80%
- Often delegated to junior staff
- Done personally at lower levels of management

- Historically 20%
- Relatively short
- Confusion of decision making with information gathering

Figure 6-3   Decision Cycle Time.

Using Proactive Intelligence

As we have seen, giving decision-makers access to information when they are planning a decision is critical: it enables them to make informed choices based on facts and not on gut feeling or anecdotes. Even this, however, may not be enough. Decisions or actions may not always be planned in advance. Actions may need to be taken when extraordinary events take place: a shortage of parts in inventory, a breakdown in the network supporting the ecommerce site, and so forth. An intelligent business must have the capabilities of alerting the business managers when these kinds of events happen. Alerts on events are not a new concept, although they usually are not spread out to a broad range of people, because they have generally been costly to implement.

What business intelligence can provide is the generalization of these techniques throughout an enterprise: allowing users to subscribe to alerts, or define the exception rules that they want to be notified on. When the event happens in the data warehouse, a notification is broadcast to the user via different kinds of devices, including email, pagers, and cell phones. This is called *proactive intelligence*. Instead of a businessperson seeking data to make a decision, the event in the data triggers the user to make a decision or take action.

Chase Manhattan, the U.S. bank, has successfully enhanced its speed of execution, implementing a business intelligence system allowing users to get to the data themselves. Using e-business intelligence allowed Chase to respond quickly to an unplanned event.

Chase Manhattan and the Malaysian Currency Crisis

During the Malaysian currency crisis in 1998, the rapid depreciation of that country's monetary system set off the collapse of its stock market and asset prices. As a result, many financial institutions in the United States found themselves scrambling for information about their holdings and investments in the volatile region—particularly since the Federal Reserve required that these institutions report their level of exposure.

However, Chase Manhattan Global Investment Bank, a division of Chase Manhattan Corp., felt that it was able to respond faster than its competition. Having implemented a business intelligence suite earlier in the year, the bank was prepared to deliver highly detailed reports, breaking out the different levels of risk to the Fed, as well as to its own users, at the height of the disaster.

Because it had its systems in place, Chase Manhattan was ready to respond instantly to an unplanned event.

Controlling the Company's Course: Balancing the Corporate Scorecard

As we discussed previously, it is increasingly important for the enterprise to enable managers and employees to have access to information in order to improve everyday decisions. At the executive level, it is also necessary to use these new techniques to control the course of the company. These techniques are important enablers for different kinds of management practices: Activity Based Management (ABM), Economic Value Added (EVA), or Balanced Scorecards.

A number of companies are now adopting the Balanced Scorecard methodology to control the course of their strategy. The Balanced Scorecard is a business performance measurement system introduced by Robert Kaplan and David Norton in 1992. In their research, Kaplan and Norton advocate for measuring at the highest levels of the organization a number of key performance indicators that go beyond the traditional financial measures of revenue and profitability. Traditionally, companies have had an "unbalanced" view of their performance as they usually have only measured financial performance. As

Kaplan and Norton explain, "The Balanced Scorecard retains traditional financial measures. But financial measures tell the story of past events, an adequate
story for industrial age companies for which investments in long-term capabilities and customer relationships were not critical for success. These financial measures are inadequate, however, for guiding and evaluating the journey
that information age companies must make to create future value through
investment in customers, suppliers, employees, processes, technology, and
innovation."

The Balanced Scorecard suggests that an organization be viewed from
four perspectives: learning and growth, business processes, customers, and
financials. (See Figure 6-4.) It advocates that organizations not only define
specific goals in these four areas but also develop metrics, collect data, and
analyze it relative to each perspective. The traditional financial measures are
important but are mostly lagging metrics, i.e. they tend to measure the past.
However, metrics assessing the learning and growth capabilities of an organization have much more predictive value. The implementation calls for building a hierarchy of objectives and giving constant status. As an example in a
transportation company, each truck driver could know what he or she is
doing to hit the company goals. His or her satisfaction and on-time delivery
ratings would be printed on his weekly pay stub.

The Balanced Scorecard approach has been recognized as one of the top
management techniques. In fact, it was selected by *Harvard Business Review*
as one of the most important management practices of the past 75 years. It
is very useful as it forces a company to establish metrics and base decisions
on fact, not gut feel, and it drives an executive team to agree at a strategic
level on what should be measured. This metrics definition process is critical
as hashing out the measures often reveals inconsistent understanding of the
goals. It prompts examination of metrics other than traditional revenues and
profits. Information is thereby regarded as a strategic management tool.
Enterprise business intelligence provides a solid foundation for creating and
maintaining such balanced scorecards.

While Kaplan and Norton advocate building a hierarchy of objectives
which serve all levels of the organization, often, it seems, enterprises turn
Balanced Scorecards into a reborn Executive Information System (EIS) that
only serves the top. Enterprise business intelligence provides reporting and
analytic capabilities and a free flow of information to all levels of a company, thereby enabling the implementation of the Balanced Scorecard system
in lower levels in the organization. True enterprise agility comes only
through employee empowerment.

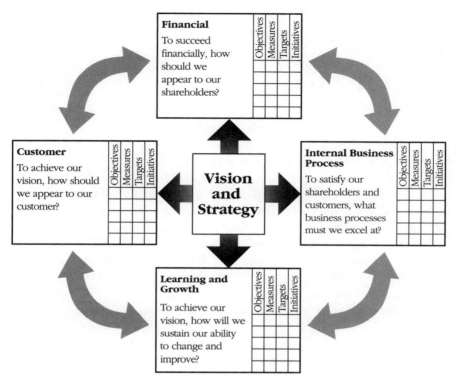

Source: Kaplan & Norton, The Balanced Scorecard, 1996

Figure 6-4   The Balanced Scorecard Model, Kaplan and Norton.

Business Intelligence, Business Benefits

Because of the wide applicability of enterprise business intelligence—intranets, extranets, or e-business environments—the business benefits are numerous and frequently enhance the bottom line. These business benefits can be summed up in four main categories:

- Lowering costs
- Increasing revenue
- Leveraging the investment in enterprise resource planning (ERP) systems
- Improving internal communication

This list is far from exhaustive, since empowered users continue to find imaginative new ways of making productive use of enterprise business intelligence.

Lowering Costs

Cost savings can be enabled by business intelligence in many areas from reductions in the IT staff all the way to a better negotiation with suppliers.

Eliminating Report Backlog and Redeploying IT Staff. Without ad hoc access to data, users have to rely on IT programmers to give them answers to their questions. Because the number of questions coming from end users is very large and is not easily anticipated, it is a never-ending task for them. Static reports designed to satisfy a large number of users only prompt them to ask more questions. (See earlier "Encourage Users to Find Root Causes of Trends.") Consequently, the IT staff is drowned in requests and cannot respond in time. They spend time on low-leverage activities that they do not like doing (eventually driving staff turnover) and that wastes money.

Once you implement an enterprise business intelligence system, business users can answer their own business questions by designing their own queries and reports. The company can redeploy the programmers who formerly performed these tasks to higher value-added, and more interesting and enjoyable, activities. This can generate significant cost savings in headcount, since sought-after IT staff can be reallocated to projects that add more value to the organization.

Finding Gold Nuggets in the Value Chain. You can use enterprise business intelligence to apply activity-based costing methods to identify hidden costs and missed opportunities, and drive new revenues. From these findings, resources can be allocated to highly profitable products, customers, and projects, thereby increasing the bottom line.

Profitability Analysis at Hertz Lease

Hertz Lease uses its enterprise business intelligence system to track and tune approximately 60 variables that govern its contract vehicle leasing business with companies. Data analysis adds hard information and fact-based forecasting to Hertz Lease's business processes, enabling it to more precisely calculate the length of contracts and fees that it needs to charge to be profitable in a low-margin business, says IT director David Shapland. Before the implementation of a Web-enabled enterprise business intelligence system, Hertz Lease suffered from classic problems of disparate legacy data stores and poor data quality and integration, all of which delayed its ability to make sound business decisions. "It was a complete mishmash, and keeping the whole thing in line was very difficult," says Shapland. "What we really needed was a way to extract the data and put it into a usable format for our own internal use and for our customers."

Today, their Web-enabled data warehouse is used by about 130 employees. This enterprise business intelligence system enables Hertz Lease to track such variables as fuel consumption, mileage recorded, length of contract, interest costs, maintenance and repair, residual values, and vehicle depreciation to build profitability forecast models, which in turn informs its pricing structures. Given the payback, the system has delivered in its first implementation in France in enabling faster, better decisions and more profitable contracts, Hertz Lease's aim is to expand the enterprise business intelligence system beyond 130 users to several hundred users throughout 12 European countries.

"It had always been an approximation—the only time we really knew whether or not we had made a profit was when we sold the car," Shapland says. "If everything stayed static from the day that you wrote the contract to the day that you sold the car, you could measure it, but in fact it changes all the time. Because events change all the time, to measure whether you are making a profit or not is very complicated."

Lessons Learned

At Hertz, the value of a set of existing information (data about leasing contracts) has increased dramatically with its use. A set of data that was badly understood and not very accessible turned into several golden nuggets:

1. Direct access to data by end users has reduced IT costs (direct savings).

2. Direct access to data by end users has accelerated decision times (better performance).

3. The leasing representatives have been able to obtain the real data on profitability, therefore focusing their marketing and sales efforts on more profitable contracts (better revenue/margin performance).

4. Expansion to more users will leverage the first benefits even further.

Volkswagen Finance

Volkswagen Finance France also handles the leasing of cars. Their business intelligence system allowed an interesting discovery that later resulted in significant new revenue. The customers of a particular model of the Audi product line had completely different behaviors than customers of other cars. Based on their socioeconomic profiles, they were thought to want long lease terms and fairly large upfront payments. Instead, the information showed that Audi customers had a propensity to want shorter lease plans—40 percent of the lease plans for the Audi were 12 to 36 months as opposed to 15 percent for the other brands—and to finance a large part of the purchase through the lease. Based on that insight, the company immediately introduced a new scheme combining shorter length of lease, larger upfront payments, and aggressive leasing rates, especially for that car model. The take up on the new scheme was immediate, resulting in millions of dollars of additional revenue.

Lessons Learned

Business intelligence can uncover previously unknown customer behaviors that can be used to create marketing programs with immediate benefits to the revenue line.

Challenging Conventional Wisdom. As we discussed before, almost all businesses rely on assumptions and rules of thumb. However, in seeking competitive advantage, it is important to challenge these beliefs through detailed analysis of data, as they can sometimes prove to be incorrect. Heuristics or rules of thumbs are often wrong, because

- They are built up over time on assumptions that may no longer be valid.

- They were never right in the first place but built around the best surrogate available.

An example is the general thinking that the highest revenue customers are the most profitable and therefore are the ones who should get the best attention. However, these customers may, in fact, consume more than their share of resources, and as a result not be the most profitable. However, if the company has no way to measure individual profit by customer, it is a reasonable surrogate (which to this day is used in many companies).

Using business intelligence, conventional wisdom can be challenged based on hard data. Managers can identify the true costs and profits associated with individual customers or products. Misdirected and wasted resources can be eliminated.

Arjo Wiggins Appleton

For years, at Arjo Wiggins Appleton, a European paper manufacturer, the rule of thumb in the sales department had been "the heavier the paper, the better the margin." So salespeople were pushing the heavy paper products. However, by spreading the use of business intelligence software and enabling finance users to look into sales information, the company found out completely different data from the distribution of gross margin per product: low-weight papers and heavyweight papers happened to be low contributors to gross margin. Instead, middleweight papers turned out to be the most profitable models. This discovery was in total contradiction with the sales guidelines in place based on the previous rule of thumb. Reengineering the sales process based on the actual margin distribution pattern per model helped Arjo Wiggins Appleton turn from a money-losing company to a profitable organization in just one year.

British Airways

Enterprise business intelligence will occasionally lead to surprises. One of British Airways' first forays into e-business intelligence came in the early 1990s, as a means of exploring its suspicion that it was suffering a high degree of a particular type of ticket fraud. British Airways' managers were concerned that a few instances of ticket fraud that had been uncovered were only the tip of the iceberg, said Peter Blundell, the airline's knowledge strategy manager. "Once we analyzed the data, we found that this ticket fraud was not an issue at all," said Blundell. "What we had suspected was fraud was in fact either data quality issues or process problems. What it did do was give us so many unexpected opportunities in terms of understanding our business. The moral of the story is that we did a post-implementation audit and found we got huge benefits, but the big fraud issue we expected was not there." That was about a decade ago, and since then, Blundell estimates that business intelligence has resulted in something on the order of $100 million in cost savings and new revenues for the carrier.

Negotiating Better Contracts with Suppliers and Customers. The key to successful negotiation is doing your homework. A solid grasp of facts and figures is invaluable when it comes to negotiating contracts with suppliers and customers. For instance, if you can analyze supplier performance—on-time delivery trends, percentage of rejects, and price changes—you are in an excellent position to discuss all aspects of the contract. The same is true with customers. This can work to the customer's benefit, for instance if you identify that the customer's spending patterns qualify him for a particular packaged deal.

A good example is Fiat Auto. The Italian carmaker had money going up in smoke, but it did not know it. Fiat Auto maintained a worldwide network of parts suppliers for its automobiles, but before installing an enterprise business intelligence system on top of a data warehouse, Fiat Auto managers had no practical way of tracking, comparing, managing, and minimizing costs for those components. A revelation on the value that such a system could provide came during its testing phase, in 1999, on a part as pedestrian as the ashtray.

During the testing phase, IT engineers detected a large discrepancy in the prices that Fiat was paying for the ashtrays in a pair of vehicles. The data warehouse enabled comparative analyses of various component prices. Curiously, the engineers discovered that the ashtray for the economy model Fiat Punto cost about 50 percent more than the ashtray for the luxury model Alfa 166.

The IT staff was the first to discover this interesting data and alerted the purchasing department. The purchasing managers could not believe it and initially thought there was a mistake in the information. Per individual ashtray, the sum of money at stake was not huge—ashtrays go for a couple of dollars—but with 650,000 Puntos rolling off assembly lines each year, the costs quickly mounted. Armed with its nugget of intelligence, Fiat was able to renegotiate prices with the supplier of the Punto ashtray and is now saving several hundred thousand dollars a year.

For conservative, old economy companies such as Fiat Auto, having such useful information at the fingertips of managers was unheard of several years ago. What little reporting capabilities that Fiat Auto managers had at their disposal had been cobbled atop transactional data systems and were ordinarily rigid and would inhibit the performance of those systems. In addition, those reporting capabilities had been built in at substantial cost by programmers, some of them having left the company and taken their knowledge with them.

Until the advent of the data warehouse and a related system for customer relationship management, the understanding that Fiat Auto managers had of their business was very weak, says Castelli, the Fiat CIO and a former professor of computer science at the University of Milan, in Italy. And with some 2200 suppliers, millions of customers and production facilities in countries ranging from Brazil to Morocco to Poland, Fiat was drowning in data overload. It needed business intelligence, and that was among the top priorities when the innovative Castelli joined the company in 1997.

"The implications of being able to predict what is going to happen is vital for production, investments, incentives, marketing campaigns, advertising—all those things are hugely impacted," Castelli says. "Trying to understand what the customer really wants can have a huge influence on the supply chain, influencing in turn the suppliers and their production capacity. Not only do you need to have an excellent system to predict what is going to happen in a functional area, but you need to look at the entire chain. You need to look at five or ten key performance indicators, rather than looking at 200,000 rows of raw data that no one is able to interpret."

Improving Operational Efficiency

Bringing real time intelligence to operational systems can bring great improvements to efficiency, and therefore lower costs and increase quality of service.

Penske Logistics

Enterprise business intelligence is driving operational efficiencies at Penske Logistics, a Penske Truck Leasing Company and one of the largest providers of transportation services in North America. The need for a system that would help Penske Logistics monitor and better manage its shipping and logistics business became clear in the late 1990s.

In response, Penske Logistics developed an internal enterprise business intelligence application that enables it to pinpoint more than 100 variables crucial to its operations, such as number of stops, duration of stop, fuel consumption, miles per gallon, average speed, and other factors.

The system's infrastructure relies on the Qualcomm OmniTracs system that provides computers installed in each of Penske Logistics's fleet of 3,000 trucks that beam data to satellites for transmission to a Penske Logistics mainframe computer. From there, the data is exported to a data warehouse that is accessed over an intranet by about 750 employees using a Web-based business intelligence tool. "The intranet is growing about as fast as our business has been growing," says Tom Nather, senior systems analyst at Penske Logistics, in Beachwood, Ohio. "We have everyone empowered in the company from the president on down, to the managers at all the field locations. It is top to bottom—we've got everyone hooked."

Penske Logistics does not track these metrics out of curiosity. It knows that in a high-volume, low-margin business, even an adjustment that that can squeeze a couple of more miles per gallon can mean a substantial cost savings. Before the enterprise business intelligence implementation, the number of miles per day was recorded on paper by truck drivers and calculated out to miles per gallon. Drivers were inconsistent in filling out paper reports, and it would be many days before managers had access to that data, inconsistent as it was.

Now, the Qualcomm system automatically records the number of miles driven, and Penske Logistics's mainframe calculates the miles per gallon before the data is loaded into the data warehouse. From there, Penske Logistics employees can analyze opportunities for improvement. This analysis can highlight a need for maintenance, or modification of a driver's driving habits—down to improvements so detailed as changing the RPMs at which he or she changes gears.

By closely tracking the comings and goings of its fleet, Penske Logistics has at its fingertips information that helps it keep its fleet running at maximum capacity, and that helps its customers move goods faster between point A and point B. The enterprise business intelligence system enables Penske Logistics to observe in near-real time a truck that is only half full, and reroute it for a quick pick up from a customer. This is a particularly powerful benefit because all the revenue is upside. Just as an empty airplane seat represents a highly perishable inventory and a lost opportunity when it goes empty, so does half an empty truck.

Lesson Learned

Tracking and analyzing data in real time in a logistics chain can bring immediate opportunities for efficiencies.

Increasing Revenue

Differentiate Your Services.   Leading companies are using enterprise business intelligence to differentiate their product and service offerings from competitors, through value-added Web-based extranets. This is especially useful in commodity industries, where a key factor in vendor choice hinges on the services a supplier provides alongside its products. Companies can give their clients self-service access to tailored reports on account activity, thereby helping them identify opportunities for cost savings.

A leading institutional investment firm realized that access to information and research was an important service to differentiate the successful investment management firms from the rest of the industry. With over $150 billion in assets, this firm now allows its customers instant Web access to a range of reports about their accounts, giving them the ability to work faster and identify more effective investment strategies for their company and their company's employees. In later chapters, we will examine case studies and strategies on how to build business intelligent extranets to better serve customers, enhance relationship with suppliers, and create new sources of revenue.

Improve Strategies with Better Marketing Analysis.   In the age of e-business, having the best intelligence is critical for marketing analysis. With easy access to ordering, accounting, production, shipping, customer service, and even external databases, marketers can find answers to the most detailed questions. Armed with the answers to these questions provided through enterprise business intelligence, the marketer can precisely tailor product launches and promotion campaigns to the targeted audience. Data mining techniques help find the most profitable customers, discover hidden trends, and predict customer reactions to specific product introductions. Using new intelligent segmentation techniques, companies can microsegment their markets and their customer base. In this way, they are able to have a much more fine-grained understanding of customer behavior and to tailor personalized marketing campaigns, thereby gaining an edge over the competition.

Belgacom, the Belgian telephone company, uses enterprise business intelligence to size up and reduce customer attrition. It is able to examine which customers place a high number of calls to a certain country for which Belgacom knows that a competitor offers a lower rate. Armed with this knowledge, the company can decide whether to proactively address this potential source of customer churn by lowering its rate or running a promotion. In a later chapter on customer intelligence, we will look in further detail at how business intelligence helps enhance customer relations and improve marketing efforts.

Empower the Sales Force. Many users can capitalize on remote access to data—particularly the sales force. While out on the road, sales representatives may want to check the system for product availability and shipping times for their clients. Through a Web-enabled enterprise business intelligence system, sales representatives are able to drill into data to determine the client's transaction history, buying patterns, contact information, problem resolution, and customer support center calls to better prepare for a meeting.

For several years, sales representatives have had contact databases and, in more advanced organizations, enterprise sales force automation software installed on their portable notebook computers. A new breed of Web-enabled sales force automation applications makes it possible for those representatives to continue to store information on their laptops, and then sync the information to the company's central sales database over the Internet. Through a business intelligence system, either integrated within the sales force application or built on top of it, mobile sales representatives can have an intelligent and complete view of their activity; they also can fine-tune their sales efforts through ad hoc data analysis. They can improve their results by analyzing their selling patterns, which allows them to compare their results to targets, to previous year's figures, and to other sales staff, and focus on high profitability customers and products.

From a management point of view, the sales managers can have an up-to-date digital view of activity in the field. And they can see which activities most drive sales success (e.g., number of deals worked, average deal size, seniority, number of cold calls made) in order to guide the behavior of new members of the team.

Innovex

Innovex, a London-based subsidiary of Quintiles Transnational that provides outsourced sales, marketing, and clinical research services to pharmaceutical manufacturers, launched a data warehouse in 1999 that has about 70 users examining sales and marketing data. It is helping the company's business users pinpoint sales and marketing efforts without involving IT, says Jeremy Broadis, Innovex's business director of decision support services.

Business intelligence is key to gaining competitive advantage in the pharmaceutical industry, Broadis said. "The old marketing model was shotgun—go out and call on any old doctor," he says. "We are becoming more advanced in how we target doctors through the use of predictive modeling techniques. Salespeople need intelligence on whom they should call on and how often. You need a sales data warehouse and business intelligence to do that. Otherwise, you are back to shotgun marketing."

The next step is to extend the system to Innovex's 1200 sales representatives over the Web.

Allegiance Healthcare

Allegiance Healthcare uses an enterprise business intelligence system called ASPIRE (Allegiance Sales, Pricing, and Integrated Reporting) to give Allegiance sales representatives the capabilities to better understand their customers' purchases.

Representatives selling Allegiance's medical and surgical supplies to hospitals and care providers can now recognize a customer's cost-saving opportunities and make standardization recommendations. "Customers like the immediate access to information and are already making cost-saving decisions," says Mark Ciekutis, Allegiance data warehouse manager, in McGaw Park, Illinois. The cost savings resulted from a reduction in administrative and technical services associated with the previous systems and from a reduction of administrative costs for support and reconciliation of multiple legacy sales force systems.

Every month, a sales representative's territorial data is extracted from Allegiance's data warehouse and downloaded to his or her laptop computer. Data marts are then created that show sales and pricing data about their territories. Using ASPIRE, sales representatives can identify cost-saving opportunities and make standardization recommendations, such as contract purchases and purchases of Allegiance's own line of "Best Value" products.

Allegiance's goals in the project were three-fold. The first goal was to reduce the IT staff that supports the sales force. Before ASPIRE, Allegiance had five IT groups, consisting of 10 people, supporting 17 sales organizations and seven different types of reporting systems. That was reduced to one IT group, consisting of four people, to support a sales force of 1100, all using the same unified system. The rest of the team was redeployed to other projects.

The second goal was to make the data both more consistent and current. Allegiance previously provided different cuts of data to various sales groups. Each cut of data originated from a different reporting system. When sales representatives from different Allegiance product lines came together to create corporatewide customer proposals, they found inconsistencies in the numbers. Using ASPIRE, which is sourced from only one data warehouse, Allegiance was able to offer its sales force the same enterprisewide data concerning customers, products, purchasing, and pricing.

Changes in pricing, which occur as deals with various manufacturers expire and new contracts are signed, happen so frequently that it results in inaccurate pricing to customers and margin erosion to Allegiance. ASPIRE keeps sales representatives informed about changes in pricing, electronically downloading the changes as they occur. This advance notification gives customers plenty of time to update their purchasing and accounts payable systems. This allows for prompt payments to be made without incurring added administrative expenses to either the customer or Allegiance. Credibility with customers has improved and so, too, have the efficiencies that allow for expenses to be minimized.

The third goal was to make training of sales representatives easier and to make collaboration among them a possibility. Rather than constantly having to learn new systems as they moved from one sales group to another, sales representatives now use the same sales force automation tool. Trainers, too, only need to learn one system and can train any combination of sales representatives, regardless of the product lines involved. ASPIRE's common user interface also has allowed sales representatives to identify opportunities in their customer base and to share applicable ones with the rest of the Allegiance sales team.

ASPIRE was part of a larger business systems overhaul implemented by Allegiance called the *Horizon project*. Allegiance replaced its key business systems with an SAP ERP system for managing data and built a separate decision-support data warehouse for enterprise business intelligence. Since implementing Horizon, Allegiance has been able to save $10 million per year in IT expenditure and deliver a better level of service to its business users. ASPIRE itself was a $1.7 million project finalized in August 1999, after taking two and a half years to implement.

Lessons Learned

1. Integrating business intelligence in a sales force automation application enables the sales organization to be much more responsive to customer requests.

2. Providing a common system that is shared by the whole sales force and that integrates data from multiple sources ensures better collaboration between the salespeople.

Leveraging Your Investment in Your ERP System

Financial, budgeting, and accounting systems, manufacturing, engineering, product planning, inventory control, shipping and logistics, human resources—the systems backbone of many companies—have all profited from the introduction of software specific to their application areas. These software packages have helped companies achieve efficiencies in automating and streamlining a multitude of nuts-and-bolts processes that years ago were conducted via what now seem to be prehistoric means—paper and communications in person and over the telephone. However, the automation of these processes has been only an early, first step in helping businesses transform themselves into lean, agile operations. Mission-critical as it is, the information stored in these ERP applications and transactional systems has, for the most part, not been liberated and effectively exploited for the intelligence that it holds.

Ironically, many of these packages have been purchased by customers with the ultimate goal of having a better understanding of information or improvements in data sharing. First, the customer focused on the back-end systems. An organization would implement an ERP to have a complete understanding of their supply chain and analyze data across manufacturing, sales, inventory, etc. More recently, companies have set their eyes on implementing front-office systems. These issues were introduced earlier in

Data Overload. For instance, a company would purchase a sales force automation package, because, previously, salespeople kept their customer data in a spreadsheet on their PC in their own format, and no sharing would be possible. If that salesperson left, or if his or her territory was to be divided among several salespeople, all that information would either be lost or mostly unusable. However, these systems for the most part are not designed to leverage information; instead, they are designed to automate process. They automate the supply chain process, the order-entry process, the customer support process, or the procurement process.

In many cases, companies that implement large packaged applications tend to lose track of their original goal. The act of putting in place these operational systems tends to accidentally put people on a course of the endless task of optimizing the operations. The initial goal of getting better information has been lost. And there are very practical reasons for that. An implementation of financial, human resources, and product planning applications can require many months and millions of dollars. Quite often, companies have lacked the financial and personnel resources to couple these systems with complementary enterprise business intelligence systems that would enable data analysis.

And the vast resources that companies brought to bear on remediating the Y2K problems, real or imagined, diverted time, energy, and money from initiatives to incorporate this transactional data into enterprise business intelligence systems just as companies had begun to recognize that it would be a fruitful endeavor.

To boot, ERP applications are notoriously complex—a number of these applications have thousands of tables and a proprietary format that takes programmers years to master. Just the process of extracting data from ERP applications and transforming it into another format has spawned a cottage industry of vendors with tools designed expressly for that purpose. But increasingly, we are witnessing a drive to evolve these operational systems beyond automation into realms of intelligence—what might be called *intelligent ERP*.

One study found that businesses now have their sights set on data warehouse integration of data from ERP and other operational systems with data from ecommerce applications, for a broad view of the business. With more companies evolving into click-and-mortar operations, some 46 percent of respondents to a query by market research outfit Survey.com in 2000 deemed it extremely important that these two data sources be blended.[1]

[1] Survey.com, "ERP, BI, and ecommerce: Where Are the Winners?" 2000.

Liberate Your Operational Data

Enterprise business intelligence systems liberate the operational data in enterprise resource planning applications and make it available across the organization for analysis. A company that deploys a costly and complex enterprise resource planning system usually wants to leverage intelligence from the ERP applications as quickly as possible to go beyond process automation, maximize return on investment, and extend the visibility and reach of the ERP applications within the organization.

There are generally three phases toward a full-fledged exploitation of ERP applications for intelligence:

1. *Limited access against the operational data store.* This kind of implementation lets selected users access the data directly in the production ERP application. Shortly after an ERP implementation is up and running, some instant gratification is delivered to users with an urgent need to access and analyze the data directly against the data store. This solution is attractive because it delivers results quickly and does not require an intermediary data structure. It is often seen as a solution that cannot scale, because the security and performance of the ERP system is mission critical to the customer; the IT staff does not allow many end users launching long ad hoc queries directly into the system, potentially risking the functioning of the system. It is hard to get good performance for analysis activities without crippling the ERP application. In addition, the ERP system has been designed for transactions not for decisions and, therefore, it makes it very hard to build a system simple enough to use by business users. However, as we will see in the BOC Gases example below, some companies have obtained huge benefits from this approach. It has proven to be a fast and efficient solution in many situations.

2. *Scheduled reports.* Reports are run during off-peak hours directly against the ERP system. This solution solves the performance issue of the first solution. It is limited to giving predefined, prescheduled reports to the user community and, as such, it is a rigid implementation where business users cannot ask any question they want, when they want. However, for a large group of users who only want to receive predefined reports and do not want to perform their own analysis, it has proven to be a perfect solution.

3. *Design and deployment of a data warehouse.* Here, data is extracted and moved from the ERP application into a data warehouse for analysis and report generation. This is the preferred way to implement a robust business intelligent system on top of an ERP. It enables the company to design

the warehouse for the purpose of information access by nontechnical users. The process of transformation and extraction from the ERP to the data warehouse can be managed and scheduled regularly, allowing better control of the data available for the users. Finally, it enables the creation of data warehouses that mix data coming from different environments, different modules from the same ERP system, or ERP data with CRM data coming from a completely different application.

BOC Gases

BOC Gases, a multinational supplier of industrial gases based in the United Kingdom, decided against immediate implementation of a full-fledged data warehouse, after ERP applications from the German software giant SAP to run its core transaction processing took two and a half years to implement. BOC, a unit of the BOC Group that employs about 35,000 people and has $5.5 billion in annual revenues, did not want to undertake a large warehousing project that could tie up nearly as many resources as the extensive SAP implementation.

Instead, BOC Gases opted for a flexible enterprise business intelligence system that would pull data directly from SAP applications. The implementation of a user-friendly enterprise business intelligence tool would insulate users from the complexity of SAP applications, avoid maintaining a staff of programmers adept at SAP's proprietary ABAP language to generate reports for the business staff, and provide business users with self-service access to the information they needed.

BOC Gases concentrated first on delivering information from SAP's sales data application. An enterprise business intelligence tool was provided to about 350 sales and marketing people in Europe. Through laptop computers, these sales and marketing people gained access to product and customer information specific to his and her areas of responsibility and are now able to drill into the data for details. The acceleration of business processes was substantial. Whereas previously they had to wait weeks after month's end prior to receiving paper-based reports, they now had easy-to-use information available electronically in a couple of days.

After the sales data implementation, BOC Gases followed up with an additional system for materials management, using enterprise business intelligence to create a snapshot of inventory levels that fall below predefined thresholds. Inventory reports are run nightly against SAP and published on the company's intranet. Another implementation used exception reporting—a means of highlighting outliers—to keep tabs on key business processes and quickly addressed problem areas. For instance, BOC was able to determine whether an interplant transfer order issued at one site had been completed at the corresponding site.

Lessons Learned

Contrary to conventional wisdom, it is possible to gain great benefits by implementing a basic business intelligence system directly on top of an ERP, bypassing the need to create a data warehouse.

Novartis Crop Protection

Formed by the merger of two major pharmaceutical companies—Ciba-Geigy and Sandoz—Novartis is one of the world's leading life sciences companies. Novartis Crop Protection is one of the companies in the Agribusiness division. Novartis Crop Protection manufactures a broad range of agricultural chemicals and has manufacturing facilities and sales units throughout the world. Crop Protection's commitment to sustainable agriculture focuses on the research and development of products to control the weeds, pests, and diseases that harm and reduce harvests.

One of the primary challenges of producing agricultural chemicals is that the production planning is done with a five-year lead time. This implies the integration and analysis of a great deal of external information, such as long-term market and sales forecasts. In addition, there are seasonal cycles that have to be managed. Most sales are realized from December to April. However, production has to be maintained at a constant rate throughout the year. Whereas the long-term planning is based on market forecasts, short-term planning is based on actual sales data from the group companies. Also, the management of production and distribution processes is complex, because it implies the combination of multiple materials and substances and involves numerous suppliers. Because of these constraints, having control over all relevant data is critical to Novartis Crop Protection success.

The company had standardized on SAP R/3 for both its finance and its supply chains, implementing many modules including *Materials*

Management (MM), *Production Planning* (PP), as well as *Warehouse Management* (WM). The company decided to implement a data warehouse and standardize on a single business intelligence environment to access data across all data sources within SAP, and therefore cover most facets of running an agricultural chemicals company, including purchasing, production planning, sales and distribution, materials management, and finance.

One of the principal requirements was that the business intelligence solution had to be useable by anyone in the organization, regardless of position or technical skill level. It had to be able to do cross-process reporting, i.e., reporting across several modules of SAP. As we have described earlier in the Value of Information model, the value of data increases as users from different departments can access the same information, since they can then start cross analyzing that information with data from their own business area. At Novartis, the business intelligence implementation also had to isolate users from the complexity of the underlying SAP R/3 system. The tool had to be open to all sources of corporate data, including both SAP and non-SAP data. An additional requirement was to be able to produce a wide variety of reports from simple, ad hoc reports up to more elaborate EIS-style reports.

Because the implementation of a business intelligence solution was made in parallel with the SAP implementation (as opposed to being an afterthought), Novartis was able to implement the system in a short amount of time. Then, once the system was implemented, users throughout the enterprise were able to access data across all SAP modules and get much faster results than in the past. Enterprise business intelligence had compressed the reporting time from weeks to days.

Lessons Learned

1. Implementing a single business intelligence environment through a data warehouse allows access to data coming from multiple business processes at the same time, and consequently results in better understanding of the overall business

2. In the case of a complex system, consider starting the implementation of the business intelligence at the same time as the implementation of the ERP.

Improving Communication

Develop a Common Language, Leading to Goal Alignment. Implementing enterprise business intelligence across a corporation's activities requires departments to agree on basic business terminology. For instance, different departments may not define a customer in the same way. Discussing and defining common vocabulary can help divisions align not just their business terminology but also their work processes.

The first part of the process is to ensure common semantics. A good business intelligence system allows you to define and store business terminology that members of the same business entity should share. For instance, a term like *sales revenue* can be complex to define. It involves pricing information, discounts, potential rebates, and the quantity of items sold—all at the same time. Members of a marketing group, for instance, should share the same definition for sales revenue. However, the accounting department may use the same term when referring to a different definition, as it distinguishes bookings from recognized revenue. The time of sale and criteria for revenue recognition are key to the definition. It is vital that business semantics be defined for the different business areas of your organization. As part of this process, there needs to be an agreement on a set of corporate terms that will span across departments. The term *customer*, for instance, may need to be used consistently throughout the entire enterprise. If so, all departments need to use the same semantics for it.

Having an agreement on business terminology goes a long way in improving the company's agility. Users from totally different departments can communicate in a much better way and share common goals. The second part of the process concerns *data consistency*. High-quality data and consistency among disparate data stores help ensure that decisions are made based on accurate information.

Walter Nelson, senior vice president of core engineering at Ventro, a business-to-business online trading exchange in Mountain View, Calif., is a big believer in data quality. Data quality was a large issue when he served as an IT manager at Fair, Isaac, a large credit scoring and financial consulting company in Marin County, California. "If you do not have a quality data set that is well behaved, you lack that fundamental base for analysis," says Nelson. "At Fair, Isaac, the nature of the data we received was highly variable. The data we got contained a lot of junk, and we spent a lot of money just to build the tools to scrub the data. And now at Ventro we spend a prodigious amount of energy in cleaning up our data and making it appropriate for our end users. But once we have it scrubbed and in our repository, it is an extraordinarily precious resource."

Promote Accountability and Efficiency. A common issue within companies is that other departments take too long to communicate information. For instance, the finance department, a perennial whipping boy, is often faulted for not providing reports as fast as business managers would like to see them. Since enterprise business intelligence dramatically speeds up querying and reporting time, internal requests can be satisfied much faster, thereby improving relationships among departments, as well as employee accountability and efficiency.

Stimulate Curiosity. Some of the most interesting discoveries made by companies using enterprise business intelligence originate in ad hoc, cross-departmental queries. In other words, using enterprise business intelligence across multiple steps of the value chain generates the greatest benefits. The discoveries made are often the result of the curiosity of one individual making inquiries on the borderline of his or her official job description, affirming that positive results can be obtained from giving free rein to users' autonomy and curiosity. With enterprise business intelligence tools, users can leverage and enhance their own intelligence and creativity.

Successful Strategies for Implementing an Enterprise Business Intelligence System

As for most strategic projects, the success of an enterprise business intelligence initiative is not guaranteed. Its success depends on a number of essential factors: its role as part of corporate strategy, the involvement of business managers in its purchase, a careful implementation, and a federated approach.

Enterprise Business Intelligence Must Be a Part of Business Strategy

While enterprise business intelligence allows the identification of hidden costs or of new revenue opportunities, these benefits are achieved only once action is taken, i.e., costs are cut or additional revenue is pursued. The enterprise business intelligence system is part of a process, and its returns are included in those of the process as a whole. The enterprise business intelligence project brings value as part of a larger business strategy, and the value of the project can only be measured along with that of the strategy.

The guiding criterion of an enterprise business intelligence system should be, Does this system help our company achieve its strategy?" To answer this question, several intermediary questions must be asked. First, *What is your strategy?* For instance, become the market leader in a given segment, be number one or number two in all markets the company operates in, increase revenues by 20 percent, or increase market share by 30 percent. Next, *What are your objectives set to fulfill that strategy?* Divest from nonleading activities, improve customer service and customer retention, improve the bottom line, decrease costs in the IT department by 10 percent, improve customer retention rates by 5 percent, or reduce procurement costs. Lead a successful business reengineering program to transform the company into an e-business. The more precise these objectives[2] are and the more they actually define and support the overall strategy, the more effective the related business intelligence system will be in helping achieve that strategy.

Third, *What are the key performance indicators your company should track to measure success in meeting the objectives?* A balanced scorecard initiative may help your company develop these metrics, though you need not implement a full-fledged, corporatewide, balanced-scorecard approach to start getting the benefits of business intelligence. Even starting with a handful of well-rounded indicators that are tracked only at the first few levels of an organization can put you on the right track. They must be agreed upon at the highest level and shared with everyone in the organization. For instance, if the company has strong goals in learning and growing, it may focus on how well employees are financially motivated to be creative. And finally, *How can you use enterprise business intelligence to meet those objectives?* Improve business efficiency by identifying opportunities or waste, access information that was not easily available, improve customer service, measure the progress made in reaching your objectives, take corrective measures as soon as you start deviating from goals.

Business Managers Should Drive Enterprise Business Intelligence

Business managers drive the success of enterprise business intelligence. As one detailed analysis showed, the companies that were most successful in implementing enterprise systems were those that, from the start, had "viewed them primarily in strategic and organizational terms," as opposed to focusing on technical aspects.[3]

Gopal Kapur, president of the Center for Project Management, a project management consultancy group in San Ramon, Calif., argues that an effec-

---

[2] Large organizations tend to define their strategy, then related goals (nonquantifiable targets that support the strategy), then objectives that define each goal. Smaller organizations tend to define the strategy and then directly define objectives. In either case, objectives must be S.M.A.R.T. (specific, measureable, achieveable, relevant, and time bound).

[3] Thomas H. Davenport, "Putting the Enterprise into the Enterprise System," *Harvard Business Review* (Cambridge), July–August 1998.

tive business sponsor is the single most influential ingredient in the recipe for success of any IT project, enterprise business intelligence included. According to Kapur's checklist, in order to champion the project, the project manager, and the team, an effective business sponsor should:

- Empower the project manager with appropriate authority
- Remove high hurdles and keep the team out of political minefields
- Support the team in resolution of cross-functional policy issues
- Formally manage the project scope

Business managers are also in an excellent position to provide input into the front-end business intelligence tool with which users will interact. Companies invest large sums in data warehouses, enterprise systems, or other forms of databases, only to encounter dissatisfaction among users, because the tool they use is too complex or too difficult to use. Achieving a return on the investment depends heavily on how the users "take" to the system.

If business users find that the enterprise business intelligence tool is adapted to their needs, and makes their life easier, they will make return on investment happen. This is why it is crucial for business managers and users to drive the initial design, implementation, and training of the enterprise business intelligence system.

Maximizing Return on Investment through Implementation

To ensure maximum business utility, the enterprise business intelligence system must be carefully rolled out. In particular, the users must be involved in the planning phase, the system must be as easy as possible, the users must be trained thoroughly, and management commitment must be ensured.

Involve the Users in the Planning Phase.   Business users must be involved from the beginning, in the planning and design phases, to ensure the system responds to all of their needs. It is also critical to involve users in the pilot phase to ensure that the terminology and standard reports are meaningful to them.

Allegiance Healthcare took care with the design and implementation of its ASPIRE system. For each component of ASPIRE—sales analysis, deal pricing, and customer proposals—groups of 10 to 12 users were identified to participate in the development effort for the project's full life cycle. These users participated in requirements gathering, user-acceptance testing, and pilot rollouts. During the construction phase, users were shown either prototypes or up-to-date progress reports, to make sure the developers were meeting expectations. The user groups, for example, helped refine the customer proposal component of ASPIRE by showing the development team formats of proposals that had been in use.

Each of the three ASPIRE deliverables involved user acceptance, as well as pilot phases that were conducted in similar fashion. After receiving the software in CD-ROM format, conference calls were held with the user groups. The pilot phases also gave the IT development team a chance to better understand the capacities of the communication networks and database servers.

Planning was the only way to successfully accomplish a project the size of ASPIRE, says Ciekutis. Each development team created project plans, all of which flowed into higher level group plans. These plans then were rolled into an even higher level plan for the larger Horizon Project. Progress-to-plan was measured at the team level weekly, with progress, as well as actual spending-to-budget, measured at the manager level monthly. Weekly team meetings were held at all levels of the organization, from senior management through subteam levels.

Make the System as Easy to Use as Possible.   The most successful enterprise business intelligence systems allow users to readily access data and to perform analysis with a graphical user interface that is relatively nontechnical, easy to use, and easy to understand. The number one success criterion for the implementation of a business intelligence system, mentioned over and over again, is ease of use. Make sure that you pick a solution that your users are comfortable with. The ease of use of the system will also depend on how meaningful the data is for the business user. Ensure that the terminology used by the system corresponds to the business terminology of the business users. Finally, make the data as simple as possible.

The Belgian telephone company Belgacom took pains to ensure that its users were insulated from the complexity of the data warehouse that they would access through enterprise business intelligence tools. "If top executives have to work with complex tools, they will never use them" says Koen Vermeulen, director of IT business analysis. "They need quick information that is easily accessible."

Train the Users.   While the best systems today are extremely user-friendly and intuitive, enterprise business intelligence is a new way of thinking; regular, customized training, based on users' own business problems, will help them extract maximum benefits from their data.

Most of the training will need to revolve around the data itself. Training on the use of software tools should take no more than a day or so. The critical path lies in educating the users about the data. What data is available? How is it categorized? What do the various business terms, such as *customer* and *monthly sales revenue*, mean? How often is the data updated? Data training should last about two days—understanding your data is about twice as difficult as understanding the tool.

Ensure Management Commitment.   The importance of management commitment in the success of these systems is critical. Because enterprise business intelligence is a new way of doing business, management has to lead the way in relying on the new tool. Also, as we have seen earlier, the introduction of such a system can be a significant departure from traditional business methods and may challenge conventional thinking. To battle common misperceptions, the highest level of management will need to sponsor the initiative.

One car manufacturer implemented an enterprise business intelligence system to help guide the allocation of funding based on the profitability of a project. The factory director made a rule whereby any project manager attending management meetings without a summary report generated by the system would not be given a chance to defend the project. This ensured that the data was kept up-to-date. In this instance, it took managers less than a month to become regular users of the enterprise business intelligence tool.

Implement a "Federated Business Intelligence Systems" Approach

A first look at enterprise business intelligence benefits may lead company executives to demand IT to create a centralized corporate data warehouse that incorporates all data needed at all levels of the company. The promise of a *pure* architecture and a *single version of the truth* may sound very attractive, but is highly unrealistic, and experience has shown that this approach will most likely fail. Integrating all data at all levels into a single environment is too formidable a task. Its implementation is too long and too costly. A preferred implementation is to accept the fact that many smaller business intelligence environments, based on many smaller data marts, will be built throughout the organization. By being smaller and closer to the data they manage, and to the users who are the most involved in building and interacting with that data, these business intelligence implementations tend to be successful in a short amount of time.

Although these systems are not fully integrated, if they are built properly with an open technical foundation, they can be linked effectively. As we saw in Chapter 3 on the value of information," when users of other business areas can access the business intelligence environment of another business area, hidden facts are discovered, and consequently, the value of information is significantly increased.

A company implementing a federated approach can enable these disparate business intelligent environments to share common corporate metrics while letting them have their own local measures. Such an approach also trains the company on how to deal successfully with the unavoidable future addition of other back-end systems. As the company progresses in its information systems strategy, more applications will be built to automate certain business processes, and more data warehouses will be built on top of these applications. As market pressures such as hypercompetition and globalization increase, companies consolidate through mergers and acquisitions at a rapid rate. These acquisitions often force companies to embrace the business applications and data warehouses of the acquired company. A corporation architected around a federation of data warehouse systems that is used to efficiently open and link these systems will be much more able to integrate to the new environment.

However, in order for such an approach to succeed, it is imperative that the federated systems be built around a single standardized business intelligence solution. The product set needs to be open so it can embrace data coming from as many databases and applications as possible. Standardizing around one solution across the enterprise will enable users to communicate easily, to navigate across many departmental systems from the same system, and to adapt to changes, reorganization, or business model changes extremely efficiently.

Fiat Auto's enterprise business intelligence, a Web-based system with 600 users and growing, is a great example of the federated approach. The main data warehouse serves as the hub for a network of interconnected data marts specific to business areas, such as finance, engineering, production, purchasing, human resources, sales, marketing, and others. "It has already paid for itself," according to Fiat CIO Castelli. Fiat Auto has spent about $10 million on the warehouse, but the company has already realized some $45 million in returns, says Castelli, largely as a result of the sort of cost comparisons that led to a lower price on the Punto ashtray.

As a summary, the federated business intelligence approach is more viable than any other for the following reasons:

1. Each of the smaller environments has a much better chance to succeed.

2. Incremental linkages are feasible and enable a progressive and less risky road toward building an enterprise view of the company's information.

3. Departments feel more empowered.

4. Companies are ready for inevitable consolidation.

As Douglas Hackney said in his January 2000 column, The Federated Future," in *Data Management Review*: "A federated environment .../... does not try to swim against the Tsunami of market and business forces driving nonarchitected/nonintegrated systems. Instead, it facilitates the integration of these systems, thereby avoiding the certain political death of opposing a powerful executive's tactical agenda."

Summary

The widespread use of information technology generates tremendous amounts of data within a company. This data contains information that is invaluable to decision makers throughout the organization. The issue for most businesses is that the data is inaccessible to all but the IT department or the executives through complex systems. While most IT departments can run queries and produce reports at the request of business users, a self-service approach to information undoubtedly will provide the greatest benefits. With direct, easy access to information, users can find answers to all the questions that are raised by their activities. Armed with precise, up-to-the-minute information, users can develop effective responses that help their company attain its goals.

The key to leveraging this wealth of data is to implement an enterprisewide business intelligence strategy. Once that is completed, business users at all levels of the enterprise can pinpoint what drives their business activity. They can help reduce costs, increase revenues, improve customer satisfaction, and improve cross-company dialogue. While many of these benefits are clearly quantifiable, some of the more intangible ones—such as improved communication throughout the enterprise, improved job satisfaction of empowered users, or sharing of intellectual capital—will give your company the greatest edge over the competition.

7
Customer Intelligence

There is no greater truth than what your customer is telling you.
Guy Abramo
CIO
Ingram Micro

With fancy words and acronyms like *one-to-one marketing, personalization, customer churn, lifetime potential value, customer relationship management* (CRM), *market-basket analysis, cross-selling,* and *target marketing* buzzing about in companies that are endeavoring to become "customer-centric," one wonders what the customer—you know, that person who is always right—would make of all the noise. In this chapter, we discuss the concept of customer intelligence and offer detailed recommendations on how to leverage your data in order to better understand and serve your customers.

A fair bet is that most businesses do not know much about their customers. Even companies furthest advanced on the journey to achieving profitable customer intimacy are still struggling with what to make of the tidal wave of information they are collecting on their customers. They are struggling to understand who the customer is, what the customer wants, when, how, and *why* the customer wants it—the fundamental questions that all companies should be seeking to answer.

Most businesses are now on a mission to become more customer-centric. The emphasis is shifting from transactions, processes, products, and channels to the ultimate source of immediate and long-term profitability—the customer. This change is driven by intensified competition, deregulation, globalization, and saturation of market segments. Last, though not least, this change is driven by the Internet, which offers a bonanza of choices online, thereby raising customer expectations. Product differentiation is eroding. The competition is just a click away, and the switching costs for customers are becoming ordinarily negligible.

Companies find it harder and harder to differentiate on factors that prevailed in the 1980s—product quality, operations, logistics, and business processes. The quality of many products has improved, many businesses have streamlined their supply and distribution chains, and companies have benefited from the widespread business process re-engineering exercises of the 1980s and 1990s. In this new ruthless environment, it has become essential for companies to find new ways to attract new customers, to maximize the value of each existing customer, and to retain the most profitable ones. Numerous studies show that it is easier and as much as six times less expensive to sell to an existing customer than to acquire a new one.

This can be achieved by

- Knowing the customers better than the competition does—not only knowing who they are and what they have purchased, but also understanding what they want at a particular moment in time

- Exploiting that knowledge to create the best possible customer interaction—informed, personalized, and insightful, but not intrusive—and then increase customer satisfaction

- Building switching costs into the customer relationship

To accomplish all of the above, you will need to collect and analyze all the pieces of information available to your organization that relate to the customer. This will allow you to understand the customer's profitability, as well as his or her expectations and preferences. With this knowledge you can then determine the customer's lifetime value to your organization. Note that to understand the value of the customer, you must look not only back in time, but also forward in an attempt to predict his or her future potential.

Once you understand the lifetime value of the customer, you can then define and take the actions required to materialize that value. It is this collection and analysis of information, and the resulting actions based on our intimate understanding of the customer, that we call *customer intelligence*. Customer intelligence will ultimately allow you to deliver the best service and interaction with the customer.

A study by the Meta Group analyst firm in March 2000 revealed statistics showing that business has a long way to go to solve this multifaceted customer riddle. (See Figure 7-1.) In Meta Group's survey of 800 business and IT executives, 83 percent of respondents answered "no" to the fundamental question, *Does your company know who its customers are?*[1] And the survey found that 67 percent did not feel that their companies were effectively using client data to understand their customers. But efforts are intensifying to get to know these customers—56 percent of Meta Group's respondents counted improving customer intimacy as among the top three priorities of their companies.

Achieving customer intelligence ultimately involves two very important objectives:

- The *360° view of the customer,* i.e., the ability to aggregate in a single view all the data you have about a customer

- The *segment of one,* i.e., the ability to segment the customer base in such a fine-grained way that you can implement pure one-to-one marketing.

First we will review these two concepts and the challenges of putting them to work, and then we will discuss the basics of customer relationship

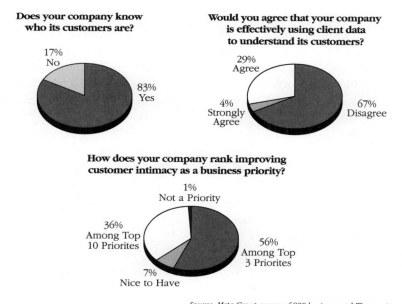

Source: Meta Group survey of 800 business and IT executives

Figure 7-1   Know Thy Customer.

---

[1] Meta Group survey, reported in *Information Week*, May 1, 2000.

management and how customer intelligence enables a more intelligent CRM. Finally, we will discuss the concept of *Customer Value Management*.

The 360° Relationship

Understanding your customer base means knowing much more than their demographic distribution. It means having a full view not only of their purchase history, but also of all their interactions with your company. Interactions can happen through multiple sales channels (direct sales, online purchases, resellers, etc.) and through multiple points of contact or "touch points" (customer support center, marketing programs, sales force interaction, and so on). By tracking, observing, and analyzing these interactions, you can gain great insight into the customer's needs and desires at any given moment.

Traditionally, the various departments in contact with customers have a good understanding of their own communication with the customers, but rarely know much about the other interactions. A salesperson knows how many calls she made to a customer for a potential new sale. A customer support representative knows how many times that customer has called to complain about product problems. A marketing manager knows how many times he called that customer to serve as a reference. Typically, none of that information is shared across these different functions, leaving all employees involved with only partial information. To address their expectations effectively and efficiently, each of the company's representatives who interacts with a customer needs to have a clear and complete picture of that customer's activity.

This holistic picture of the customer is what we call the "360° view." The business intelligence software implementation of this 360° view can take several forms, including a dashboard of business indicators on a screen, a set of business reports accessible via a Web portal, or an environment that delivers direct ad hoc access to the customer data. The key is to integrate in a single environment the related data that comes from all points of interaction with the customer. Achieving this is critical to

- Converse with the customer in a fully informed way, and therefore provide the best possible service

- Measure the customer's actual profitability

- Determine what programs should be implemented to maximize the revenue opportunity from each customer

Telecom Italia

One of the ways that Telecom Italia, the large Italian telecommunications provider, optimizes its customer care and marketing is by tracking the call records of its 25 million customers and integrating that information into a customer-oriented data warehouse. Telecom Italia empowers some 9000 call center employees with access to the data warehouse, giving them insight into customer behavior that may be summoned up while in conversation with the customer. "The real big focus now is on the customer," said Maurizio Salvi, customer care and development IT manager, in Rome. "We are able to understand whether the customer can use other services and products. We need to understand who needs what, and then target those customers with new services. We analyze the traffic to understand what the customers do, and can build a customized offer depending on the customer's traffic patterns."

Why Most Companies Do Not Have the 360° View

Most companies do not have a 360° view of their customers. The reason for this is that they have yet to integrate the disparate departmental systems, the data silos that we talked about earlier. In this age of multidivisional companies, business units, decentralization, mergers, and acquisitions, it is often impossible for the left hand of the organization to know what the right hand is doing.

Add to this the challenge of dealing with inconsistent data—the credit card division might use its own call center software and a certain customer numbering convention, while the mortgage division may use a different one. The credit card system may contain a Ben Jones of 321 De Anza Drive as Customer #127, while the mortgage system contains a Ben Jones of 321 Deanza Ln as Customer #235. It is difficult for the company to realize that Ben Jones #127 is the same person as Ben Jones #235. Disparate systems and inconsistent identification methods are the primary deterrents to attaining a 360° view.

The parent company must therefore balance the requirement for common data conventions with the need to maintain the autonomy and empowerment of each of its business units. To accomplish this, it will need to enforce at least one of the following:

- The business units will have to use a common information technology infrastructure, including common systems and common customer naming and identification methods.

- The businesses will be required, on a frequent basis, to load their customer information to common, enterprisewide data warehouses in which the data will be cleaned up and consolidated.

Customer Profitability: A Tale of Two Customers

How should your credit card division handle a $15 disputed fee? From a business perspective, the answer should depend on the business value of the customer making the inquiry. Look at customers A and B below. When you look at the whole table, it is readily apparent that A is a far superior customer for whom you would literally bend over backward. B, on the other hand, is not a great customer. Now look only at the third row of the table, which represents the perspective of the individual business unit that runs credit cards. From the business unit perspective, A and B are identical. You might deny the adjustment to both and might deeply regret having done so when customer A takes her business elsewhere.

It was once thought that Pareto's Law applied to profitability—20 percent of the customers generate 80 percent of the profit. As organizations started to focus on customer profitability, many realized that Pareto's Law should be reversed: 80 percent of the customers generate 120 percent of the profit. The other 20 percent of the customers actually cost you money, and you would either be better off without them, or at least you would be better off restructuring your offers to make the relationship a profitable one.

Customer A	Customer B
Has $100,000 in CDs	Has a basic checking account only
Has $350,000 mortgage at above market rate and has not yet refinanced	No mortgage
Pays credit card bills on time, runs a low balance, and does not generate interest and fees	Pays credit card bills on time, runs a low balance, and does not generate interest and fees
Has brokerage account with $150,000 invested and trades frequently	Uses another supplier as his broker
Never calls your customer service number for help	Constantly calls to inquire as to status of outstanding checks

The issue is that most companies cannot discern the difference in profitability between customer A and customer B. Most organizations can only see customer information within their stovepipe or business unit—the credit card division, for example, can only see customer interaction within that division. With the 360° view of the customer, the person, or computer, interacting with that customer at a given touch point—order entry, email response management, call centers, customer support systems, the Internet, kiosks, and in person—can know everything about the customer's relationship with the business.

Another common problem is that companies often use only lag metrics—such as past sales, or past costs generated through calls to the call center—to define the profitability of a customer. This method can only give an idea of the past profitability of a customer and does not necessarily give great insight into what the potential future profitability of that customer may be. Future profitability is the most important metric to track, but it is hard to identify, because it is based on prediction. By combining different sources of information, not only past transactions, but current interactions and behavior, the forward profitability is a metric that can be estimated and therefore acted upon.

Beyond the 360° View, the 360° Relationship

Achieving the 360° view of the customer is very important, but in some ways, it is not enough. A company does not simply want to be able to see all aspects of the customer relationship; it wants to be able to *act* on that information and to act in a consistent manner regardless of the customer interaction or touch point.

What is needed is not simply a 360° view of the customer, but a 360° *relationship* with the customer. Once your organization has achieved a 360° view, you can then see that only one Ben Jones exists in the company records, although his name appears under two slightly different addresses, in the mortgage and the credit card divisions, respectively. You want to be able to not only recognize Ben Jones consistently across multiple divisions, but to take consistent actions with him, regardless of the point of his interaction with your company. For example, if you have decided that Ben is a good target for a home equity loan, then you would like to (1) mail him an offer, (2) discuss this possibility with him next time he visits a branch, (3) pop up this idea the next time he visits your Web site, and (4) discuss this idea with him the next time he calls your call center.

Conversely, customers expect the companies they do business with to be knowledgeable about them, regardless of what communication channel they choose to use. If a customer has ordered a sweater through an online store and a defective piece of merchandise arrives, she expects to be able to call an 800-number and speak with a customer support representative who has details of the transaction at his fingertips. A 20-minute telephone ordeal with a support representative who has to request information that the customer supplied on the Web site does nothing to earn repeat business.

While this 360° relationship makes a lot of sense, few organizations are able to both recognize a customer across multiple divisions and perform consistent actions with that customer regardless of the interaction point. Putting the infrastructure in place necessary to do this is a requisite first step to reaching customer intelligence.

The Utopian Segment of One: Segmentation 101

The second key concept in customer intelligence is *customer segmentation*. The way companies have traditionally tried to get closer to their customers is through realizing that customers are not all the same, and that each of them has potentially different needs and desires when it comes to the use of products and services.

In the early days of the industrial era, when production and distribution ruled, this was not the case. Henry Ford famously proclaimed on the availability of Model T's: "Any color you want as long as it is black." Such arrogance would be punished today, of course. Customers are not the same, and they want different things from a product or service. If they cannot find satisfaction from your company, they will go to your competitor. Some people will buy a Mercedes Benz as a status symbol, others for durability, and others for resale value. Knowing which customers are buying for what reasons can help in focusing your marketing and business strategy.

Because customers are different, companies have long known that they should attempt to group similar customers into *buckets*, or *market segments*, in which the customers have common characteristics or interests. The goal of customer segmentation is, of course, not only to group the customers into common segments, but also to treat them in a way that meets the unique needs and interest of the segment. Pitching a senior citizen a skateboard, or pitching a preteen a new Mercedes is a waste of everyone's time and effort.

Sometimes, you might think that the segment and its needs are obvious. But it does not always work that way, and segmentation can sometimes surprise you. A case in point is Mobil Oil. Mobil assumed that buyers of its highest grade of gasoline would predominantly be affluent people who drove expensive vehicles—a Lexus, a Mercedes, a BMW. These people would be discriminating motorists certain to feed their cars with the highest-octane fuel to maximize performance and extend the vehicle's longevity, or so the thinking went. Based on this assumption and a limited degree of data analysis, Mobil's target audience for advertising and marketing its premium fuels would be people who watched televised golf and PBS, read Conde Nast and Esquire, and shopped at Nordstrom.

Guy Abramo had a surprise for Mobil. The oil company hooked up with the Center for Data Insight—a research center created in 1997 through a partnership between Northern Arizona University and the consulting firm KPMG—for which Abramo was working as managing director of marketing intelligence. He later joined Ingram Micro, the $29 billion computer distributor, where he now serves as CIO. As a proof of concept, the center ran data from Mobil's retail stores division through a series of data mining exercises. The researchers at the center took about a year's worth of customer point-of-sale data from credit cards, and enhanced it with demographic information from a third-party provider. The results upended Mobil's belief that buyers of its highest-grade fuels would be affluent people.

Abramo and others from the Center and KPMG presented their findings from this proof-of-concept exercise at a meeting in the summer of 1997 at Mobil's headquarters in Fairfax, Virginia: "Our data showed it was just the opposite," said Abramo. "They expected to see Lexus and Cadillac drivers, but what we found was that people buying superunleaded owned older model vehicles and tended to be part of the blue collar demographic. They were the '69 Buick drivers. That was not what they expected. I think the biggest impact was recognition of what they did not know and the fear of creating multimillion dollar advertising campaigns on the basis of perception rather than reality."

Further analysis upended another assumption—that buyers of premium fuel would tend to be loyal to the Mobil brand. In fact, they were not as loyal as Mobil thought. Customers of Mobil's regular unleaded gasoline had much higher loyalty scores. Armed with intelligence from data that had remained unexploited in its data stores, Mobil was now prepared to tailor its advertising and marketing accordingly to target markets, build customer loyalty, and drive revenues.

The Limits of Demographic Segmentation

Many companies use demographic segments—segments based on standard demographic measures, such as age, income, geography, gender, and marital status—to divide up their customer base and create marketing programs. The problem with demographic segments is that they tend to be very large or coarsely grained. If you have 8 million customers, as do many phone companies, retail banks, and consumer ecommerce companies and you place them in eight segments, you would end up with an average of 1 million customers per segment. While you have segmented your customer base in recognition of the fact that not all customers are the same, you have done so at an extremely coarse granularity.

The problem is that you may be missing major marketing opportunities in much more finely grained or smaller segments in the customer base. Because of the coarse-grained segmentation, major differences among individual members of a segment—say, the 1 million people who own minivans and have kids who play soccer—are overlooked. Clearly, many customers are interested in many different things. Telling them apart and finding much finer-grained segments become a new goal.

In fact, the inability to get beyond very coarse-grained segments is a key reason that standard response rates for direct marketing, such as direct mail, are only about 2 percent. For every 100 promotional mail pieces sent out, only two responses, on average, are received. As one direct marketer stated: "You can say no to me. I have very thick skin. Ninety-eight percent of the offers I make are rejected and thrown away." Clearly, there is a huge opportunity to eliminate waste and improve productivity. This can be accomplished by delivering better focused marketing campaigns through finer grained segmentation. Doing so will result in significantly higher response rates.

One example is British Airways. The airline's customer intelligence system helps it determine how to best serve its customers, reduce its costs, and boost revenues by analyzing multiple variables. The airline analyzes routes, market share data, and bookings through travel agents and computerized reservation systems to calibrate its routes and schedules. Analyzing market share data against British Airway's internal information gives the company interesting insights into who its competitors are and where the passenger feed comes from for particular routes, says Peter Blundell, British Airways' knowledge strategy manager. Understanding changing market dynamics enables marketing campaigns to be launched into areas likely to be fruitful.

"You want to segment your market so that you do not flood the market with deals that nobody's going to take up," Blundell says. "Getting the right offer to the right group is very important. Customer intelligence enables us to understand what our booking profiles and customer profiles look like, so that we can make the right offer to the right person."

"A student, for instance, is time rich and cash poor. A student might have a huge lifetime value, and if you can capture the student's business at that point with the right offer you have been successful," Blundell says. "The offers that a student would be interested in are much different than the offers you would make to a businessperson who is cash rich but time poor. That person is much more interested in having the best possible schedule, maximizing his or her time, and having high quality service. A businessperson is not really interested in saving a hundred dollars."

The 1:1 Future

In a bold attempt to address this rather desperate situation, Don Peppers and Martha Rogers introduced the notion of one-to-one marketing in their hit book, *The One to One Future*. In this book, the authors argue that businesses should move away from coarse-grained segments of one million customers toward fine-grained segments, with the ultimate goal of reaching the segment of *one*—to treat each customer as the individual that he or she is. They argue that the business world should move from one-to-one million marketing to one-to-one marketing.

The key recommendations of the 1:1 future were to treat customers as individuals, based on a holistic view, with consistent actions across touch points, and to think in terms of share of wallet, not share of market. Fundamentally, the book "turned sidewise" many classic ideas based on product-centric marketing concepts, such as positioning and the drive for market leadership in product categories. While those concepts are still quite valid, Peppers and Rogers reminded marketers to think simultaneously across two dimensions—the classic product dimension, as well as the newly conceived customer dimension.

In practice, the primary result of the one-to-one movement is seen in the personalization of ecommerce Web sites and the widespread use of personalization engines to deliver content that has been tailored based upon an analysis of available customer data. (See Chapter 8, on ecommerce intelligence.) However, the basis of personalization is all too often only ecommerce data and not data gathered from customer interactions with other touch points, such as the call center, customer support, and store sales.

With an understanding of the 360° customer view, segmentation, and one-to-one marketing, companies are ready to explore ways of acquiring, building, and caring for customer relationships.

The ABCs of CRM

At its heart, CRM is about doing three things to maximize the lifetime value of customer relationships.

1. *Acquire.* Attract new customers intelligently. An intelligent CRM implementation can enable your company to

   - Target the right kind of prospects through segmentation techniques

   - Develop the right marketing campaigns with personalized offerings to the proper segments

   - Follow the leads through the sales effort

   - Close the loop on the effectiveness of the whole process.

2. *Build.* Build your customer's value over time. Once it has acquired a new customer, your company must work hard to increase the value of that relationship over time. This means understanding your customers enough so that they are enticed to repeat business, through cross-selling or up-selling programs. And it also means having the ability to measure and track that customer value over time.

3. *Care.* Provide the best level of service to customers. Good customer care translates into customer retention. With a solid informational infrastructure built on customer intelligence, you are able to better understand their needs, make your company easy to do business with, and provide customers with a multichannel self-service environment.

Optimizing the value of a customer relationship is like moving through a three-dimensional chart (see Figure 7-2). The y-axis of this chart is the number of customers that your organization has, the z-axis is the value of the relationship, and the x-axis is the duration of the relationship. Customer acquisition (acquire) moves your company up the y-axis. Maximizing the value of the customer relationship through techniques such as cross-selling and up-selling (build) moves your company along the z-axis. Caring for customers over the long term (care) moves your organization along the x-axis, increasing the duration of the relationship. Customer intelligence can help

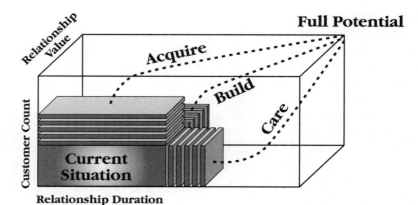

Figure 7-2   CRM Is about Maximizing Customer Potential over Time.

your organization take steps to move from wherever you are to the upper right-hand corner of this chart.

A for Acquire: New Customer Acquisition

When we talk about acquiring customers, we are fundamentally talking about optimizing the "target-to-conversion" loop. Key questions include

- Who are our best prospects for sales and marketing?
- How can we use promotions most applicable to the segments we are targeting?
- What is the best combination of programs and sales calls to convert the prospect into a sales lead?
- How can we efficiently move the prospect through the sales cycle?
- What is the measurement of return on the original marketing programs that drove the lead?

Targeting

Targeting, as the name implies, is figuring out the desired target audience for a marketing promotion. In the context of marketing to existing customers, targeting is typically done using the segments that you have created for your customer base—you select a few of the predefined customer segments as the target for a promotion, or you perform some basic operations on those segments to create a target. For instance, you may seek to target the number of high-value customers who have not bought recently. To do so, you will need to identify the intersection between the segment of high-value customers with the segment of customers who have not bought recently. This is obviously a very important target, as these are high-profit customers whose inactivity could be a sign that they are defecting to another supplier. A timely promotion—a "love letter"—along with a nice coupon with an incentive for them to make a quick repeat purchase may be just what the doctor ordered to keep them in the corporate fold.

Once you have segmented your customer base, you are in a position to improve your targeting practices. You may evolve from the standard approach of having *customer marketing* personnel running programs to existing customers to having *market segment managers* who manage the company's relationship with customers in one or more segments, and to maximize the revenues and profits derived from those segments. Therefore, the targeting process will be driven by a market segment manager who has specific revenue and profit objectives for a segment.

The most traditional way of targeting is to define the target audience for either a new marketing program, or more broadly, a new marketing campaign that consists of a series of integrated programs. For example, say you are launching a new telecommunications switch and wish to build an integrated campaign that uses direct mail (both email and snail mail), advertising (both print and banner), and trade shows to inform the target audience (network designers in telecom companies) about the new product.

Because you know your market well, you know there are a large number of trade shows, magazines, Web sites, and mailing lists available to use in the product launch. The question is which trade shows should we attend, which magazines and Web sites should we advertise in, and which mailing lists should we rent?

Customer intelligence provides value in this context by giving you the power to analyze the results of historically similar programs. On the mail side, and even on the advertising side, you can drill into this information to see which subsets of the total mailing list you mailed to, which cuts worked best, and which demographic versions of a magazine your advertisements ran in. Armed with this information, your marketing managers are in a strong position to make good decisions when targeting their marketing programs.

Another way to perform targeting is to exploit relationship networks. Savvy realtors will ask a purchaser if they have friends interested in selling a house, and car salespeople will ask a similar question about cars. *Network penetration* refers to the idea of "building out" from a single customer to reach his or her family and friends, or in the business-to-business realm to start with a single department and then branch out to other departments, and then other divisions. Businesses such as Amway have had great success exploiting these relationship networks. Now, new techniques known as *affiliate networks* are emerging on the Web to perform the virtual equivalent of Amway—using relationships to penetrate people's business or personal networks.

A simple example of this is Amazon.com's affiliate network program, under which tens of thousands of affiliates have signed up to sell books on Amazon. The affiliate simply joins the program and places a few links on its site that either list, or more powerfully, recommend various books. When a customer of the affiliate's site is persuaded to buy a book, the customer presses the link, gets directed to Amazon, and has his or her order taken and filled. Then the affiliate is given a finder's fee (typically in the single-digit percentage point range). This model is very powerful because it provides true added value. If someone is visiting his or her favorite management consultant's site and reading information on leadership, what better time and place for that management consultant to recommend the person's favorite readings.

Enterprise Marketing Automation

Once a marketing department runs a campaign, the question becomes what to do with those people who respond. In some cases, such as a direct mail campaign pitching a child's CD, life is simple—you take the orders and mail the disks. In most cases, however, particularly in business-to-business environments, life is much more complex. No one orders 10 aircraft engines or mainframe computers as the result of a direct mail piece. That is not to say that direct mail is not valuable in the sales of those products. It is just more difficult to measure, because the industrial sales cycle is complex, in that the purchasing decision is made by a group of people within the targeted organization, and a company will interact numerous times over an extended period with each of those people.

An operational CRM system known as an *enterprise marketing automation system*, or a *campaign management system*, provides a systematic means of handling the responses from marketing programs. No matter what technology or implementation approach is chosen, the business goal remains the same—to handle the influx of leads, score them, and then place them into a process as a result of the score.

For example, customers who "have budget and are going to buy in the next 30 days" might immediately be sent to sales. But what do you do with customers who are "just looking" and who indicate no intent to purchase? You may have spent $50 to $150 to get the response. Do you throw them into the virtual bit bucket because they are not ready to buy right now? Of course not; you place them into a process, often known conceptually as "the incubator." From here, they may be periodically contacted and reminded of your company's products.

Customer intelligence plays a key role in enterprise marketing automation, because it allows you to measure not only the effectiveness of your targeting, but the relative effectiveness of the different incubation paths into which you place customers. Say that all A leads are passed to sales and all B and C leads are incubated, and that you try four different processes for incubating the B's:

- Send a postcard every month with different messages around the benefits of your product.

- Invite to a seminar, make a telemarketing call, and follow up with a ten percent price promotion mailer.

- Mail the business benefits brochure, wait two months, and make a telemarketing call.

- Mail video or CD, followed by monthly postcards.

Customer intelligence will let you analyze the relative effectiveness of these incubation methods. As many things in marketing still remain a "black art," the enlightened marketer is driven by the desire to constantly experiment, and then to measure the variances driven by that experimentation. Customer intelligence provides marketing with the information systems backbone to do just that.

Sales Force Automation

Say the lead has been successfully incubated and is now ready to be passed to the sales organization, and that, depending on either the size of the opportunity or its location, you might pass it to your sales force, or to one of your distribution partners. A number of questions need to be answered:

- How do you know if sales has followed up the lead at all?

- How do you know if sales is executing the agreed-to follow-up process for a lead of its type?

- How do you get it back and give it to another rep if they do not?
- How can you see if the deal is won or lost?
- How can you see which competitors are in the deal?
- How can you know if the deal got put "on hold" and the prospect needs to be reincubated?
- How can you see if any forecast revenue exists this quarter from the opportunity?
- How can you know who else inside the target company is involved in the same opportunity as the lead you found?
- How can you see if the lead became a customer?
- How will you find out the lead's new address if the lead changes buildings?
- How can you keep tracking this individual if the lead changes companies?

Answering these problems is the province of *sales force automation* (SFA) systems. SFA systems take leads, assign them to sales representatives, help them execute a sales process and methodology, help to track attributes of the deals (e.g., competition, application), and help to keep track of individuals and their relationships within companies and when they change companies. They also assist with forecasting and commissions generation.

Business intelligence is often used for standard and ad hoc reporting and analysis, against the underlying SFA database. While the real power of business intelligence is unleashed in a 360° customer warehouse, using it to access the SFA database will lead to answers to the preceding questions.

That is the practice at Heineken's beer sales operation in Madrid, Spain. Some 150 salespeople for Heineken's *El Aguila* brand of beer are outfitted with handheld devices to manage taking orders, deliveries, discounting, and routes while in the field. The data they collect is entered into a sales force automation application. There, through a Web-enabled customer intelligence solution, the information is accessed by the Heineken sales managers and administrative personnel to measure efficiencies, assess profitability, size up sales performance, and track problems and issues that affect customers.

"Our vision has been to provide tools to the sales force that allow them more time to dedicate to customer management," Darrell Proctor, information systems manager, says. "As they must manage their sales routes profitably it is important they have the most up-to-date information about their customers including deliveries, pricing and discounts, and any incidents that have occurred and impacted the customer."

Measuring Marketing Effectiveness

One of the most powerful ways to use business intelligence for customer analysis is to apply it to the particularly nasty problem of evaluating marketing effectiveness in complex business-to-business sales cycles. This can be done standalone or as part of a broader effort to measure customer profitability. The key problem is that business-to-business sales processes are not as simple as filling in a card and giving a credit card number. Multiple programs touch multiple people over an extended period of time that result in an initial order and then follow-up purchases.

What is needed is a way to look at a set of individuals in an organization over time, the marketing programs that they experienced, and then the net resulting revenues for the organization. Only in this way, by aggregating the costs and benefits of business-to-business marketing, are you able to get a realistic picture of the return on investment (ROI) of business-to-business marketing programs. Evaluating such programs in isolation is often done, but the results are questionable as they ignore the greater reality of business-to-business selling.

Often, in performing such ROI analyses, it is better to start backward. That is, rather than ask the question "what happened to all the leads I generated in Q1," the ROI analysis is more effective by looking at the question backward: "Of all the sales in Q3, tell me the marketing I did to these organizations." The power of set-based analysis, explored in the next section, is very useful in doing this type of analysis because you can identify a set of individuals, perform a series of actions on them, and watch the evolution of that set of people over time. One interesting analytical test to perform on a single program, however, is to look at which was the final marketing program that "pushed the prospect over" into becoming a customer. So, rather than calculate ROI based on this figure, you are actually trying to determine the correct sequencing for marketing programs as a function of where someone is in the sales cycle.

Finally, we should add that this whole analytic process may be further improved through integration of third-party data with your internal data. A number of firms provide third-party evaluation of the evolution of customers down the demand pipe for different industries, by measuring items such as awareness, positive opinion, consideration, trial, purchase, and repeat purchase. Moreover, they can calculate standard conversion ratios for each movement along the demand pipe. For instance, these analyses can evaluate what percentage of those who were aware of a product offering actually considered a purchase. This sort of third-party data is useful when analyzed standalone as a sanity check to look for "leaks in your demand pipe" and common causes for them. It becomes more powerful when combined with your own analysis of your lead funnel and demand pipe, or with additional third-party data, such as advertising expenditures.

B for Build: Maximizing Customer Value

Once acquired, you need to ensure that you maximize the value of the customer over time. This is where most of the heavy lifting of marketing segmentation is actually performed, because you will first wish to segment your customers, and then to perform additional marketing to them as a function of their segment.

Segmentation for the Elite: Data Mining

As we saw in the market analysis example of Chapter 5, there are two basic techniques for customer segmentation: data mining and set-based analysis.

Data mining is the high-end approach to customer segmentation. Ph.D.s in lab coats use rocket science techniques such as neural networks, chi-squared automatic interaction detection, case-based reasoning, and genetic algorithms to determine segments inside the customer base. These advanced techniques are used in industries such as credit card management, for complex analysis such as credit card fraud.

The purpose of data mining is to build a mathematical model that represents accurately the attributes of the customer base. The idea is that if one can find a model or hypothesis that describes well the characteristics of existing customers, the same model could be used to identify future prospects or opportunities. A frequently cited example of such a data mining model, almost folklore in the data mining industry, is the model which predicted that grocery store purchasers of diapers were also very likely to buy beer.

Building the model involves a great deal of time and effort—neural networks, for instance, need to be trained on an existing set of data, and only after a significant amount of training will they attempt to predict future behavior or do segmentation. The task also requires a great deal of expertise. It is not uncommon to have a staff of statisticians spend six to nine months to build a data mining model. These models are then deployed to help make marketing and operational decisions, such as whom to target for promotion and predicting who is likely to churn.

Data mining models are very powerful, and they have delivered great value in addressing high-end analysis problems. The problem, however, with data mining is that it is inaccessible to most people, and it has not yet been adapted to a marketing campaign that needs to be designed and implemented quickly.[2] The models are built by a small group of specialists, meaning that relatively few models may be made, they take a long time to build, and the models are usually "black box"—there is no easy way to understand what the model is or how it was built.

Segmentation for the Rest of Us: Set-Based Analysis

What is needed is a more accessible segmentation technique that can be practically applied and used every day by mainstream marketers, without the assistance of Ph.D.s. What is needed is a democratization of the ability to do segmentation, much as a general democratization of data access was needed 10 years ago. Managers need to be able to define their own segments and quickly determine

- How many customers belong to a particular segment (e.g., customers who buy diapers from the grocery store every Friday)

- How different segments interact—how many customers who belong to a different segment are also members of this segment (e.g., how many customers who buy beer from the grocery store every Friday also buy diapers?)

- How membership of the segment evolves over time (how many of the customers who buy diapers today were also buying diapers last year?)

Set-based analysis provides just such a technique—a way of performing segmentation that is easy to understand, and regular marketing staff can easily be trained to do it. Through new techniques like stepwise queries and visual selection, marketers can create sets, or customer segments that can be reused throughout the organization by the individuals who interact with customers. Because segments or sets are easy to build by the marketing people

---

[2] Decision trees, a data mining technique illustrated in Chapter 5, are an exception to this rule. They are easier to understand and help describe the properties of relatively small sets of data, for example, data within a business report. Several desktop data mining tools are available for this purpose in the market.

themselves, marketing programs driven by these techniques tend to be built faster and be more accurate.

A very useful approach when analyzing customer segments is a technique known as *stepwise query*. This method lets marketers take a gradual approach when defining their customer segments. The idea is for them to take simple steps and sequence their construction of segments. For example, a marketing analyst might want to create a segment that consists of all airline "frequent flyers" who fly out of Chicago's O'Hare Airport. This segment would also include all other flyers who use one of three named U.S.-based airlines, but excluding any customers who fly oversees or travel with children. The marketing manager would

- Start with all frequent flyers, regardless of which airline they use

- Add all flyers who use one of the three airlines in question

- Keep only travelers with flights within the United States

- Exclude any flyers who travel with children

As organizations learn more about their customers, marketing analysis inevitably becomes more complex. With stepwise querying, the selection process remains quite simple, however complex the final query to the database. It is also much easier to deal with exclusions, which are important for marketing. Stepwise querying makes it easy to plan a marketing activity along the following lines, for example:

- Step 1. Select two random control groups of 5000 prospects

- Step 2. Select the 1000 highest-earning customers, skewing the results so that 75 percent are male

- Step 3. From this group, select customers spending more than a certain amount during the past 12 months

- Step 4. Exclude people who were targeted last month

- Step 5. Exclude people who bought products during the last week

The power of stepwise querying is greatly strengthened when used in combination with a technique called *visual selection*. Visual selection is an important step in the understanding of customer data. It allows marketers to see a high-level overview of their customer information before they begin a query process. For example, a customer service manager may create a query

such as "how many inbound calls to my service center in Seattle went unanswered after two minutes?" After the query is run, the manager learns that
only 30 of its thousands of calls exceeded the two-minute limit. Using visual
selection, this same manager could have seen at a glance that while 30 calls
languished at the Seattle call center, a much higher percentage exceeded the
two-minute limit at the company's Miami call center. Instead of wasting time
querying data about the successful call center in Seattle, the customer service
manager could act upon the graphical representation of hold-time information and quickly focus her efforts on fixing the problem in Miami.

Visual selection lets the marketer take the structure of the data into
account when defining and refining the request for data, and to change
direction in midcourse if appropriate. However complex the criteria used to
build the segment, the user always knows how a decision will affect the final
counts of customers in the segment.

Visual selection gives users an overall grasp of the data at the outset so
that they do not go down blind alleys. With a visual selection tool, the user
can see how many customers fit a given criterion before running any queries.
If some groups contain very few or no customers, and are therefore not useful for further analysis, this is immediately obvious. The total number of
queries is therefore reduced. Errors in data entry, such as the real-life example of a company whose customer database contained 30,000 people who
had not yet been born, can be detected before any more time is wasted.
Visual selection helps users to decide what questions they should ask based
on the structure that they can see and streamlines the processes of segmentation and analysis.

A major advantage of set-based analysis is that it makes it easy to arrive
at a result of a known size and structure. Marketers often know the structure
of the answer at the outset. They commonly ask questions such as *I can
afford to print 1000 brochures. Whom should they be sent to?* Visual selection
enables the user to see how each step in building a query affects the final
count. At any point, it is possible to define a sample that fits the requirements of the results in terms of size, content, and structure. Sampling therefore makes it possible to tailor the selection process to arrive at the desired
number of customers. Similarly, it is easy to fulfill requirements—such as
choosing an equal number of customers in each sales territory, by skewing
the results into the desired form.

One 2 One.   The mobile phone market has grown incredibly fast over the
past decade, and the introduction of new networks and services will further
fuel that growth. With high rates of churn and the constant introduction of

new services, mobile phone companies have to work hard to create a personal relationship with each of their customers. One 2 One, a mobile phone provider in England, uses customer intelligence to support a range of customer services and operational requirements—from fraud management and supply chain evaluation to customer relationship management and the creation of products and services to meet customer needs.

One 2 One uses a customer intelligence system to exploit a data warehouse that includes information from customer care systems, telephone switches, prepaid vouchers, and external geo-demographic data. One role that customer intelligence plays is in helping One 2 One identify customers to include in a specific promotion, and then to monitor the success of promotions. "It enables us to refine our customer segmentations," says Adrian Daniel, One 2 One client team leader. "It ensures we can get the right population groups and then run queries on that group, enabling us to refine the product or promotional offering."

For example, One 2 One was able to produce a customer segment that included all customers who had opted for prepaid phones, but who had bought only one voucher and made few calls. "We mailed them to let them know that vouchers no longer expire, and then track the success of that promotion based on an increase in calls made over time," Daniel says. One 2 One's finance department also uses customer intelligence to track customer churn patterns. The company takes a group of customers that joined in a specific month and discounts those who leave at the end of a one-year contract, concentrating on the rest to see why they are leaving or staying. Daniel goes on to say that "Churn is a fact of life in the mobile market. By applying filters we can cut the total five million customer population down to a very small group, enabling us to answer specific questions about that segment."

Types of Analysis

Once you have created your customer segments, you then are in a position to perform a number of common techniques and analyses to help increase customer value. Customers may be segmented by a variety of characteristics—profitability, risk, revenue generated, geographic areas, lifestyles and life stages, length of time as a customer, and income, for example.

Segmenting customers by profitability can help you understand which groups tend to purchase high-profitability items frequently and which groups produce only a marginal profit—or no profit at all. Factors such as transaction history, income, and "recency and frequency" of purchases may be fed into a customer segmentation model that includes spending bands of high, medium, or low, and propensity to purchase by various categories. From this information, forecasts on future customer purchases and profitability are developed.

Recency, frequency, and monetary value are key characteristics in customer segmentation, taking into account how people buy over time and the value of their transactions. Customers may be segmented by the sequence in which they buy products, by the channel by which they came to do business with you or by which they conduct the bulk of their business, by sales force territorial region, or by customer needs.

Another segmentation model may examine customers at a given time in a given year to assess customer turnover. Many companies use dozens of segmentation models that are evolving to include more finely grained data points. In a parallel to our analogy in Chapter 5 likening a business intelligence system to one of local water distribution, the customer base may be compared to a lake. A lake may remain fairly level, but its contents are always changing, with water constantly flowing in and out of the lake. Segmentation enables companies to examine the changes in the composition of the lake and to take appropriate, intelligent action.

The example on page 159 shows several segments and the sorts of objectives that a company might build around them.

Analysis and measurement may be conducted on various customer segments, with the following types of specialty analysis often used:

- *Interaction analysis* allows you to measure how different segments interact. You can use this type of analysis to compare two different segmentation models—for instance, compare risk to recency or value segments to product segments.

- *Dependency analysis* shows how the members of specific segments exist within other segments. You can then see how alike different segments might be. The process, also known as clustering, simplifies the task of understanding the customers' complex buying behaviors.

- *Cross-segment migration* is ideal for identifying how people change over time. You can track how specific high-value buyers have moved to become medium- or low-value customers and then take relevant action as a result.

- *Cross-time migration* allows you to look at a specific segment and see how it changes over time.

- *Category management analysis* allows you to define how you track and measure specific product-related activity. By creating segments of prod-

Segment Name	Goals for Members of This Segment	Potential Offer/ Activity	Measurement
First–Time Buyers	Repeat A customer who has bought once might be encouraged to buy again.	Send the customer a welcome pack Customize an offer relative to their first purchase Promote items that customers may have viewed on your Web site or even added to an unchecked cart.	Leave the First–Time Buyer segment
Quarterly Buyers	Intensify A customer buys quarterly might be encouraged to buy monthly.	Schedule a call to discuss how they plan to use your products to explore repeat business opportunities Work to get an understanding of their total buying requirements for your product range	Join the Monthly Buyer segment
Book Buyers	Cross-sell A customer who buys books might be encouraged to buy videos.	Offer a promotion on videos relating to the subject of books that the customer has bought Recommend videos bought by people who have bought the books they have bought	Join the Video segment
Video Buyers	Up-sell A customer who buys videos might be encouraged to move up to DVDs	Offer an aggressive promotion to buy a number of other DVDs featuring the same stars, films, or genre Provide an incentive to the customer to move to DVDs by lowering the entry price	Join the DVD segment

ucts, stores, time periods, and customers, you can simplify the visual communication to help extract consistent meaning from your data.

- *Promotion analysis* allows you to track and measure the relative performance of groups of products, customers, and time periods. You can measure the relative performance of promoted and nonpromoted products for control and index the performance of different time periods.

- *Market-basket analysis* enables you to determine which products consumers tend to buy in concert with other products, providing clues for cross-sell and upsell opportunities. For instance, an online sporting goods retailer may find it productive to show a pop-up window offering athletic socks to a person who buys running shoes.

- *Survey analysis* allows you to track the relative responses of different groups of customers to a questionnaire or survey. You can compare and contrast these groups to a larger population and to each other. Seeking feedback from customers and then measuring and acting on the responses is an integral part of a multi-channel strategy.

C for Care: Customer Service That Qualifies as Care

Once a company acquires customers, segments them, and performs actions that build customer value through increasing frequency, upselling, and cross-selling, it is well on the way to maximizing customer value. Now it needs to do a good job of servicing the customer and building his or her loyalty. The third dimension of the CRM cube is the duration of the relationship. Several factors influence the duration of a customer relationship:

- Leveraging the 360° view to resolve disputes and address problems

- Providing self-service customer care

- Predicting and preventing customer churn

The surest and most obvious way to lose a customer is to make the customer angry. The most effective way to permanently lose a customer is to see only a part of the total relationship and, based on that, make a bad customer service decision that alienates the customer.

The way to ensure a long relationship is to deliver service that delights the customer. That means not only providing a 360° relationship, but also allowing customers to serve themselves. As numerous studies have shown, self-service customers not only are happier customers, but they cost less as well. In a CRM context, that customer care might mean anything from providing a searchable database of problems and solutions to technical problems, to allowing someone to see the status of an order, or even to the more sophisticated case of allowing someone to analyze her historical orders and bills. The last example is what we call a *customer care extranet*, one of the fastest-growing areas of customer intelligence. Organizations are flocking to develop extranets and self-service data access and analysis as a way of reducing their customer service costs and differentiating their products and services. (We cover this topic in greater depth in Chapter 10.)

Finally, the last way, and the most defensive way, of prolonging a customer relationship is to anticipate its end and take preventive action to avoid it. This is the realm of *customer churn* and has been a typical application of high-end data mining within the highly competitive telecom business. But customer churn does not need to be only used in high-end data mining applications. There are a number of simple steps that can be taken to ensure that you are avoiding churn:

- Generate reports of customers who are not actively using any subscription services you offer.

- Generate reports of customers who have not used your product for more than twice their average interpurchase interval.

- Periodically survey customers, mailing them a link to an online survey to simply ask them their future intentions regarding the purchase of your products.

- Generate reports of customers who have experienced an unusual number of problems, and deliver those contacts to your telemarketing system. A company representative can then follow-up on the customer, apologize, sympathize, and learn the person's current problems and future intentions.

New Forms of Customer Value Management

If you follow the advice presented so far, you will be on your way to building strong customer intelligence. Few organizations are at this level today, but among those which are, where are they today, and what problems have they encountered when implementing these ideas? For all its value, the one-to-one marketing theory put into practice presents some practical obstacles:

It does not work well for very large customer bases, for example, and it does not deal with fluctuation over time in an efficient way. To solve these problems a new class of analytic applications is emerging, called *customer value management* (CVM) applications. In the context of a customer base of 8 million, the impossibility of creating 8 million discrete segments is a classic example of the difficulties of turning theory into practice. Sure, lots of segments sound great, but how do you manage an environment of such hypersegmentation? The answer is simple:

- Some segments must be managed by objective. These high-value segments will have assigned market segment managers with revenue and profit objectives, who manage the segment on a daily basis. There will be relatively few of these—hundreds or a thousand, at most.

- The other 7,999,900 must be managed by exception. Measures and triggers on these segments can automate responses to actions.

Customer value management (CVM) applications are starting to provide these abilities by allowing companies to build the segments, attach measures to them, and then assign action rules on each measure, such that the segments can largely be ignored unless a material change is automatically detected. Another issue concerns how dynamic the customer segments are over time. Indeed, experience shows that people migrate through and among segments. A customer segment that may look stable because its size is not changing, may undergo considerable changes as the people who belong to it come and leave regularly. Effective marketing often depends on the ability to look at how the same customers change over time. For example, an analysis of churn and the factors that affect it is of central importance for companies wanting to address the issue of customer loyalty. Change is also the mainstay of *event-based marketing*: People are receptive to offers when their circumstances change, although this receptivity seldom lasts very long.

To measure change, it is necessary to take a "snapshot" of a set of customers at a given moment in time, and record it for comparison with future snapshots. There are two aspects to this process:

- Tracking a group of individual customers over time, in order to see, for example, whether they buy more after your marketing activity than they did before

- Taking successive snapshots of a segment that meets particular criteria, to see how the membership changes

To capture the required information using these tools, it is necessary to plan a specific data structure in advance. For instance, you would want to identify the people who were good customers in February, and then to identify those who join and leave that group in March. Similarly, you may want to identify individual customers who have recently married or had children.

Summary

Customer intelligence is a process that leverages the capabilities of business intelligence in the context of customer relationship management. It entails developing a 360° view of the customer and using not only the traditional business intelligence techniques, but also more sophisticated segmentation techniques. Customer intelligence is a key enabler, helping you know your customers better and helping you exploit that knowledge to anticipate their needs and deliver on their expectations. By focusing on the customers with the highest value potential and providing the best service to them, you will be more able to realize that value effectively and more likely to retain these customers in the future.

8

Ecommerce
Intelligence

*For pure-play dot coms, business intelligence is absolutely the critical element
for turning an unprofitable company into a profitable one.*

Scott Carl
Vice President of marketing
Outpost.com

Ecommerce companies whose business is purely online face many unique
challenges. Their customers are expensive to acquire, faceless, impatient,
and can switch to another supplier at the click of a button. At the same time,
these companies collect an extraordinary amount of information about their
customers' demographics, expressed preferences, past transactions, and
observed behaviors. Using that information intelligently can make the difference between a doomed unprofitable dot com and a successful leader in the
new economy. Ecommerce intelligence brings tremendous value but must be
implemented incrementally: first by analyzing basic Web traffic and transaction data, then by implementing personalization technologies and segmentation techniques, and finally by using clickstream information and
third-party data. Using this process, a company can build a real understanding of its customer base and adapt its offering to meet the needs of the most
profitable customers. To put it more bluntly, got data? Dot coms do. They
are practically drowning in it.

Every day, tidal waves of data are generated by surfers and shoppers paying a visit to online merchants. Not only are all the purchase transactions
recorded, but every button pressed, every image downloaded, every review
read, and every single click is stored in massive log files—What book did the
consumer consider buying before purchasing? What Web site did the person

165

come from? Where did that individual go after leaving your site? How did the consumer move through your site prior to the purchase? The net effect can be overwhelming—and lucrative. What does one do with a terabyte of data consisting of the digital trail of the customer's Internet protocol address, pages of entry and departure, pages viewed, length of session, links followed, banner ads clicked, and points of shopping cart abandonment? Online retailers have back-end transaction systems that record purchases of products and services. How does one integrate the Web-generated click-stream with the back-end transaction data to learn more about the customer, and translate that information into more precise and profitable marketing?

These questions are very much on the minds of business and IT managers, as they deepen their commitment to e-business. They recognize that they are sitting on mountains of data that are richer and deeper than businesses have ever captured. This data can provide businesses with insight into customer preferences, shopping tendencies, and product affinity. With this data, an e-business can go beyond what click-and-mortar businesses have been able to achieve in terms of customer intimacy and marketing effectiveness.

Traditional and nontraditional businesses are starting to recognize that bringing intelligence to bear on this data can pave the way for them to attract and retain customers with tools, such as marketing campaigns, product placements, and cross-selling offers. They are exploring information on both customers and visitors and segmenting the data into groups for target marketing. They are examining how the insights produced by analyzing data can be used to enhance personalization and to improve the online experience. They are looking to clickstream for clues on how to improve Web site design, offer placements, and the overall stickiness of their sites—making sites more attractive and engaging enough so that people stick around.

In this chapter, we will explore the unique particulars of doing business over the Web, then investigate why there is such a need for intelligence in an ecommerce environment. We will examine the different steps companies can take to progressively gain insights on all the data acquired through their online activities. And we will finish by examining the overall benefits of harnessing data in a pure ecommerce environment.

Performing without a Net: The Particulars of Web Business

The stakes for dot coms are high. Conducting business on the Web is a very challenging task, because consumer behaviors in cyberspace are dramatically different than in the physical world:

- Switching costs for the consumers are extraordinarily low. A customer is able to hop from your Web site to a competitor's and make purchases in just a few seconds, for reasons that may or may not be obvious. A lower cost offered by a competitor is one possible reason, but there are many others—poor response time or cumbersome order forms, for example. Regardless of the reason, however, a shunned online merchant is left only with the Web data the customer left behind to try to figure out what went wrong.

- Internet shoppers are notoriously impatient. A Saturday morning visit to a retail store in a shopping mall entails a greater investment of energy than a leisurely surf to a Web site. While at the store, a consumer may well wander around and purchase something that was not on the shopping list. On the Internet, with the consumer a click away from the door at any moment, dot coms need to provide a rewarding, informational session to the visitor by recognizing his or her likes and dislikes and catering to them in a personalized manner. If a Web site is a little too slow, or the user interface is not intuitive, a potential customer will quickly lose interest and visit another site.

- Price comparison is available at the click of a button. Once they have found the product they are interested in, consumers can now research better prices via an automated agent.

The result is that e-tailers are performing on a tightrope without a net. In a selling environment with fickle customers, low switching costs, and instant price comparisons, one mistake may be your last. That said, there are two additional factors that are seemingly unique to e-business: purely information-based relationships and extraordinary customer acquisition costs.

Purely Information-Based Relationships

Online merchants face an irony unique to e-business. On one hand, the only thing they know about their customers is the information that exists in the data they capture about them. They have no stores where executives can practice MBWA (management by walking around), in order to chat with customers, observe their behavior, and hear what is on their minds. On the other hand, online merchants have an ability to record data that is unheard of among more traditional retailers. In one sense, they know less, but they can remember much more. So, the issue becomes how to extract intelligence from the massive amounts of data. How to get the best of both worlds—

knowing a lot about the customers, remembering it, and acting on it when the time is right.

The automation of customer contact minimizes the factor of human intelligence in the business equation. A well-trained bank representative will seize on an offhand customer comment regarding a home equity loan to steer the customer to the home equity department, or see to it that literature is mailed or an email sent. An alert travel agent, when facing a price flinch, will use her wits to suggest a lower priced package vacation and in turn build customer loyalty. An insurance agency representative may see in a customer file a month-old inquiry on a life insurance policy, and take the opportunity to raise the topic in a conversation on an unrelated matter.

Online merchants cannot readily benefit from this human observation and intuition. They have no way to leverage their interaction with the customer into a profitable, relationship-building transaction, except by exploiting and analyzing the data captured while the customers were online. They no longer have human customers, only digital ones. It makes Scott Carl, vice president of marketing at online high-tech e-tailer Outpost.com, think back to the days of the quaint mom 'n' pop corner store: "You walk into your local mom 'n' pop butcher shop and the guy knows that he sold you a really nice piece of steak last week, and the first thing he says to you is, 'How did that steak work out for you?'" He's trying to understand what makes you tick—did you like that steak. In his mind, he's keeping track of his best customers, the people who come in again and again. In a sense, e-business intelligence gives us the ability to mimic that behavior. Ultimately the goal is to become familiar enough with the customer so that the customer gets products and service that he or she wants, and is treated in a manner that leaves them feeling comfortable and wanting to come back."

Online retailers cannot enjoy the same degree of intimate banter with their best customers as the local butcher or department store manager can. In another sense, however, the online retailers do have an advantage over their offline counterparts, because they are able to track and "remember" the activity of customers in ways the more traditional retailers cannot match. Because every single purchase is recorded immediately in a database that also includes profile information, retailers have at their disposal all the information they need to move to the next level in customer relationship.

Extraordinary Customer Acquisition Costs

The second thing that is unique about the Web as a business environment is that by historical standards, customer acquisition costs are very high.

That is because online merchants offer a wealth of information on products and services that present the customer with an electronic bazaar. The Internet as a whole is the world's largest catalog, enabling product comparisons with a handful of mouse clicks. By viewing online catalogs for office supply distributors, for instance, it is easy to determine which offer the lowest price on a printer. With this key information in hand, the consumer is halfway home to a purchase.

The proliferation of product browsing, however, seldom results in a purchase. The abundance of choice and information leaves consumers ever more fickle and merchants ever more in need of customer loyalty and marketing programs to drive profitable return business. Companies trying to sell automobiles and trucks over the Web, for instance, find that the vast majority of visitors appear to research vehicles for style and horsepower, but make their actual purchases at the dealership.

A McKinsey & Co. study in early 2000 found that less than 5 percent of visitors to a business Web site actually purchased a piece of merchandise.[1] And some two-thirds of them do not return to make a second purchase. With customer acquisition costs running approximately five times greater than the average customer purchase—McKinsey puts the average customer acquisition cost at $250—Web merchants need to make strong efforts to build loyalty and drive repeat business. (See Figure 8-1.) It is therefore absolutely essential to create a loyalty effect with the customer and make sure he or she returns loyally, and frequently, to shop on the site.

Getting consistent, repeat business of even a small percentage of customers can have a large impact on the bottom line. Frederick Reichheld, a management consultant at Bain & Co. in Boston and author of *The Loyalty Effect*, estimates that keeping just 5 percent of customers who would otherwise defect can improve profitability by as much as 50 percent. Reichheld sees the Internet as both raising the stakes for business and providing a vehicle for measuring customer loyalty: "Now more and more companies recognize that lifecycle value of the customer is the right way to think about the economics. More and more people see that customer loyalty is vital and will be more intelligent about managing it. The other thing is a lot of people could not even measure customer retention rates. I think 15, 20 percent maximum of the companies I have seen measure retention. With the Internet, there is no excuse for not tracking which customers come back for more, what the average ticket is, what the average penetration is. The tool is there—it's a weapon. Some companies are going to use that weapon and some are going to get shot with it."

---

[1] *The Industry Standard*, March 20, 2000.

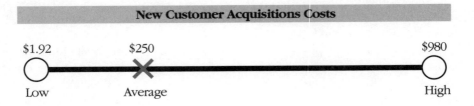

Figure 8-1   Ecommerce Site Costs per Customer.

Who Will Survive?

The odds are not so good: many industry analysts predict casualty rates above 75 percent for the 30,000 or so dot coms. Access to capital has dried up for many as the IPO opportunity has come to a halt, and late-stage investors are in a wait-and-see mode. For the lucky ones who went public before the fall, stock prices that enjoyed lofty valuations have come back to earth, or gone underground. Many casualties have happened already. Ghost sites now populate the Internet frontier with shutters flapping in the virtual wind.

Second to securing the next funding phase, the biggest challenge for dot coms is new competition on the Web from established merchants who bring strong brand names to Internet sales. For those click-and-mortar companies, the Internet is for the most part another sales channel—not the only one on which their futures rest.

In spite of the growing pains and highly publicized disappointments, there will be profitable survivors. Online spending from the consumer sector enjoyed a health surge in 1999, rising to $16.2 billion from $4.5 billion the previous year, according to the Internet consumer tracking service Bizrate.com. Bizrate.com's research also found that 47 percent of online traffic was driven to merchant sites from Web referrals, far ahead of the 19 percent of traffic prompted by printed marketing material.

For many B2C dot coms, the ability to analyze their data and take action on the results will figure prominently in whether they survive, are acquired, or go bankrupt.

The Need for Ecommerce Intelligence

Any dot worth its com has quickly come to regard e-business intelligence as mission-critical, and recognizes that conducting e-business without deriving intelligence from the data that is captured is tantamount to flying blind. Dot.coms need to capture and use their information in order to survive and prosper. In fact, you see this need already in the way Wall Street values dot com companies—the value of a typical dot com company centers more and more around the value of its customer base and how well it knows these customers. As Patricia Seybold, CEO of the Patricia Seybold Group and author of the best-selling book *Customers.com* rightfully pointed out, the AOL-Time Warner merger positioned the value of each AOL customer at about twice the value of each Time Warner customer. The difference? Because of its frequent customer interaction, AOL has vast amounts of knowledge about its customers, whereas Time Warner knows very little about its customer base.

The correct approach to dealing with customer data and applying business intelligence is different depending on your organization's overall approach to ecommerce. Pure-play business-to-consumer (B2C) dot coms, which do business exclusively on the Web, are implementing e-business intelligence systems to help them make sense of their data—which provide their only clues as to critical information, such as visitor behavior and customer preferences. Dot com's strategic goals are to convert browsers into buyers, and then to build customer loyalty by implementing targeted lifecycle marketing programs. They need to focus on the most profitable customers and the most profitable products in order to reach their financials goals. In order to achieve these goals, the surviving ecommerce players will need to have a nearly perfect handling of their customer and sales information.

The B2C click-and-mortars, which are established companies with retail outlets or catalog distribution mechanisms, have embraced the Internet as an additional sales channel. They have a challenge that is not faced by the pure-play dot coms—integrating the data generated by e-business with data from other sales channels to achieve holistic views of customers across all channels. In addition, the B2C click-and-mortars generally already have sophisticated back-end systems that have been built with a specific business model in mind. Now that the business model is changing, the back-end systems need to be adapted in order to integrate the online component. Their ultimate goal is to reinforce the customer relationship and to improve customer service.

The Ecommerce Evolution

Moving to e-business intelligence technology is the second phase of Web commerce evolution. The first phase has been building robust, reliable, and high-performance Web sites that are easy enough for visitors to navigate.

Phase I: Getting Up and Running

- *1997–Being Unique.* Pioneers and visionaries test online shopping concepts. The primary focus is offering online catalogs and taking basic orders. (See Figure 8-2.)

- *1998–Being Available.* As online business begins to grow, dot coms focus on building a site that can handle the entire order-taking process, can scale to support large volumes, and is available 24x7 with minimal downtime.

- *1999–Being Productive.* Dot coms are focused on building affiliate partners, deploying basic personalization, and working out the kinks out of their basic orders.

The early work in the shift to online purchasing has involved deploying systems that manage interaction with the customer. Online businesses have followed the triage approach of companies that deployed back-office enterprise resource planning systems to automate business processes—a pragmatic philosophy captured by the statement, "get the system running first, we'll optimize later." In the gold rush of the Internet economy, few dot coms have had the time, personnel, or money to implement e-business intelligence systems in parallel with the construction of the basic, workable online operations.

During the first phase of Web commerce, many online businesses have been born, but few are providing true intelligence on their operations, resulting in disappointments in managing the customer base. Stories of consumers receiving duplicate catalogs from the same retailers, receiving mailers to apply for credit cards from companies with whom they already have accounts, and offering to buy books they already have purchased, are rampant in discussions of the weaknesses of the new economy.

The second phase is now upon e-business—to derive intelligence from all the data captured during the customer interaction, to make the interactions as personal as possible, and to create value by reaching the highest levels of loyalty. In short, to make e-business truly intelligent.

Phase II: Getting Smart

- *2000–Being Intelligent.* Dot coms focus on streamlining fulfillment, improving and automating customer service, customer relationship management, and building closer relationships with their suppliers. They are starting to deploy intelligent e-business systems that incorporate the analysis of transaction, clickstream, and customer profile information into merchandising and promotions.

Analyzing collected data to better inform customer relationship management and personalization technologies, to improve the precision of target marketing, and to hone the ability to make decisions can have make-or-break implications. It is not enough to simply build good and user-friendly online systems; it is now critical to build intelligent ones.

Because of the sheer amount of data they capture, ecommerce companies are being challenged with the task of handling some of the largest data stores in the world. Data warehousing guru Ralph Kimball predicts that clickstream warehouses will dwarf conventional warehouses in size within the next

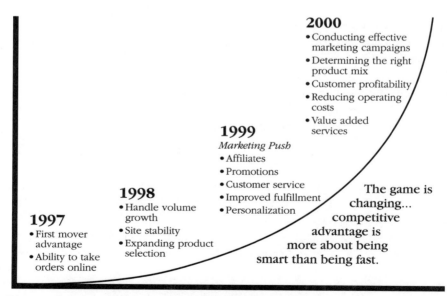

Figure 8-2   Achieve Competitive Advantage Online.

decade.[2] Some already have. A company called MatchLogic, a Colorado-based subsidiary of Excite@Home that provides digital marketing services to companies such as Procter & Gamble and General Motors, has a warehousing system that contains dozens of terabytes—and climbing. That is approaching the size of the largest warehouses run by retail stores. So far, the world's largest databases were point-of-sales datastores containing records of each line item on a cash register receipt. Clickstream databases are quickly becoming about two to five times bigger because they record not only everything someone purchased, but they also record every virtual aisle they walked down and every product they virtually picked up, looked at, and put back.

Fortunately, e-business is recognizing its crying need for data analysis just at the point at which the data warehousing and business intelligence industry has reached the level of maturity necessary to make sense of this new and potent source of data overload. The back-end databases that serve as a platform for an analytic data warehouse have profited from the performance and scalability enhancements through the late 1990s that have made them capable of handling terabyte-sized data loads without choking. Database vendors such as IBM, Microsoft, and Oracle have tailored marketing messages specific to dot coms moving into e-business intelligence and data warehousing—or Webhousing, as it is called.

Front-end e-business intelligence tools, of course, have been adapted to run over the Web, enabling broad deployment and a consistent Internet platform for e-business. And significantly, the many hard lessons that the retail, financial services, and insurance industries learned in constructing and leveraging terabyte-sized data warehouses are being applied to warehouses that are swiftly filling with inexorable streams of clickstream data, helping to guide explorations into uncharted territories of high-end data warehousing.

The tools are ready—bring on the clickstream.

Building Intelligence Step by Step

Building an intelligent system that optimally leverages all sources of information an online company has captured about its customers does not happen overnight. It takes several iterations, a significant investment in technology, and an accumulation of knowledge that comes only with experimentation, trial, and error. Companies that are new to the online game usu-

---

2 Ralph Kimball, The Special Dimensions of the Clickstream, *Intelligent Enterprise* magazine, January 2000.

ally are at stage zero and use almost no data at all, whereas companies more advanced in e-business intelligence are able to integrate data coming from transactions, clickstream, and other sources to build powerful consumer relationships.

There are four primary types of customer information that are leveraged through e-business intelligence:

- *Demographics.* This describes the basic attributes of the customers: who they are, what neighborhood they live in, what their income bracket is, their marital status, and so on.

- *Expressed preferences.* This describes what topics customers have expressed an interest in (e.g., types of books or music they like, stocks they track, sports teams they follow). The preferences are usually captured through form-based questionnaires when the consumer registers for a site or a service.

- *Past transactions.* These are the records of past transactions that the consumers have had with the company (e.g., what books they have purchased, what auctions they have conducted). These are recorded when the consumer actually conducts his or her purchases.

- *Observed behaviors.* This is information derived from observing the navigation the customer follows in using the Web site, as well as where he came from and where he went afterward. This data, called *clickstream information*, is coming from every single click throughout the consumer online experience, and it is collected in large log files.

As the ecommerce company gets more and more sophisticated in building an intelligent e-business, it should progressively leverage these different types of information in an efficient way.

Let us now look at the typical steps ecommerce companies typically follow in leveraging their information, in the order in which they typically evolve as they get more and more skilled in exploiting the power of e-business intelligence.

Step 1: Basic Web Traffic Analysis.   The very first type of analysis of any Web activity is the measure of Web traffic. In the early days of the Web, hit counters were the rage. Marketing executives of fledging dot coms would crow over surges in the hit rate and dutifully report at board meetings that the site's number of hits had risen from 1 million to 2 million hits per week. It provided a riveting number that could help a Web site sell advertising space. This was the time when the hottest buzzword in the industry was eyeballs (i.e., the number of eyes that were looking at the site on a regular basis), which had the convenient by-product of allowing some executives in the hyperbole-ridden dot com space to multiply the actual number of visitors by two (for each eye). Web traffic information that sites have at their disposal ranges from soups to nuts and varies in its usefulness.

BASIC HITS AND PAGE VIEWS.   Hits and page views are the lowest level of clickstream data, the sequential record of pages visited. This data provides a record of entry and exit points into a Web site, what pages were visited, which links were followed, how long a person viewed a particular page at what time on which day, the browser type, the visitor's Internet protocol address, and other information. This type of information is often used to help secure advertising dollars. It can also point to problems at a site—a problematic page, for example, where people drop off, because response time is too slow. It can help a Web site tailor its quality assurance and systems maintenance practices to ensure that the site is able to absorb high traffic times.

At Business Objects, for instance, by doing basic analysis of our Web site operations, response times, outages, top pages, and top downloads, we made an interesting discovery: What we thought was an out-of-date white paper with a not-so-exciting title of "How to Evaluate BI Tools" was, in fact, one of the top downloads on our site. We were about to kill the piece when, thanks to the Web logs, we realized how popular the paper was; we decided to rewrite it instead. The problem with this data is that it is mostly anonymous and tells the Web site little about customer behavior, customer loyalty, or customer profitability. It might be used to serve up an advertisement for a sporting goods product, if the clickstream reveals ESPN.com to be a regular entrance or exit point; but for the most part, it falls far short of providing a Web site with the intelligence that it needs to be successful.

The number of page views and hits amounts to little more than digital turnstiles. It is as if a retail store were to count the number of people entering the store, without bothering to examine how much they had spent or what they did when they were inside. Nevertheless, these basic metrics remain the principal quantifiers of online sites activity today. A Forrester research study in late 1999 found that more than 80 percent of respondents from 50 companies relied on hits and page views to assess their business.[3] Forrester found that far fewer used look-to-buy ratios (12 percent), registered user visits (24 percent) or sales and revenues (34 percent). Similarly, the pre-

---

[3] Forrester Research, "Measuring Web Success," November 1999.

dominant use of the metrics (42 percent) was to report overall traffic levels. Twenty-eight percent used the information to report on site sales and leads, and 18 percent used it to adjust site content. However, Forrester's study found that this situation is swiftly changing: Eighty-four percent said they expect heavy demand for intelligence from the clickstream in two years, up from just 26 percent at the time of the study.

Step 2: Customer Interaction Analysis. The next step is to go into more details about customer interactions with the Web site. The first type of measure is the conversion rate from a browser to a customer (either a registered user or a buyer). Conversion rates have been viewed as a key indicator of the Web site effectiveness—as well as one to convince investors to participate in the next round of financing! However, conversion rates do not provide any insight into the customer patterns. Ecommerce companies need to know the frequency of interactions, the average purchase, and the categories of products purchased.

REGISTERED USERS ANALYSIS. Registered users are the people who have had to register for site usage, often by filling out a survey form. The *New York Times*, for instance, is a free site, but requires the user to complete a registration form. Depending on the questions asked, this data could allow a Web site to size up its visitors and customers by profession, education, age, gender, race, leisure activities, merchandise purchasing, and so forth. Through the registration process, the site is able to get the demographic as well as the preference information as referred above. Recorded email addresses provide a way for the site to communicate with these registered visitors.

This data may then be used to help to inform personalization engines to serve up content relative to the visitor's interests. It enables the site to display the person's name when he visits, in a bid to build intimacy. A visitor with an expressed affinity for golf or gardening, may then be served advertisements or content specific to those interests. Combined with clickstream data on the visitor's site usage habits, the Web site is able to develop a fuller picture of both individual visitors and its visitor population as a whole.

BUYERS AND TRANSACTIONS ANALYSIS. Once users have become customers, the site is now able to analyze the historical transactions to identify their most loyal customers and their purchasing patterns, as well as the segments they fall into with respect to interests, frequency, or profitability.

A dot com company should start by producing a series of standard reports that can be executed automatically on a regular basis, in order to provide business users with answers to the basic questions about the business:

- Who are my top 20 percent customers? What percentage of my total revenue do they generate?

- What is the trend in the buy/view ratio—how effective was our site redesign?

- Which portals referred the greatest number of visitors?

- How many orders did we get this week?

- What was the average order size?

- What is our weekly sales volume?

- Can the production volume of my suppliers support sales fulfillment?

- How much ad revenue are we generating with the new site design compared with the old one?

One dot com turning its transaction information into actionable intelligence is Outpost.com. The Internet seller of PCs and other high-tech merchandise from Kent, Connecticut, has been growing quickly through 1999 and into 2000, recording 4 million visitors per month and growing beyond 500,000 registered customers. Outpost.com is going beyond the simplistic measurement of page views and now is embracing metrics that are less technology-oriented but more business-oriented. The company is tracking metrics such as the average number of items per order, back-order dollars, frequency over six-month periods, and so on.

A large factor in the lack of exploitation of Web information in the past has been the low-level nature of the software tools used to analyze the data. Many companies only used basic Web log analysis products or homegrown applications. Now, many advanced Web companies are graduating to established e-business intelligence and data warehousing software and methods to maximize their return on investment. To maximize the value of analysis of Web data in a Webhousing environment, the technology components are largely the same as they are for a data warehouse in a brick-and-mortar implementation:

- A relational database to serve as a data warehouse analytic platform

- An extraction, transformation, and loading tool to move data from Web servers (where the clickstream log files reside), transactional data stores (where purchases are being stored), and back- and front-end applications into the data warehouse

■ Front-end e-business intelligence tools to analyze the data

Step 3: Real-Time Personalization. Personalization is the ultimate realization of the one-to-one marketing dream. Customers are recognized when they come in, can tailor the way they interact with the merchant, and receive promotions and marketing programs that perfectly fit their personal requirements and preferences.

Leading Web sites have deployed some form of personalization for some time. Sites like Yahoo! and Amazon.com, for instance, use personalization engines to greet a returning visitor by name and to propose specific products or promotions tailored to his or her personal needs. A personalization engine in use at a music and video retailer is able to recognize a customer who has purchased new DVD releases in the comedy genre, and serves up information on the latest available comedy releases when the customer returns to the site. The system makes an educated guess that the customer will be interested in the latest releases, and makes it easy for her to purchase the sort of comedy DVD films that she has in the past. It is a win-win for both the customer and the retailer.

The four primary ways of performing personalization are *greetings, customization, narrowcasting,* and *recommendation.*

Greetings are the most basic form of personalization: the consumer is greeted by name and welcomed back when he or she comes on the site. Personalization engines recognize a visitor's Internet protocol address, or cookies stored on his personal computer, and correlate that information with past visits in order to recognize the visitor.

Customization allows a consumer to tailor the service he is receiving from an ecommerce site, or to configure the products he wants to buy. As an example, any Yahoo! user can customize his use of the popular search by creating a MyYahoo! environment which is more adapted to his needs. The MyYahoo! page will, for instance, show only stock quotes for your portfolio, and the particular news subjects you are interested in.

One great example of customization is the American Airlines Web site. Once logged into the site, customers are welcomed by name, and they are shown the number of frequent flyer miles they have on their account, as well as customized information and special offers based on their profile and previous travels with American. The customer can provide American with a large choice of preferences, including home airport, preferred destination, hotel and car rental companies, and preferred seating choices.

Narrowcasting is the delivery of time-sensitive information personalized to each consumer. Instead of being sent messages that apply to large numbers of consumers, customers can declare particular events they want to be alerted about. These kinds of personalized messages can be sent through email, phone, or pagers and allow the consumer to be informed without having to connect to the site. Yahoo! Finance, for example, enables a customer to define an alert that will be delivered if a stock price fluctuates more than a certain percentage. United Airlines also provides flight paging services via various wireless devices. Flight paging provides customers automatic notification of flight delays or cancellations so that they can remain informed of any changes in the status of United Airlines flights.

A *recommendation* enables a site to propose products that are tailored to the customers' requirements, whether they have been explicitly expressed by the consumer or implicitly calculated by the ecommerce engine. Recommendation technology has evolved dramatically in the past few years. It used to be based only on the preferences that a consumer would have explicitly expressed at registration time. Now it can be done in real time and predicted automatically by the personalization engine using different types of information: observed real-time behavior, purchase histories, and expressed preferences. Finally, it can match that data with information regarding other consumers who share similar interests, using a technique known as *collaborative filtering*. The system is then able to make recommendations that are quite accurate.

CLOSING THE LOOP.   One element that is often overlooked in setting up the personalization is to conduct after-the-fact analysis. It is easy to get so wound up on everything happening in real time that you forget to step back and evaluate how the overall system is performing. Indeed, the engines provide recommendations. But how well do they work? Were the products that were recommended ever bought? Is the purchase rate on the recommendations much higher than on the other products? Is this a profitable activity? Provided the data is captured properly, all these questions can be answered by applying standard business intelligence analysis on the feedback information.

Step 4: Getting to Fine-Grained Segmentation.   Despite its value, an out-of-the-box personalization engine goes only so far. Because it operates in real time, it works well when the customer goes to the site and engages in live interaction. However, personalization technologies are not very adapted to drive a massive marketing campaign, nor they are particularly suitable for many types of purchasing decisions with complex sales cycles and multiple decision makers. The next step, therefore, is to enhance the site's marketing power by using an e-business intelligence system performing customer segmentation. We start with the low-hanging fruit that can be picked through coarse segmentation, and we continue on to fine-grained segmentation.

SEGMENTATION FOR CUSTOMER OPTIMIZATION.   In the early days, company officials at Outpost.com were largely clueless about their customers and their behavior. They could not say which were their most frequent or profitable customers, and they were unable to specifically market the items these customers probably would be most interested in purchasing. An e-business intelligence system with heavy-duty data analysis was the ticket.

Outpost.com began with a fairly uncomplicated test in January 2000. It segmented its customers into three groups, according to how recently they had visited the site ("recency"): the active customers, the semiactive customers, and the customers who had been alarmingly inactive. Outpost.com then targeted the inactive customers with email marketing promotions or offers—offering a modest discount on products, for example—to try and entice these customers back into the fold. And it worked! Some 25 percent of the customers that Outpost.com had deemed dangerously inactive returned to make a purchase. Outpost.com was hooked.

The company is evolving its system into more sophisticated segmentation and more precise marketing. It is assessing its customers by recency, frequency, and monetary value—how recently a user visited the site, how frequent those visits are, and the profitability value of the customer currently and potentially. The data from those three variables is aggregated in a data mart and fed into a data mining tool that uses sophisticated algorithms to assign an overall customer value score.

"The company looks for their best customers and treats them very well, and pays less attention to the customers who are not as profitable," Scott Carl, the vice president of marketing says. "The intensity of a marketing campaign can be directly proportional to the value we place on going after a customer that is 170 days old versus a customer that is 352 days old. Rather than flying by the seat of our pants, we're basing our marketing decisions on an analytic process that is a closed loop."

Another compelling indication that Outpost.com's e-business intelligence system could drive profit came in spring 2000. Carl and his team had about 30,000 segmented customers who were deemed the most profitable, according to *recency, frequency*, and *monetary* value (RFM). Of those, about 10 percent were partitioned off as a control group, and 90 percent of Outpost's best customers received an email on a product promotion; the control group received nothing. Again, the results were impressive. Over the next month, the 90 percent receiving the email generated 40 percent more revenue per customer than the control group, Carl says.

The next question is to determine the magic frequency—the optimal frequency of emailing marketing messages and discount offers to consumers. The rich source of clickstream and transactional data provides a factual foundation for zeroing in on the number. "If I email someone too little, I'm not reminding them enough about Outpost. If I email them too much, they get upset with me and won't want to deal with me."

Outpost.Com, a pioneer in pure-play B2C e-tailing, is using e-business intelligence to move toward a profitability that previously had been elusive. Its parent company, Cyberian Outpost, reported net sales for the first quarter of 2000 at $64.8 million, nearly double the comparable figure for the first quarter of 1999. At the same time, losses were more than cut in half, dropping from 27 percent of sales to 11.5 percent. Sales to past customers jumped substantially, from 43 to 58 percent in the first quarter of 1999. Average order price rose to $280, while gross profits per customer rose to $37, versus $29 for the same quarter a year ago. Meanwhile, the cost of customer acquisition fell significantly, from $104 to $47. Carl credits Outpost.com's ability to know its customers, target them, and build loyalty through e-business intelligence as a key driver in the company's move toward profitability. "There's absolutely no doubt that it's led to a material improvement in the bottom line," Carl says.

MINING THE DATA MOTHER LODE.   The harvesting of Web data generates large, complex data volumes. Companies are gathering data that is more finely grained than in the past. By integrating data from various systems, they are able to go beyond the basic profile of John Doe as a 35-year-old white male who buys a piece of electronics equipment on the average of once a year. Web site activity, information on cookies, household and demographic information, online surveys, customer support calls, consumer credit reports, and other sources enable the company to collect additional details. The number of attributes associated with one single piece of data can grow by several factors.

The mounting quantity and complexity of this data often beg for the data mining. Data mining goes beyond reporting, query, and multidimensional analysis to automatically sift through large data sets to discern patterns that might otherwise be difficult to detect. It uses artificial intelligence technologies to conduct knowledge discovery—that is, it can look for patterns in large data sets and identify common elements.

Whereas a query or multidimensional analysis will begin with a hypothesis—we know that sales are down in the western region, for example—data

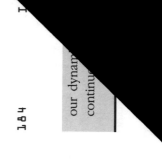

mining is more free-form. Its exploration of t
tion, but with the objective of finding correla
tical analysis. It has long been used by financi
and risk management, by telecommunications
churn, and by retailers for market basket and

Application of data mining to Web data
instance, that surfers originating from Exci
purchase products of greatest profitability. \
may decide to increase its advertising at Excite.com. Data mining can
enhance a Web site's ability to segment its customers by behavior—for
instance, that surfers who spend more than five minutes at the Web site are
three times more likely to buy a product than those with shorter visits.

eBay: Building a Better Auction

eBay is bidding for better knowledge of many of its ten million registered users of its 24 × 7 auctioning services with an e-business intelligence system designed to make sense of the vast amounts of data
generated at its Web site. The data stream is dynamic and powerful—
eBay members add more than 500,000 items to the site daily in more
than 4200 categories ranging from pottery to computers. The site
absorbs more than 1.5 billion page views per month, and typically has
more than four million items for sale at a given time.

By deriving intelligence from this data stream, eBay is looking to
become a more intelligent online auctioneer. One area the company
wants to analyze and compare is the success rate of auctions conducted via two models, the English auction and the Dutch auction. In the
conventional English auction, a good is sold to the highest bidder. In
the Dutch model, a seller sets a price on an item, and then decreases
the price in increments. The first person to place a bid takes the merchandise.

By understanding which model results in the highest percentage of
successful transactions, eBay can fine-tune its efforts to accommodate
successful transactions among its members, and that drives return business in this fast-growing online auction space. "We operate in a very
competitive marketplace, and it is important that we continually
improve the experience for our community of buyers and sellers," says
Bob Sanguedolce, CIO of eBay. Our e-business intelligence strategy
"will allow us to capitalize on the size and high transaction volumes of

ic community, to better understand our users and enable
d improvements that will benefit the eBay community."

Step 5. Going through the Streams of Clicks. Every move on a Web site, every ad banner clicked through, every page request from every visitor is recorded by the Web site owners into massive log files; this is the clickstream information.

The clickstream data contains details on customer behavior that are richer than what can be achieved in traditional channels. It moves a step beyond the department store practice of using video surveillance cameras to track customer movement throughout the store to improve merchandising.

A department store can analyze that film to compare whether women gravitate toward a rack of shoes when they are placed next to pocketbooks, or whether men are more inclined to purchase fishing rods when a sign is posted to compare the benefits of two different models. But it is not possible for the store to combine what is learned from merchandising studies with such customer metrics as demographic characteristics, past purchasing activity, and lifetime potential value (for the simple reason that the videos do not indicate who the customer is). Nor is it easy for the store to use the information from its videotapes to attract the customer with a marketing message. Nor it is possible for a video to tell you what store the customer visited before coming into your store. And it is not at all practical to track the activity of each of the tens of thousands of shoppers that visit the store every day.

In e-business, the surfer and shopper leaves a digital trail of which Web pages were viewed, how long those pages were viewed, which links were followed, the routes that visitors took before executing a transaction, the Web site they visited before yours, and the one they went to next. This data can be extraordinarily enlightening as to the path that customers followed before executing a purchase. Businesses that monitor these circuitous customer paths can glean telling insights as to what advertisements, products, and Web page content positioning is striking a chord with the consumer.

Let us consider how a dot com might use some of the information that it captures. A sporting news Web site, for instance, is able to track the paths of visitors to its site. Many of them will be loyal users who visit several times a day to check scores of their favorite teams. The trail that they leave enables the Web site to segment these users into groups that have a habit of checking the scores on particular teams on a certain threshold percentage of their visits, or by the amount of time spent viewing Web pages related to those teams.

Consider Joe, a 30-year-old single male in Los Altos, California. Joe is a regular visitor to a sporting news Web site. He provided personal information when he registered—his email address, age, zip code, gender, and annual income—in order to participate in a fantasy baseball league available at the site. The Web site can tell through data analysis that Joe belongs to a segment of people who live in California, but who regularly check the scores of teams in the New York area.

Based upon the discovery of this segment and the placement of Joe in it, the site can make offers to the "relocated New Yorkers at heart" for fairly obvious promotional items like Yankees caps and Mets tee shirts. In addition, through affiliate marketing programs (provided Joe has opted to receive such promotions), the site can promote other items that might be of real interest to this segment as well—for example, good frozen bagels, subscriptions to *New Yorker* magazine, or travel offers.

Savvy online merchants are digging into the clickstream to answer some key business questions:

- Which pages are drawing traffic that results in a purchase?

- Which ads are most frequently followed?

- What do our most profitable customers do on our Web site?

- What path is followed by those who buy our most profitable products?

- How can I tell when someone will be at the best point to propose a cross-sell or upsell?

- What navigation do customers follow before abandoning their shopping?

Answering these questions enables a Web site to take an informed action:

- Optimize placement of the page and the link to it

- Increase advertising rates

- Segment those customers' characteristics and provide a special site for gold customers

- Encourage more customers down the most profitable path

- Propose cross-selling at the right time

- Examine the shopping process for weaknesses or obstacles that prompt customers to turn away

GoTo.com

A pioneer of an online marketplace that introduces consumers to advertisers, GoTo.com focuses on delivering a network that creates a win/win scenario for both the consumer and the advertiser, by quickly and easily matching consumers with specific online providers of goods and services who advertise on the GoTo.com network. As one of the 20 most visited sites on the Internet, GoTo.com recognized the opportunity to access, analyze, and share this mass of unique visitor information, and they decided to implement an e-business intelligence system.

With access to this clickstream data, GoTo.com uses business intelligence to identify ways to facilitate the online buying process, by analyzing the browse-to-buy ratio to understand how and when a customer purchases products on their network. By analyzing the Web traffic on their site, GoTo.com is also able to make better merchandising decisions by putting the right products in front of the right customers whenever they visit their site.

Another e-tailer using e-business intelligence to analyze its customer base and turning that analysis into intelligent marketing is More.com, a San Francisco-based online merchant of health care items. More.com's e-business intelligence initiatives began with tried-and-true analysis of transactional data recorded by customer purchases, with plans to expand analysis to include clickstream data.

Using its transactional data, More.com, a privately held company, has created dozens of customer segments, built around such metrics as what products they buy, whether they take advantage of promotions, and repeat buyers over given periods of time—two weeks, a month, 90 days. It also tracks customers by recency, frequency, revenue generated and profitability, and looks at their Internet service providers through their email addresses to correlate that information with buying patterns, finding a ten-fold spending difference between customers using different Internet providers.

With the intelligence generated, More.com is able to run targeted marketing programs and cross-sell and upsell promotions. Buyers of contact lenses, for instance, are sent a reminder email when the contacts they last bought are near the end of their useful life. "The positive response rate to that particular program runs as high as 20 percent," says Chuck Drake, More.com's director of customer relationship management. The e-tailer can also deduce a customer's affliction and run marketing campaigns off that information—buyers of diabetes test strips may be offered related products, for instance. "It's telling us a lot about customer buying patterns, and that's very important to our financial forecasting," Drake says.

With a good grasp on basic transaction analysis, More.com is looking to advance into the more challenging realms of data mining, automated marketing campaign management, and real-time personalization that is driven from the results of analyzing both transactional and clickstream data—correlating customers' behavior on the Web site with historical buying patterns and feeding that information instantaneously to a personalization engine for action. "The sheer volume of clickstream and making it useful is challenging but ultimately promises huge rewards," Drake says. Clickstream and transaction records captured on individual customers may be warehoused and analyzed to produce customer profiles—a historical view of the individual's behaviors at the Web site and whatever other data may be snared on lifestyles, demographics, income, and so forth. The deeper insight into the customer may then be fed to the personalization engine, expanding on its capabilities to interact with the customer in a meaningful way. Combined with customer information supplied during a registration session, online survey, or transaction, it gives the site a rich data stream that if effectively analyzed can easily mean the difference between profit and loss. Analyzing clickstream and integrating it with other internal customer data sources is a science that few master today. Because of the complexity and its volume, few online businesses are using clickstream to its maximum capacity.

Step 6: Enrich Content with External Data.   Once a customer has made several purchases, the Web site is able to further enhance the customer profile. Demographic data from third-party providers may be appended to the profile to provide a richer view of the customer base. Analyzing that enriched data might show, for instance, that a customer who buys history books falls into a demographic segment inclined to also buy classical music. Marketing pitches in the form of emails and personalized content may then be delivered to cross-sell classical music CDs.

This data is critical in building profitable repeat business. It enables refinements in one-to-one marketing in the form of emails, snail mail, and personalized content served during site visits. The overall customer base may be segmented by a host of characteristics to better understand who is buying what. The data may be analyzed to determine an overall customer score that provides the Web site with a roadmap on which customers are their best bets for marketing efforts.

The simple rule to follow is the more data you have about your customers, the more sophisticated data mining and segmentation models you will be able to build. Using third-party data to enrich your database will help you to find segments that were otherwise undetectable. Sometimes this data must be purchased. Sometimes, you can devise business arrangements or partnerships that provide it. American Airlines and United Airlines, for example, have recognized that a great source of information that helps in their marketing efforts is the data coming from the affinity credit card businesses they have associated with their name and frequent flyer programs.

Step 7: Reaching Optimal Intelligence.   A company can reach optimal intelligence once it is able to combine historical transaction records, observed behavior via clickstream data, and preferences expressed in online surveys. Ingram Micro is in motion to become such a company.

Ingram Micro

Ingram Micro, with $29 billion in annual revenue, is the world's largest distributor of computer products. Their customers are electronic superstores, or retailers who in turn distribute the products to consumers. As the world is moving toward the Internet, and consumers can now purchase products directly from manufacturers over the Web, Ingram very rapidly responded with an aggressive Web strategy.

It is now distinguishing itself as a leading implementer of e-business intelligence with their recent launch of the "WIP" project (Web Insight Platform). The new platform fully leverages the different types of information that are made available to a company doing business online. This Internet platform allows Ingram Micro executives, sales, and marketing managers to obtain an integrated, daily view of their business. Ingram executives view the project as a critical application that will allow them to identify revenue growth opportunities, improve customer relationships and one-to-one marketing, and maximize their internal operational efficiency.

The WIP project combines data from four disparate information sources:

1. *Clickstream data:* customer behavior on Ingram's Web site, such as pages visited, path taken (from page to page), activity on page (browse/buy), and others

2. *Sales data:* transactional data on sales across channels (e.g., through partners, direct, through the Web site)

3. *Customer feedback:* data coming from the call center application which provided profile and preferences/usage information

4. *Infrastructure data:* information on system performance, such as Web site hit rates, system uptime, peaks/lows in system usage

With access to this combined data, Ingram can run a much more intelligent organization. It enables the following:

- Clickstream analysis for selling advertising space. Executives can track clickstream activity of their largest customers. With this information, they can view the 25 most popular Ingram Web site pages according to a particular customer, such as a large electronics store chain, and the five pages that generate the most sales for Ingram from that store chain. Ingram can then offer this information to the suppliers whose products are being viewed most on those pages, to incent them to advertise more on those pages, or list more product promotions there.

- One-to-one marketing, through linking transaction and call center data. A telemarketer on the phone with a customer could pull up the Web Insight Platform to view purchasing history of a customer. They might see that they tend to purchase cables whenever they also purchase monitors from Ingram. When the telemarketer is on the phone with the customer, the report would flash an icon for cables as a reminder to cross-sell these products to them while they are selling monitors.

- Tune the system for peak activity from combining clickstream and transaction data. By analyzing the clickstream data for a given week, Ingram has seen that visitors tend to browse and research products on Monday and Tuesday, with a large spike in sales orders on Wednesday, and then an increase in browsing, and research again on Thursday/Friday. With this information Ingram Micro can optimize their infrastructure and staffing to make sure their operation is prepared to handle the spike in orders on Wednesday, and provide customers with product background/information on the other days.

Other applications are related to opportunities to understand how particular customers surf their site. If they are spending a great deal of time researching a set of products but not purchasing, a telemarketer could follow up with them to answer more questions or offer a special discount or promotion.

Intelligent Scenarios: Benefits of Business Intelligence for Ecommerce

By incorporating e-business intelligence into their fundamental business processes, online companies are finding the means to move faster, achieve competitive advantage, and build customer loyalty. Several ways in which the results of e-business intelligence manifest themselves include:

- *Enhanced personalization.* The results of data analysis allow you to elevate the intelligence quotient of your personalization engine. By feeding the engine data from a customer profile built through e-business intelligence, a Web site is able to deliver content more precise than what may be offered by the basic capabilities of the engine.

- *Intelligent decision making.* Through data analysis, dot coms are able to respond quicker to changing customer demands, competitor's moves, and market conditions. Combining transaction data with clickstream data provides not only the ability to analyze what has happened in the past, but to predict future events on the basis of modeling and forecasting of historical trends, and to make the right decisions.

- *Cultivate customer value.* The results of data analysis of dot com visitors and customers speak volumes about preferences of the marketplaces and demographic groups within it. Through a fact-based, analysis-driven understanding of customer preferences and customer profitability, dot coms are able to tailor their products and services to the most profitable sectors with one-to-one marketing campaigns and intelligent advertising.

- *Improved customer service.* A consolidated view of the customer and his or her activity enables your sales, customer support, and call center representatives to speak intelligently and efficiently with the customer, leaving a positive impression and enticing that person's repeat business.

- *Fine tune the Web site.* By analyzing the patterns of Web site visitors and shoppers, dot coms are able to intelligently assess which pages and links are driving the most traffic, and adapt those for maximum value, both from visitors and from advertisers on the site.

Eventually, the real benefit of knowing your customers through ecommerce intelligence is to create a lifelong relationship and true customer intimacy. A good customer on the Web is one who will be a customer for many years to come.

A Note on Privacy

Dot coms stand to profit by analyzing the data they capture on visitors and shoppers. They can both improve their own operations and enhance the visitor's online experiences through e-business intelligence. But the data collected can be a Pandora's box from the perspective of consumer privacy. Through the capture, sale, and exploitation of consumer-oriented data, marketing databases have aroused the ire of consumer advocacy groups. A dot com that implements a forthright consumer data privacy policy will profit in the long run.

There is an obvious conflict between the protection of privacy and the convenience of personalization. Consumers want to receive a personalized service based on their personal information, but they also want to make sure that this information is not put in anybody's hands. A balance needs to be struck and the consumer should be the one to decide. As such, the capture of consumer data is best handled on a permission basis. Consumers should be presented with a clear explanation of how the data they provide is being used. They should at all moments be able to consult through the click of a button on every single site the information the site has on them. They should also be presented with a clear choice on whether the data that they provide may be resold or otherwise used—whether, for instance, they wish to receive promotional emails or newsletters at an address provided.

For privacy, many European nations already provide a model. In France, for instance, the government long ago established an organization called the National Commission on Information Systems and Freedom (Commission Nationale de l'Informatique et la Liberté) that governs the handling of consumer information. The laws protect the public by requiring companies to inform a person that information is being captured from them, and the companies must provide the person with the right to view, modify, and correct the information as well as prevent the collection of data. As we in the United

States watch the Europeans deal with privacy issues, dot coms should consider proactive implementation of some aspects of the European regulations. An online enterprise that proactively ensures the responsible handling of personal information has a bit of a competitive advantage and stands to win greater loyalty with its online audience.

Information Embassies

9

e-Business
Intelligence
Extranets

It's no longer about giving customers data—it's about giving them intelligence. The payback is huge.

Frank Colletti
Director of e-Business Solutions
Zurich U.S.

Transparency is in. Barriers are out.

Traditionally, a company's means of doing business were fiercely guarded. The company would endeavor to insulate its processes from the scrutiny of its business customers to prevent those customers from uncovering a piece of intelligence that might be used to negotiate a better price. Or worse, the information might prompt the customer to take its business to a competitor.

The Internet is forcing this to change. B2B ecommerce is rewriting those old rules. Companies are being forced to become more transparent as customers and business partners become more demanding and have more information at their disposal to negotiate optimal contracts. More and more, we are seeing companies using e-business intelligence over extranets to provide that transparency. Just as they empowered their employees with information, they are now extending their information democracies by placing information embassies within the borders of their customers (providing customer care extranets) or suppliers and partners (providing supply chain extranets). What is more, many vendors are charging an entrance fee to the information embassy, providing a paid-for information hub that we refer to as an *information broker extranet*. The details of each of these different types of extranets will be covered in Chapters 10, 12, and 13.

In this chapter, we will look at extranets as a generic group. We will first analyze the forces that are driving the sharing of information between business partners and therefore the creation of these business intelligence extranets. We will examine the evolution of the different models for data sharing from basic paper reporting to today's intelligent extranets. After taking a look at the risks and rewards of such systems, we will finally look at the key ingredients for success.

From Trading Products to Sharing Information

The Focus on Transactions

The fall of the stock market in the first part of 2000 and the disillusions that have followed regarding some of the dot com companies have shifted the public center of attention from the more visible issue of business-to-consumer (B2C) e-tailing to the less visible, and much larger, area of business-to-business (B2B) trade. Highly publicized company failures have taken some of the bloom off the B2C rose. At the same time, executives who were once afraid of being "Amazoned" in the B2C space, are now even more worried of being "Cisco-ed" in the B2B space. Cisco, and its ability not only to transact 87 percent of its orders over the Web,[1] but to greatly reduce cost in core areas such as supply chain and customer service, has become the role model for everyone.

Therefore, in the past couple of years, most of the hype and attention of the media, industry analysts, consulting firms, and vendors have been focused on how to automate transaction processes on the Internet:

- How can we sell our products over the Internet?

- How can we buy our supplies online?

- How can we implement an efficient e-procurement system?

The focus has been on how the Internet can enable the current business processes and do it well. And when companies are talking e-business intelligence, they are talking about how to make these processes more efficient, more intelligent; they also are talking about having better, more targeted marketing campaigns, and about achieving a better understanding of what the customer really wants.

---

[1] Cisco Website, company fact sheet, August 2000.

Thus far, little attention has been paid to the huge benefits that can be garnered, not only by transacting with one's customers, suppliers, or business partners, but also by sharing information in an intelligent way. Still, according to Pricewaterhouse Coopers, 60 percent of companies do not have extranets linking their own operations with key partners. While most say they will catch up in the next two years, nearly 12 percent said they have no plans in place for supplier and partnership linkage.

Imperative for Sharing Information with Customers, Suppliers, and Business Partners

B2B interactions have quite different characteristics than their B2C counterparts. Let us take the example of a PC manufacturer like Dell. For the consumer who buys online, the critical requirements are going to be the ability to purchase the right machine and to configure it properly, as well as the speed of delivery, the price, and the guarantee of quality. Once the transaction is completed, the consumer does not need a lot of information about the purchase. Now let us take the case of a purchasing manager of a large enterprise who is going to order directly from such a manufacturer. Not only does he need information on the price, the speed, and the quality of the product, but he also needs to track the interaction with the manufacturer. How many PCs were purchased? Have they all been delivered on time? Did some have defects? Were there some returns? Is the service received in line with the service agreement? Monitoring the interaction with a supplier is a key requirement for a B2B interaction. Information sharing is therefore becoming a standard requirement.

Lots of Information to Share.   Commensurate with the surge in online B2B spending is a surge in the quantity of data generated. Information that was once exchanged in person, on the phone, and over fax machines is increasingly being generated and captured digitally. Each good or service offered, each bid placed, each sale declined, and each transaction executed generates a data record. Sellers of goods maintain mounting piles of data on their activity with customers that is of immense value for those customers to access and analyze, and for which many are happy to pay.

Many of the companies that have not yet bought into the B2B ecommerce model and maintain traditional sales and distribution channels are, at least, on the Internet. Their customers are knocking on the digital door for Web-based access to information that shows them, for instance, their purchasing patterns over time, by department, by product, and so forth.

A Need for Transparency.   The new transparency, or openness, between companies has ushered us into the very early stages of Information Embassies. Pioneers in this space are turning their data warehouses inside-out, using Web-based platforms that enable customers to access and analyze their data through a browser. "You have to become transparent with the client," says Frédéric Tiberghien, CEO of VediorBis, a large temporary employment agency in Paris that is rolling out an e-business intelligence extranet for dozens of its clients throughout 2000. "We think it is a way to differentiate ourselves from our competitors. We want to increase the loyalty of our clients, and we see a lot of room for improvement through the usage of business intelligence tools. When you balance the risks and reward, we think it is better to share the information."

A Requirement for Performance through the Whole Value Chain.   In the new economy, every company in the value chain is pressed for faster decision cycles and better performance. Most companies look inward at what they need to be better and implement e-business and e-business intelligence strategies to increase their own performance. This is the same for their business partners. In order to be more efficient, suppliers need to move faster, and to move faster, they need to have instant access to information that only their customers own: inventory levels, sell through metrics, or quality levels in the assembly line. For a company to examine its performance, it needs to look not only at its own needs but also at the needs of its partners and how it can participate in improving their performance. In a business ecosystem, if each one participates in making the others better, everyone benefits.

A Key Enabler for Competitiveness.   Better service is key to customer acquisition, loyalty, and retention. Providing an environment that fosters interactive communication and enables full transparency in the relationship with the customer is a major differentiator in many industries. In order to lower their costs and control their course of action, more and more companies want to understand the relationship they have with their suppliers. Between two products, if one comes with a full customer information system as an added service, that will be the one that the customer will choose. Competition shifts from price negotiation to value of service.

Let us consider the example of a facilities manager at a large company looking for ways to optimize the purchasing of electronic supplies. In this example, we will show how business intelligence plays a role in differentiating all aspects of a B2B transaction between two business entities, including account acquisition, browsing or discovery, price negotiation, payment, merchandise delivery, collections and final settlement, and, if necessary, dispute resolution.[2]

A facilities manager decides to leverage the growing list of Internet commerce sites to make the delivery of electronic supplies to her company more timely and cost effective. While she was able to cut costs a year ago by centralizing purchasing decisions for her company's 12 offices, the most recent employee satisfaction survey revealed an increased number of complaints related to frequent delays in ordering key electronics, such as computers and calculators. In the survey, several employees stated that they interpreted the delays as an indication of lack of attention to their day-to-day needs from the company's management. Characteristic was the comment of one employee: "How does senior management expect me to succeed if they won't even give me the basic tools that I need for my job?" Senior management did notice the survey responses and, as a result, the facilities manager was directed to reevaluate the centralized purchasing program that had apparently led to more frequent shortages in the company's more remote office locations.

The new B2B extranets recently introduced by several major electronics supply distributors offered a new opportunity to improve the efficiency of the distribution to the remote offices. The facilities manager conducted a thorough review of the Web sites of three electronics supply distributors. The first distributor's Web site offered only the usual stuff: basic company information, press releases, investor relations information, and contact information—nothing that would help the facilities manager change the way she conducted her business. As a result of their weak e-business presence, the distributor, a well-known electronics supplier, was taken off the facilities manager's short list.

The second distributor offered a more advanced Web site. Customers could actually view a complete listing of all the products distributed by the vendor. They could even compare prices for certain predefined items. The site enabled the facilities manager to compare the prices of over 40 different types of computers and 52 different types of calculators. While viewing the tables that compared office supply prices was certainly useful, the facilities manager, once again, did not see something that would address her employee satisfaction problem. While pricing info was certainly useful information, at this point, product availability and delivery estimates were equally important to her.

The third distributor offered what appeared to be the best Web site. Not only did it offer customers the ability to compare prices of different items,

---

[2] The seven stages of a B2B transaction outlined here are presented in 'Trust and Risk in Internet Commerce' by L. Jean Camp.

but even more importantly, the site offered customers a full business intelligence solution. Customers were able to identify and track the criteria important to them. For example, when comparing two brands of computers, the facilities manager could compare not only prices, but also one or more of the following indicators:

- *Quantities currently in stock by the distributor.*

- *Estimated delivery times,* by location, to each of the 12 offices.

- *Statistics on what percentage of the distributor's customers had placed repeat orders for the item.* This is a good indicator of customer satisfaction.

- *Statistics on delivery times for past shipments* (by month, product, location, product price range, or delivery time).

- *The distributor's monthly turnover, by product.* This statistic gave the facilities manager a sense of whether she was about to order a popular item.

- *Customer ratings.* While customers where typically unlikely to make the effort and rate high quality items, they often did go out of their way to rate poor quality supplies. This informal indicator offered yet another level of insurance for the facilities manager that she would not be ordering poor quality supplies.

- *Alerts.* The facilities manager could subscribe to a free service that would alert her automatically via email when, based on the frequency of past purchases, the time to reorder a particular item for a certain office location appeared to be near. This service in itself could help address the periodic office supply shortage problem.

Following an order, the facilities manager could then track, on a minute-by-minute basis, the status and estimated delivery time of a shipment. In addition, she could track the status of an invoice and payment. These statistics promised to simplify the resolution of any disputes (delivery of incorrect items or quantities, no delivery, and so on), a task that typically accounted for a nonnegligible part of her time.

Armed with these statistics, the facilities manager felt that she would be able to choose the items most appropriate to her purchasing decisions. The key to selecting this site was that the distributor did not create "canned" reports attempting to predetermine for her which criteria would be important to her purchasing decision. Having spent over 10 years ordering supplies, she knew that while low price may be the most important indicator for one purchase, timely availability, quality, or even (for public relations reasons) country of origin, may be the criterion for another purchase decision.

The electronics supplier was thus able to win the account acquisition battle by offering two simple things: a rich set of purchase decision support information and the flexibility to use it as the customer sees fit.

Evolving Models for Data Sharing

For many companies and their customers, Information Embassies improve on processes already in place. The processes built to exchange information have traditionally taken the form of paper reports, electronic file transfers, or electronic data interchange (EDI) systems.

Paper Reports

Today, most of the information that is provided to customers, suppliers, or business partners is still in the form of paper reports. The problems with that approach are numerous:

- The data usually arrives with an important delay.

- It is costly to print many of these reports, so the distribution is limited to only a few.

- The data on paper is static and therefore quite limited.

- Finally, the environment suffers, as we need more trees, not less.

It should be mentioned that providing static electronic files (e.g., PDF files) has precisely the same limitations of canned paper reports, with the sole exception of killing fewer trees, provided the reports are not printed. On paper or on the screen, a report that cannot be modified, refreshed, or changed is static, which limits its flexible use to a business user.

Electronic File Transfers

Transferring electronic spreadsheets or computer diskettes with customer activity poses its own limitations. Preparation of spreadsheets and diskettes can be labor intensive, and the data is usually dated by the time the customer receives it. Using that information in a meaningful way also involves complex loading and transfers into the company systems or rekeying the information.

Electronic Data Interchange

Another frequently used information exchange system is provided by *Electronic Data Interchange* (EDI). EDI dates back to the 1960s in its earliest incarnations, providing a data link between two large B2B companies through a dedicated, proprietary network—a digital tunnel of sorts between two companies that might be used, for example, to order seats for the month's anticipated production of new cars.

An obvious advantage of EDI systems is that they spare the necessity of manually transmitting documents, faxes, and rekeying large volumes of data into spreadsheets and other systems.

However, the following are some of the problems with EDI:

- It is proprietary and expensive and thus has been only used at the high-end of the market, such as in high-end manufacturing.

- It involves establishing proprietary, point-to-point networks for pair-wise information transfer between companies. It is not suited to the creation of information hubs.

- It is often implemented on a static scheduled basis that sacrifices agility in information transfer.

- It tended to be purely operational in nature; providing data transfer necessary to support operations, such as automatic reordering, but it did not provide data transfer aimed at analyzing and improving operations.

The EDI environment as a whole, though worthwhile, has tended to be clunky, very costly, and not well suited for volatile business climates. The Web-enabled e-business intelligence extranet improves dramatically on the EDI model by eliminating the physical data transfer and the necessity of deploying and maintaining desktop software, and by providing access to data in near real time.

e-Business Intelligent Extranets: Tomorrow's Information ATMs

An e-business intelligent extranet is built on the basic premise that customers, suppliers, and business partners should be provided with instantaneous, flexible, and ad hoc access to information. It is based on the same philosophy as an enterprisewide business intelligent system: As opposed to trying to predict what report each user needs, the information system is open for self-service. In the case of the interaction between a company and its business partners, it becomes even harder to predict what information each of the customers or suppliers are going to be interested in at a given point of time. It depends on a number of parameters that are specific to the customer or partner at that time and that the company has no knowledge about (e.g., the marketing strategy of that supplier, or the new purchasing policy of the customer).

Instead of pushing customers and suppliers various forms of predetermined data reports through paper or electronic forms, an e-business intelligence extranet acts as an entry point to the company's information system. It is usually a secure portion of the company's Web site. When the business partner logs in, they cannot only see a personalized environment with information tailored to their needs, but they also have the ability to query and analyze the company's datawarehouse. As such, the e-business intelligence acts as an ATM of information. Before going to the movie theater, if you realize that your wallet is empty, you do not go to a local branch of your bank and ask an agent for money; instead, you go to a standardized ATM and help yourself to the cash you need. The benefit for you is that you get what you need immediately; the benefit for the bank is that they do not need to maintain offices open late to respond to that demand. The extranet acts according to the same principle: it offers a standardized way (through the Web) for customers and partners to serve themselves with the information they need when they need it. For the company that provides that extranet, they do not need customer support people on the phone 24 hours a day to respond to specific questions.

An e-business intelligence extranet adds a dimension of interactivity with data that EDI systems lack in their exchange data. It also enables the hosting company to incorporate personalization technologies that adapt swiftly to changing business conditions. For instance, the extranet can, like Amazon in the consumer world, greet the purchasing managers by name and provide them with a view of orders placed within the past 30 days.

VediorBis has offered an EDI-like application called TempOffice to its larger clients for several years. While the system has proved fairly popular and useful, Robert Vesoul, VediorBis's vice president of marketing and e-business, is looking forward to rolling out VediorBis's new Web-enabled e-business extranet in 2000. One reason is the time, trouble, and expense the business intelligent extranet will spare VediorBis and its clients in getting the TempOffice system deployed and running. During a meeting in late 1999

with about 40 human resource managers of a large client of VediorBis's temporary employment services, Vesoul was asked about the TempOffice system. The client had about five installations that had proved worthwhile and
was interested in acquiring more. Vesoul winced at the number—the client
wanted 200 more! Installing that many copies of TempOffice would be an
ordeal. "They said, 'Yes, it is a great system, and we have 200 subsidiaries
that would be interested in it,'" Vesoul recalls. "To roll out that much software is really a large cost. You have to go on the site, install everything and
parameterize the software so that it can work with the client's tools. And you
would have to do training."

In response to the inquiry, Vesoul had a nice card to play: VediorBis's
forthcoming extranet, which would make life easier for VediorBis and customer alike.

Risks and Rewards
Staking a Claim

By opening your data stores to your customers and business partners to
those customers via an Information Embassy, you are able to

- Create competitive advantage through differentiation from competitors

- Help your customers save money

- Reduce the number of customer support calls

- Improve customer satisfaction

- Build customer loyalty and "lock-in"

- Reduce costs for generating paper and electronic reports and supplying
  them to customers

- Generate a new revenue stream

- Enjoy the perception as a forward-thinking technology leader

As we have discussed previously, the philosophy of an e-business intelligence extranet is much the same as an e-business intelligence intranet. Each
empowers knowledge workers with self-service and autonomy to make better business decisions. The beauty of the Information Embassy concept is that
many companies are able to leverage the lessons learned through an internal
e-business intelligence implementation, avoiding past mistakes and speeding

time to market. The fundamental technology architecture and business model has already been laid. Adoption of the business intelligent extranet becomes a logical step in the continuum of e-business intelligence systems, providing to the customer functions that range from basic internal reporting to the more powerful tools of ad hoc query and multidimensional analysis.

As we have seen in the "Value of Information" model in Chapter 3, this is a way to get an extra return on an information asset that is already captured in the company's information system and used internally for analysis purposes.

Companies at the vanguard of this movement have, in many cases, deployed e-business intelligence extranets as a value-added service and are able to charge customers and realize revenue gains that in some cases can be substantial. Though young, Information Embassies are quickly moving up in the CEOs priority list. In a recent study by Booz Allen and Hamilton, customers' and suppliers' extranets were shown as the biggest areas of Web site deployment in the next three years. In North America, the deployment of extranets is estimated to go from less than 40 percent to more than 70 percent for customers, and from less than 35 percent to almost 60 percent for suppliers.

Information Embassies are also being driven by the growth in outsourcing service. An e-business intelligence extranet layered on top of service-level agreements associated with outsourcing contracts enables the parties to track contract metrics, analyze the root cause of problems and make information exchanges more efficient. With a proliferation in outsourced services and service level agreements, Information Embassies are emerging as a means for managing many of the tricky intricacies of outsourcing.

Improving Your Own Lot

Implementing an Information Embassy elevates a company's internal processes and results in a better-oiled business, too. For instance, consider the example of an office supplies manufacturing company maintaining a sales order database. Part of a salesperson's job is to manually enter specific types of information into a customer order form. But as busy, road-weary, and harried as they are, salespeople frequently give their tedious data-entry chores short shrift. The job is often not done well, if it is done at all.

Under the new systems, though, if the customer of the office supplies manufacturer has secure, private access via an Information Embassy to its portion of the sales order database, it will spot inconsistencies in the data. An address may be wrong, a contract person's name misspelled, and quantity incorrectly entered. And, of course, the customer will call attention to the error, occasionally loudly.

The fact that the *customer* is complaining about sloppy data entry gives a manager at the office supplies manufacturer a potent weapon in haranguing his or her salespeople on the need for diligence in accurate data entry to the sales order database. The result is higher quality data and consistent business processes.

Challenges

Launching an e-business intelligence extranet can be a daunting plunge for a company to take. There are risks involved that must be tended to carefully, and cultural and philosophical changes that need to occur. Any company pondering an Information Embassy will worry that customers can use the newly available information to their advantage and to the detriment of the company supplying it. A customer's historical view of purchasing data, for example, may reveal that it is overbuying for several regions, and that those regions can easily ship their surplus inventories to another region, which would represent a lost sale. The proposition is that a short-term sales loss is worth the reward of customer satisfaction and customer retention.

Transparency means that flaws, glitches, and unseemly processes in a company are exposed. Business relationships between companies built up over decades can be called into question. An Information Embassy upends many conventional assumptions and practices. Disruptions and problems are inevitable, but so are rewards. "You're basically wearing your business on your sleeve," as Tom Nather, a senior systems analyst at Penske Logistics, puts it.

Yet the digitization of commerce is inexorable. Customers and business partners are clamoring for information, and all the while doing business on the Internet in all industries is fast becoming a commodity. The differentiator is the ability to provide customers with access to data on the business that they do with you for analysis on cost savings, efficiencies, and so forth. The data generated by those digital transactions will demand analysis, transforming the data into information and intelligence.

One bit of compelling reasoning comes from G. Gilmer Minor III, chairman and CEO of medical distributor Owens & Minor, which runs a successful e-business intelligence extranet called WISDOM. Says Minor, "The customers really own the information—it's a byproduct of their transactions."

How Much Functionality?

Companies will also find themselves wrestling with gnarly issues of how much functionality to offer external users. Basic reporting is mandatory, but should you extend those capabilities to include ad hoc query and multidimensional analysis? Additional functionality is likely to mean a higher processing overhead, meaning more cost for hardware and software licenses. More complex functions are likely to result in more users of your Information Embassy phoning into your customer support line, which adds costs. And ad hoc query and multidimensional analysis, in sufficient degrees, can extort a performance penalty on your system.

One thing an Information Embassy does not want is its external users suffering from degraded response times because a user decided to launch the dreaded "query from hell." These users, having become accustomed to a search engine such as Yahoo! (or another search engine) returning results in five seconds, may well be disenchanted if your system does not offer the same speedy response. The best answer to the question is perhaps to let the customer drive the decision, with consideration given to the requirements it places on the Information Embassy hosting company.

An Information Embassy implementation best begins with basic reporting capabilities, providing end users with predefined reports that may be run with several clicks of a mouse. The immediate introduction of ad hoc query functions, which take more time to master than basic reporting, has been known to discourage users from making the most of the system. Some external users at a given company, though, will likely be "power users." They may have used e-business intelligence software in the past, and they may be frustrated if limited to functions that to them seem simplistic. In any event, it is reasonable to expect a graduation effect in functionality expectations in a given user community, be that community external or internal.

Displacing the Competition by Analyzing Their Data

Zurich U.S. provides commercial insurance. Owens & Minor distributes syringes, surgical gloves, and catheters. Hertz Lease rents vehicles. A couple of years ago, officials at these companies would have laughed at the thought that they would be in the business of providing outsource data analysis services. Yet, that is exactly what is happening. These companies are gravitating toward an intriguing twist on the Information Embassy model. They are discussing with their customers the prospect of supplying Web-based access and analysis, not only for data generated by transactions with Zurich, Owens & Minor, and Hertz Lease, but for other companies as well.

The idea works like this: A Zurich customer we will call Acme International makes it a condition of business with another insurer that the insurer's claims and policy data on Acme is supplied to Zurich. Zurich would then house this third-party claims data, alongside its own, in its RiskIntelligence data warehouse. The value-add to Acme International is that that customer now has a single data source with claims and policy information associated not just with Zurich, but with its competitors as well. As a result, Acme International may be able to save resources on its own e-business intelligence system, relying instead on Zurich as an outsource provider. The benefit to Zurich is that they now provide the single analytic "face" to the customer, putting them in a position of strategic advantage relative to the other insurers.

Frank Colletti, Zurich's director of e-business, explains: "Let's say a customer buys its workers compensation and general liability from us, but it buys its auto insurance data from someone else. We can interface that auto insurance data into RiskIntelligence and give the customer a consolidated report of all its insurance. In the insurance industry, we all share data as long as the customer signs off. That's a common practice."

Hertz Lease is proceeding along the same path. It has a large governmental customer that does business with four leasing companies, but which does not maintain a data warehouse. Hertz Lease's ability to offer this customer access to and analysis of data on its business with Hertz Lease was a significant factor in Hertz Lease's negotiations for business with this customer. Now Hertz Lease has taken its Information Embassy a step further. Its proposition is that the governmental agency stipulate that all of the agency's vehicle leasing suppliers provide their data to Hertz Lease. Hertz would then consolidate the data and give the agency over an extranet a single point of access and analysis to information on all of its leasing contracts. Hertz Lease would realize a new revenue stream and gain advantage over its competitors.

"They said it's a very good idea—they don't want to build an IT department just to process data from these different leasing companies," said David Shapland, Hertz Lease's IT director. "It's a huge advantage for us. It means they would be very closely hooked into us, that we have a good business relationship with them."

Hosting with an ASP

ASPs, or *Application Service Providers*, have swiftly planted a stake in the e-business landscape. These companies offer to host enterprise applications for clients, ranging from back-office inventory control, financial and human resource data-management and automation software to front-office systems for sales force automation and marketing campaign management. Customers would then access and manipulate their data over the Internet. The value proposition put forth by ASPs is that they are able to spare customers from the need to maintain internal applications, and they keep on board expensive staff in times when it is challenging to find loyal, qualified technical personnel. The analyst firm International Data Corp. predicts that the ASP market will burgeon to $7.8 billion by 2004.

Organizations that are intrigued by the notion of e-business intelligence extranets, but concerned about their ability to deploy and manage them (especially on the 24x7 basis that is often required for customer-facing systems) should be aware that ASPs provide a convenient deployment option for a business intelligence extranet system. Periodic data transfers to the ASP (or outsourcing the underlying operational systems) can move the relevant data to the ASP's site. Then the ASP can provide the operations and network support required to handle the demands of the e-business intelligence extranet.

An Information Embassy in Your Hand

A future wave of the Information Embassy is its deployment over the wireless Web. In certain businesses in which data delivery speed is of critical importance and translates into dollars, companies are exploring ways to provide data to their customers when they need it, wherever they are. They are looking to the Web-enabled telephones and handheld wireless devices as the delivery vehicles, particularly as these technologies evolve. The smaller devices are growing more functional as their developers brainstorm for ways to pack more punch and overcome physical size limitations.

Accessing an e-business intelligence extranet over a Web-enabled phone cannot allow the same degree of data interactivity as can a desktop computer. Limited data interactivity may be built in, however. An Information Embassy may be configured to broadcast an alert to a sales manager's phone according to predefined thresholds that, for instance, call for immediate notification of any sale of more than $100,000. Through prebuilt queries, the sales manager would then be able to drill into the data over his phone to determine the purchasing company, the successful sales representative, and so forth.

Commercial insurer Zurich U.S. is considering broadening its successful RiskIntelligence extranet with wireless access. Ellen Feliciano, a senior project manager at Zurich U.S. headquarters in Schaumburg, Ill., envisions that speedy notification of significant events would be a big bonus for Zurich customers who use RiskIntelligence. A broadcast report of potential damages resulting from a weather event, for instance, would enable the insured to mobilize that much faster.

Feliciano also believes that driving RiskIntelligence wirelessly could provide an advantage over competitors who have caught up with Zurich in offering their own e-business intelligence extranets. "We're really excited about it because it's truly the next level. This is just what we need."

Ingredients for Success

Companies beginning to consider an Information Embassy should bear several things in mind:

1. Make it a partnership.

2. Make it secure, make it functional.

3. Think creatively and be inclusive.

4. Be prepared for a new business.

5. Build it to scale.

Make It a Partnership.   Opening your data stores to customers and business partners can be like airing dirty laundry. The records you expose to your customer may contain embarrassing errors or omissions—the CEO's name misspelled, for instance. Pioneering companies have successfully positioned their Information Embassies in a positive light, as an opportunity for the customer to contribute to the quality of information relevant to both parties. Customers usually are accommodating; after all, many are familiar with or have their own data quality problems, too. Striking a cooperative balance is mutually beneficial in improving your overall data accuracy.

Commercial insurer Zurich U.S. has seen users of its RiskIntelligence e-business intelligence extranet welcome the opportunity to promptly correct errors and omissions. Before Zurich U.S. rolled out its extranet, customers would receive a disc-based claims data report supplied by Zurich. Any errors in it would, of course, be a month or more old. And then the customer would need to wait many weeks before Zurich was able to supply a copy of a disc with accurate information. "With our monthly system, if data got coded wrong or didn't get coded, it could be anywhere from a day to 45 days before they even knew it from seeing it in the report, and even after we fixed it, it would be a month before they could view it," says Feliciano. "Now, they see a mistake, they call and it's fixed the next day, or they dial in and fix it themselves."

Make It Functional, Make It Secure.   Successfully implementing security and encryption technologies that ensure that customers see only their own personal data must be made the highest priority in the new economy. The security technology exists to make an e-business intelligence extranet effectively bulletproof. The last thing you want is for one of your top customers to be rooting around in a data repository on your transactions with one of the customer's rivals.

Balance the desirability for a speedy deployment with the need to assess and select appropriate software tools and infrastructure built to last. Resist the temptation to put tactics before strategy.

That was one of the debates among officials at B2B trading hub Ventro, in Mountain View, Calif., as they developed an Information Embassy for sellers and buyers doing business via their marketplace. "One argument was: pick anything—even if it's wrong. We don't want any analysis to slow our process. But we didn't want to go with a low-end solution just because it was speedy. We wanted to make sure that it was an investment with a strategic dimension."

Think Creatively, Be Inclusive. Building an Information Embassy involves many of the same fundamental processes as an internal e-business intelligence system. Solicit feedback from the users, the customers, on what data they need most often. Build reports that deliver that information in an easy-to-use format. Think creatively about what information may be of value to which customers.

VediorBis has an obvious constituency for an e-business intelligence extranet: the companies that engage temporary workers through VediorBis. It also has another, less obvious constituency—the temporary workers themselves. By extending extranet access and Web-based training to the temps, VediorBis hopes to fortify good will and loyalty with its most valuable asset. "We have to address the temps really as customers," says Robert Vesoul. "We need to built loyalty and have very aggressive marketing strategies with our temps, to give them social advantages and entice them to come and stay with VediorBis."

Be Prepared, This Is a New Business. While the benefits are great, deploying an extranet is a new challenge for an IT organization. So far, IT had been mostly focused on delivering applications to internal customers (i.e., different divisions and employees within their own company). In the context of an extranet, however, IT gets into the business of delivering and hosting software applications for external customers, which by the way are the core customers of their company's business. The margins for errors are small. Building an extranet means inserting software in the middle of an existing business process or an existing business relationship. This requires an expertise that may not exist yet in the company. IT organizations should partner with system integrators, applications system providers (ASP), or extranet service providers (ESP) to help them build such capabilities and implement a smooth application delivery.

Build It to Scale.   The phenomenon of *build it and they will come* observed in internal e-business intelligence deployments applies to external systems as well. In fact, the rate of adoption and number of users may exceed those of internal systems—these customers and business partners have money on the table.

Commercial insurer Zurich U.S. has already outgrown its RiskIntelligence extranet, and among its top priorities is increasing the number of concurrent users the system can support from 50 users to 250 users. The need to do so was painfully obvious in spring 2000, when Zurich officials were unable to give a live demonstration at an insurance industry event. The demo was coincidentally scheduled for the first Monday of the month, a day of heavy use by customers. The high volume of concurrent users had shut Zurich out of its own system, and it resorted to a canned presentation. "We totally underestimated how big it was going to be," says Colletti, at Zurich. "If we had known, we would have spent more money right up front."

Summary

Business intelligence extranets can apply to the interactions of a company with virtually all its external constituencies, ranging from direct customers to channel partners to suppliers, and this applies to virtually all industries. Credit card companies are communicating better with their card issuers. Banks are communicating better with their enterprise customers. Telecommunications companies are able to build intelligent billing statements to send to their largest customers.

Extranets also are becoming a fast-growing way for companies to interact with each other. In 1999 alone, more than 150 Business Objects customers started to implement business intelligent extranets, compared with just two in 1998. Progressively, the Internet is displacing the business lunch and water cooler as the medium for information exchange.

In the chapters that follow, we will review specific examples of such implementations in customer care, in supply chains, and in the new online trading exchanges. We will also review how companies can create brand new business opportunities by turning themselves into sellers of information.

10

Customer Care Extranets

With this extranet, our clients are likely to stay very close to us for a very long time. It's building loyalty—or even more than loyalty.

Robert Vesoul
Vice President of
marketing and e-business
VediorBis

Country club golf outings and five-star restaurants still work to woo business customers. A nice meal of filet mignon, blackened sea bass, or broiled scallops at a world-class eatery goes a long way in winning the loyalty of your business customers. But more and more, these customers are passing on the crème brulée in favor of a smorgasbord of information.

Information is fast becoming the dish that tempts the appetite of business customers. As customers begin to demand more transparency in their dealings with business partners, they are looking for information on some very basic points—how much business was conducted, with which departments, at what cost, and over what period of time, for example. Customer expectations have risen beyond receiving such information in the form of a paper report or electronic spreadsheet. And their expectations will continue to rise. By providing access to information through a customer care extranet, companies are enabling their clients to cut their spending costs.

Such transparency can be perceived as troublesome, because some companies would think that making customers fully informed of their purchases may end up reducing the revenue stream. Indeed, in the race for maximizing customer value, no company wants its customers to buy fewer products or services. But pioneering businesses are finding that their ability to build customer loyalty and win new business through technological leadership and information transparency far outweighs the risks of a small revenue loss.

The acceleration in professional and personal lives has left many managers accustomed to instantaneous access to information. Today's manager is likely to have at her fingertips daily access to fresh data on sales, shipping, inventory, or other business processes internal to her company. And personally, she has come to expect real-time information over the Internet on stock prices, airline travel, entertainment listings, and sports scores. The days of checking the next morning's newspaper for a stock quote or baseball score are fast becoming a thing of the past.

With this surplus of information on a manager's own company and own interests, the next frontier requires better, faster, more interactive information on dealings with business partners. Speedy, accurate information access is quickly emerging as an integral component in the care and feeding of a valued customer. The vehicle for this informational nutrition is the e-business intelligence customer care extranet. In industries ranging from insurance to financial services to telecommunications providers, companies are envisioning and realizing substantial competitive advantage and incremental revenue streams by providing their customers with access to valuable information over a secure extranet.

Belgacom, the Belgian telephone company, has impressed its large corporate clients with an extranet it calls Bill Manager. The application provides companies with a consolidated, flexible view of their telephone bills, into which they can drill and slice and dice for better understanding and ultimately cost savings. Bill Manager, launched as a prototype in late 1999, replaced a system by which Belgacom sent companies a file of their billing data. "The customer satisfaction with the program is very high," says Koen Vermeulen, Belgacom's director of IT business analysis. "They have much better insight into their telephone costs and can control those costs much better. They have an overview of all the metrics, and can drill down into the data."

For example, if Belgacom customers can analyze phone calls by job function, they can use that information to budget more accurately next year. They are able to see distinctions between phone expenses from a computer analyst who seldom uses the phone, to a sales representative who makes dozens of calls a day. In the case of cell phones, they can also compare the phone bills of employees who use a company-negotiated provider that bills directly to the company, with those of employees who submit expense claims for their phone usage.

The concept is not entirely new. Suppliers have always provided their customers with some form of informational synopsis. A billing invoice on paper, faxed or mailed to a client, relates the highlights of what items a customer ordered, when they were ordered, and how much they cost. But the value of such an invoice is woefully one-dimensional.

A year's worth of invoices piled on a purchasing manager's desk does not lend itself to the sort of analysis that would enable that manager to look for cost-savings opportunities and new efficiencies in the procurement process. And in a sizable company, numerous managers may be receiving invoices that end up scattered across multiple departments and hierarchies, filed uselessly in cabinets or discarded altogether. There is no way for the company as a whole to easily arrive at a clear picture of its purchasing from a key supplier from such a rain of paper reports. A senior purchasing manager with authority over multiple departments would have his work cut out for him to gather, consolidate, and analyze the information contained in those documents.

The customer care extranet makes such processes appear archaic. Indeed, a well-executed customer care extranet will provide the business customer with a single point of access to data on its business with the extranet host company. In addition, the extranet provides the ability to run standard reports that may be shared throughout the customer company and the power to query and analyze the data store of the business partner.

In this chapter, we will first examine the benefits of such customer-centric extranets for both the companies implementing the extranet and the customers using the information system. We will then review the case stories of three successful extranet implementations and draw some lessons from each of them.

A Win-Win Relationship

Developing a customer care extranet enables a true win-win relationship between a company and its customers. Through an intelligent sharing of information, both sides of the firewall are finding great benefits to the extranet implementation.

Benefits for the Information Enabler

From the standpoint of the company that enables the extranet, the solution adds a new level to the three dimensions of Customer Relationship Management: Acquire, Build, and Care. (See Chapter 7 on customer intelligence.) By differentiating its offering with new services, it creates a competitive edge to acquire new customers, and it enhances the customer relationship by creating a partnership based on trust, which should enhance loyalty as well.

Acquire New Customers.   An extranet solution creates a new level of service to a customer. It creates a differentiator for the core product of the information enabler, and as such, it is a valuable sales weapon. A telecom company like Belgacom will use its Bill Manager extranet as a way to differentiate against its competition. It will rely less on pricing to win a transaction with a large enterprise customer.

Create a Partnership with the Customer.   Sharing information with customers creates a partner relationship, rather than a simple customer/supplier relationship. All B2B relationships will undergo a certain amount of friction from time to time—if there is a "transparent" system between customer and supplier, customers have the reassurance that both parties will be able to see exactly what has been happening, when, and why. The common ground of the fact-based extranet elevates the playing field for informed choices and decisions by all parties, rather than squabbles about, say, whether terms of a service level agreement were met.

Increase Switching Costs.   As companies that have deployed customer care extranets have discovered, the demand for such information is great, and it continues to grow. They have been able to cultivate customer loyalty by making the value of such data practically indispensable to the customer. With such valuable information available to a customer, and progressively becoming part of its internal business process, that customer's switching costs will become much greater.

Reduce Support Costs.   Companies that deploy customer care extranets often drive down their support costs, because it is no longer necessary to maintain a large customer service organization to respond to customer information requests and complaints. Every time a customer can get support through the Web, the cost is tiny compared with a voice response unit or a member of the support staff. Indeed, the cost of a typical customer service transaction is several dollars for a live call agent, versus several pennies over the Web.

Increase Competitive Position by First Mover Advantage.   A company that is first to market with a customer care extranet stands to differentiate itself from competitors at a critical time in the evolution of information sharing. External users of customer care extranets have quickly come to regard them as essential to doing business with their business partner.

Here again, first mover advantage is prominently in play. The media and investment communities are driven by news—the first company to introduce an extranet in its field is able to benefit from large amounts of free publicity in industry magazines and at conferences. (See the Owens and Minor example in Chapter 13.) The second-to-market receives about as much attention as the second man on the moon—it's Neil Armstrong that most people remember, not Buzz Aldrin.

Enable a Potential New Source of Revenue.   An extranet may be so valuable for customers that it can be accessible at a fee only, therefore creating a new source of revenue and transforming a data warehouse from a cost center to a profit center. Whereas the extranet will most likely be offered as a free service to the largest customers, it may be marketed at a price for the larger number of small- to medium-sized ones. (This idea will be explored further, in Chapter 12, "Information Brokers.")

Benefits for the Extranet Customer

The customers who are provided with extranet capabilities from their supplier or business partner are getting great benefits. They can

- Monitor service-level agreements

- Get fast, self-service access to information

- Optimize the value of the service

- Benchmark the company's performance

  Let us discuss each of these in more detail.

Monitor Service Level Agreements.   In complex business relationships, it is important for the customer, once the purchase transaction is complete, to manage the contractual aspects of the new relationship. The purchasing manager often has the duty of determining the value of the contract they signed. Through an extranet, the customers' purchasing manager will be able to track the contract performance and monitor the supplier's compliance to service-level agreements.

Get Fast Self-Service Access to Information.   Instead of relying on static paper reports or spreadsheets, which often arrive late and do not allow flexible analysis, the customer can at any moment have up-to-date information as he or she digs directly into his or her supplier's or distributor's information system. As an example, an editor who has a book featured by an online bookseller will not want to wait for monthly or weekly sales reports. Instead, the editor will want to access the information daily. In addition, he will want to be able to analyze the data according to many dimensions: In what state did the book sell most? What are the demographics of the buyers? How do the sales break down during a week? Answers to these questions directly through the Web will eliminate the need for requests to a sales or support hotline.

Optimize the Value of the Service.   With the value-added information provided by a business intelligent extranet, the customer can get more intelligence on using the services or products and therefore optimize the relationship.

VediorBis, discussed earlier in Chapter 9, is rolling out a customer care extranet for about 150 of its largest clients. The TempOffice Online extranet helps companies that use VediorBis's temporary employment services to track expenses, qualifications of the temporary employees, and areas of specialization, by tapping into VediorBis's data warehouse. A human resources manager at a large company can have a single view of all spending with VediorBis on temporary employment, which frequently is done by individual departments on an as-needed basis. With that single view, the manager is in a good position to look for cost cutting and efficiency opportunities. The manager can size up the effectiveness of the temps and his company's value for the money.

"Our clients ask, 'How can we better organize ourselves, how can we get more productivity from the temps, how can we modify our organization to be more efficient?'" said Robert Vesoul, vice president of marketing and e-business at VediorBis. "Our clients are demanding more information, and to provide that we need business intelligence."

Benchmark the Company's Performance.   Extranets can provide to the customer not only a view of how they are using a particular product or a particular service, but also how their performance is tracking versus the rest of the market. For that purpose, the extranet combines the customer data with an aggregate view of the customer base or with external market information, and provides comparisons. The customer can then instantly view where efforts need to be placed and where resources need to be spent.

Following, we will examine three cases of companies that have implemented customer care extranets and have shared the benefits with their customers: Zurich, a large insurance company; Instinet, an electronic brokerage company; and MasterCard, the credit card company.

Risk and Reward:
The Zurich U.S. Case

Zurich U.S., a commercial insurer in Schaumberg, Illinois, with $6.2 billion in annual revenues, vouches for the value of the customer care extranet it offers to its corporate clients. The extranet, called *RiskIntelligence*, began with the objective of meeting client demand for faster information delivery, and in short order it became a strategic initiative that now figures heavily in the company's sales and marketing success.

RiskIntelligence provides Zurich clients with access to claims and insurance data, along with capabilities for reporting and analysis. RiskIntelligence, launched in late 1998, replaced a system called Risk Manager Workstation through which Zurich would provide its risk management customers with a proprietary desktop software application and mail them diskettes carrying claims data once a month. Because of the high support costs of the program, Zurich actually lost money with Risk Manager Workstation. It now breaks even with RiskIntelligence.

RiskIntelligence provides clients with mission-critical data with a lag time of just a day, compared with as much as 45 days with the old system. And it provides them with more than 100 predefined reports, such as claim summary, claim detail, lost time, lag days, and historical views and trends, compared with just six reports with Risk Manager Workstation. The breadth and depth of the available data is enhanced, and so is its interactivity and speed of delivery.

The driving force behind RiskIntelligence was the need for timely access to data. Zurich customers carry premiums averaging $1 million and more, and since premiums are directly related to a company's loss, risk managers at Zurich look for ways to decrease premiums by identifying risks and making workplace adjustments—like altering the height of a work table to reduce back injuries—in order to eliminate or decrease these risks. By having access to claims data that is timely, risk managers can identify trends more quickly and make changes before many similar incidents occur.

"Our clients want to know loss trends as soon as possible so they can make adjustments, because it's hitting their bottom line," says

Frank Colletti, Zurich's director of e-business. "If a manufacturer is getting back strains on an assembly line, it used to take them a long time before they could recognize that. But now, as those things happen, they have a report that shows them these are the things that are happening, here is the number and the cost associated with it. They can see that back strains are a problem in Kansas City and other manufacturing plants, and they can do something about it right away."

A problem with back strains may suggest the purchase of forklifts. An excess of truck accidents may indicate the need for more driver training. A spate of fires may prompt an electrical inspection in buildings. In commercial insurance, a consolidated view of historical data and trends can have profound implication on the insured's bottom line.

Zurich involved users at customer sites during early focus groups and in a pilot phase with 20 customers in late 1998. The focus groups made clear that what customers wanted was the most up-to-date data possible, regardless of how frequently they went online to view the data. Even if they were accessing the system monthly, customers wanted the ability to see loss trends, for instance, from the day before.

Customers also wanted to view claims information from a variety of perspectives. Zurich set about developing 30 different reports to meet this need. The reports were previewed during the pilot and were ready when the system debuted. A "lag days" report, for instance, was created to show customers how long it took Zurich to handle a specific loss. The report would tell a company's risk manager when an injury occurred, when the employee returned to work, how fast Zurich paid the claim, and the date when the claim was officially closed. Focus groups also revealed that customers wanted to have the option of having customized reports developed. To date, Zurich has built 300 of these customized reports for customers. Report customization is emerging as a leading-edge feature at Zurich and other extranets, as they help customers make their internal processes more efficient. For instance, customized reports streamline the distribution of different reports to multiple levels of a client's hierarchy and to different areas of interest.

Customers often prefer the autonomy and flexibility of building their own reports to suit their own needs, rather than submitting standard requests to customer service representatives that may require a few days for a response. And by the time the report is made available, it may be in a form that is not exactly as expected, or is no longer relevant since the decision it was intended to support has passed. Query based e-business applications have self-service benefits for both organizations and their customers.

Clients have seized on RiskIntelligence faster than Zurich anticipated. Zurich had some 200 individual users at 125 companies using the diskettes and Risk Manager Workstation software. With RiskIntelligence, the user population has skyrocketed for 1000 individuals at 400 companies. "The reason is that these companies see the value they are getting daily from that information," Colletti says. "We used to deal with CFOs and risk managers, and once they saw the product they wanted other people in their organizations to see the reports." The rapid uptake caught Zurich off guard. Zurich managers envisioned that RiskIntelligence would have 250 users, but that number was quickly exceeded. One customer inquired about access for 50 people. The onslaught strained the capabilities of the technology architecture behind RiskIntelligence, prompting the company to add more hardware servers and switch from Microsoft's NT operating system to a Unix version from IBM. "We totally underestimated how big it was going to be," Colletti says. "We would have spent more money on servers right up front." By the end of 2000, Colletti anticipates that 1500 to 2000 users will be logging on to the system. And because of its success in North America, Zurich Financial Services Group, the $45 billion parent company of Zurich U.S., has begun to roll out RiskIntelligence to its customers on a global basis.

Besides helping Zurich win business, RiskIntelligence also reduced costs by enabling Zurich to eliminate the creation and distribution of the diskettes that carried claims data, as well as training and supporting users on the Risk Manager Workstation software. Colletti estimates the savings at $400,000 in the first year. It also created revenue: Zurich charges a flat $5000-a-year fee, plus $250 per year for an individual user. Despite the relative ease of use of a Web-based system, Colletti and his team found that the RiskIntelligence deployment brought new issues to contend with. Firewalls, for example, posed a significant challenge. About a third of customers blocked their users from accessing a secure site, which was the case for RiskIntelligence. Zurich's IT team had to work around these firewall issues.

Another issue commanding attention was response time. It can take a customer up to a minute to run a report, and Zurich wants to reduce that to 10 or 15 seconds. It is currently investing $1 million in new hardware and software to improve performance. "We took a system that used to deliver information in 45 days and brought it down to a day. But a typical report runs for about a minute, and customers are pushing us to get it faster."

Lessons Learned

- Build the solution for rapid growth. An extranet that proves more successful than expected is a nice problem to have, but it will benefit a business to ready itself for such a contingency up front.

- Security is paramount in importance and needs to be dealt with early in the process.

- Provided the service is enough value, it can be marketed at a price, hence making the operation a break-even or a profitable business.

Show Me the Money: The Instinet Case

With investment bank customers that traffic in millions of dollars, Instinet, a subsidiary of Reuters, put a premium on customer care when it launched its fixed income electronic brokerage service in early 2000. The new system would service bond traders—traders of securities that deliver a fixed income—with a minimum trade size of $1 million. With the new service, Instinet aimed at expanding on its core competency as an electronic communications network with value-added services, including an e-business intelligence customer care extranet.

Instinet's fixed income initiative brings a new electronic dimension to bond trading. Unlike Instinet's largest area of business, equities trading, bond trading has traditionally been conducted over the telephone and in person. By offering an electronic medium for bond trading, Instinet managers aimed to leverage technology to bring much-needed efficiency and transparency to the market, by providing professional investors worldwide with online trading capabilities. The business-to-business e-brokerage offers live, real-time trading and greater control to investors. But at the same time, it cannot afford to skimp on the customer intimacy that is a hallmark of the bond-trading community.

Instinet designed a back-end system that could handle bond trading globally 24x7, and which could scale and perform in real-time. It invested heavily in transaction-processing systems and security to ensure that trading is conducted anonymously, and turned its attention to e-business intelligence.

Later in 2000, Instinet will roll out the extranet to as many as 700 users at roughly 60 client sites in the United States and Europe. The extranet will enable bond traders to report on and analyze their own trading activity—bids entered, bids accepted, latest prices, size of transaction, prices paid, liquidity, and exposure. It will also provide them with aggregated views of market-level activity for benchmarking and performance measurement.

The extranet is replacing a time-consuming and inflexible system under which Instinet brokers prepare electronic spreadsheets on client activity and e-mail them to customers. Self-service access for clients will liberate Instinet brokers from menial data-entry tasks. "It's a chore," says Duncan Johnston-Watt, Instinet's managing director of fixed income technology, in London. "The answer to that is to give the clients business intelligence so they can trigger around with the data to their hearts' content, and they can integrate it with their own systems the way they want. It's a very valuable thing to offer to our clients, because otherwise you end up emailing them a lot of data or spending time on the phone, and it becomes very labor-intensive."

Demand for such information will be high among traders, as bond markets evolve from telephone transactions to electronic transactions. "They want every single datum of information that we have," Johnston-Watt says. "Investment banks are just voracious for information. We'd much rather give the clients the capability to do it themselves. It's a very simple idea, but it turns out to be profoundly powerful." The data warehouse that clients will access through the extranet is also used internally by about 200 Instinet staff members, including brokers, salespeople, and marketing personnel. It provides the brokers with an easy means of monitoring client activity.

Lessons Learned

- Giving the customers extra access to their information is likely to increase customer activity (in this case trading of bonds) a win–win for your company and customers.

- Giving customers access to data frees staff from menial data access tasks. As that information is bound ultimately for the customer, examine the viability of letting customers access the information directly, and therefore remove your support staff from the process. The more information-intensive the customer interaction is, the more direct the link between the customer and the data should be.

- Systems do not have to be complex to provide real value for customers. Simple intelligence on the customer's activity already goes a long way. You can then build up the system from that base foundation.

- Plan on deploying the extranet system to both internal and external users—your customer support staff needs to have the same access and interface as your external customers, so that they can discuss the data using the same workflow.

Credit Where Credit Is Due: The MasterCard Case

Another company that is helping its customers do better business through an extranet is MasterCard International. In mid-1999, MasterCard launched a system called Quality Advisor that enables its member banks to track their operational performance and benchmark it against peer groups, with the objective of maximizing revenue generated by card usage and arresting problem areas.

The system uses a set of predefined reports together with a powerful customized reporting capability. Quality Advisor customers can run this against MasterCard's comprehensive data warehouse to track a range of operational performance metrics. They can examine information on the speed of card-processing terminals, rates and sums associated with chargebacks in cases of consumer dispute, approval rates and authorizations, percentages of special telephone-authorized transactions, causes of transaction failure, credit risk, and recruitment and set-up of accounts. With more than 5.4 billion transactions worth $727 billion processed in 1999, MasterCard has a bountiful data flow to harness and analyze.

With the business area working hand in hand with the data warehouse technology team, Gareth Forsey, MasterCard's vice president of franchise operational performance, has delivered a valuable information product to member banks. Quality Advisor runs against a data store that combines transaction-processing systems data with information generated by consumer surveys, and supplies insight into performance characteristics of cardholders and merchants. Bank users have at their disposal some 55 predefined reports to run against the data, and may request customized reports as well. "The basic goal of the unit is to help the banks improve the performance of their operations through understanding their business processes and through analyzing those business processes and benchmarking the metrics that are driving the business," Forsey says. "We've built a series of optimization models to show the banks what's not working and what they would need to do to improve and what the financial benefit to them would be if they did make an improvement. There's a huge incentive for the bank to improve their performance."

A key area of interest for banks is chargebacks, when a consumer disputes a charge on his or her credit card. MasterCard maintains a series of metrics associated with chargebacks that Quality Advisor bank members may examine to determine weaknesses in their systems, and how they compare against data aggregated on peer banks. Despite the large sums of money at stake with chargebacks, many banks don't heavily invest in chargeback mitigation, Forsey says. "There is a binder of rules on how and when you can charge things back, and basically a lot of banks don't invest sufficiently in understanding the mechanics of the process. As a result they take chargebacks they don't need to and process ones they shouldn't be processing," he says. MasterCard's own analysis of chargeback data related to one large bank showed that the institution could have saved between $1.5 and $2.3 million if it had modified its chargebacks process. In another case, MasterCard worked with a North American bank to pinpoint a problem that stemmed from a gas station chain misprocessing transactions on defective cards. The savings amounted to several tens of thousands of dollars a month once the problem was isolated and corrected.

Over 12 months, the Operational Performance Program, of which Quality Advisor is a key component, has enabled banks to achieve performance improvements to the tune of $175 million around the world, he says. MasterCard derives a significant benefit from Quality Advisor as well. Better performance at all points in the credit transaction lifecycle translates into greater satisfaction for individual cardholders and MasterCard's 22,000 member banks. Quality Advisor, through data analysis, contributes to brand quality and integrity, and to greater market penetration. Cardholders often tend to blame MasterCard, rather than the offending bank, for any problems, Forsey says. The take up of Quality Advisor, by banks and by MasterCard staff, keen to understand more about their customers' operational needs, has been well beyond expectations.

Lessons Learned

- The ability to give customers comparisons between their performance and benchmarks is extremely valuable. Lower-than-average performance or unusual differences will trigger immediate action, which in turn may generate large savings.

- Customer care can drive new business. Because MasterCard Quality Advisor gives banks more control over the cards they issue, they can make operations more efficient and ultimately increase the value of each card issued, giving the banks more information leads to more cards issued and ultimately more business.

Summary

Customer care extranets can provide extraordinary value in the pursuit of maximizing the customer relationship. The customers most interested in a customer care extranet are likely to be your largest, most profitable customers—those with whom you already share a good amount of information, through costly telephone, electronic data interchange (EDI), email, paper, and fax interactions.

Where does the drive for a customer care extranet originate? It may be either with the IT team or business management, but regardless of the origin, the champion stands to elevate his or her personal stead, and the given department, with advocacy for such a strategic initiative.

12

Information Brokers

Every company possesses data, or information about their data, that can be converted into a revenue source. The trick is to do it right—find your market, follow privacy guidelines, and align it with the business of your customer.

Andrew Clyne
Vice President, systems development
MasterCard International

Information generated as a by-product of a company's core business need not go unexploited for commercial value. The information that many companies maintain is valuable to other companies and can bring in a healthy stream of revenue. Properly aggregated and packaged, with due respect to privacy and security issues, information can be an asset to be leveraged and sold like another piece of merchandise. As the Internet economy continues to grow and competitive business pressures intensify, information is becoming a currency in its own right.

Companies are finding new ways to cast themselves as what we call *Information Brokers*. Businesses that have invested the time and money to create a mature e-business intelligence system, with high-quality data and sound security, may be in a position to market their information to other companies. They are turning their data warehouses into profit centers and gaining visibility in their given industries. The information they supply can help other companies become more productive, efficient, and cost effective and can better target the right product to the right customer. And in the process, of course, the company hosting the Information Broker stands to strike up new business relationships and win deals for its principal lines of business.

Although this business model is in its infancy, it is gaining traction in a number of industries and will inevitably proliferate in the coming years. Look around your own company. Do you have information assets tucked away in a corner or right under your nose that would be of interest to third parties? The Information Broker model will not apply to all companies, but forward-thinking managers are coming up with innovative uses for their data. For instance,

- A drug retailer sells prescription data to drug companies
- A health maintenance organization sells clinical data to drug companies
- A supermarket sells sales data to food products manufacturers
- An oil company sells gas-station beverage sale data to beverage companies
- A car rental company sells vehicle performance data to manufacturers
- A wholesaler markets sell-through data on end buyers to manufacturers
- A magazine sells detailed demographic reader profiles to advertisers.

Design and Circumstance

Information Broker extranets come in two forms: those created by design and those which result from ingenuity and circumstance.

Information Brokers by Design

Examples of information brokers by design are data providers such as Acxiom, Experian, A.C. Nielsen, Polk, and Dun & Bradstreet. Their principal business is the sale of information on consumers and businesses, and they have been at it for years.

These old-line information brokers have moved quickly to the Internet.

As an example, National Data Corp. (NDC) in Atlanta specializes in the sale of data related to health care and electronic commerce markets. With about $165 million in revenue per quarter and 6000 employees, the company offers a number of business intelligence applications for the health care sector. For instance, a system called Intellect Q&A enables health care providers, researchers, marketing and advertising professionals, and pharmaceutical companies to tap into a multiple-terabyte data warehouse of retail drug prescriptions over the Internet. A unit called *NDC Health Information*

Services buys information from 36,000 pharmacies on 2.4 billion prescriptions covering more than 220,000 pharmaceutical products. NDC says the data help sales and marketing decision makers identify new markets and track consumption and prescribing habits.

Information Brokers are proving to be of interest not only to multimillion-dollar companies: One small data provider, HotData, in Austin, Texas, has information offerings suited for small- and medium-sized businesses that cannot afford to spend tens of thousands of dollars. HotData sources customer information from Experian, Polk, the U.S. Postal Service, and others and sells access to the information for as little as $20 a month. HotData products involve customer and demographic information that subscribers can use to bring added precision to sales and marketing campaigns. The company keeps current with changing telephone numbers and addresses of prospective customers.

To the kinds of companies just described, an extranet is simply a better solution for delivering information to their customers. As opposed to creating complex proprietary workstations, they can open up their data store and let their customers dig around in the data (for a fee, of course), from standard PCs over the Internet. These companies give more flexibility to their customers, who are now able to ask any kinds of questions and drill through the most up-to-date information directly stored on the information broker servers. The system eliminates the need for back-and-forth communication to get to the right piece of data. In the business of marketing lists, for instance, a customer typically would apply different selection criteria, such as "list all companies of more than $100 million of revenue in a given city." The marketer would decide if the list corresponds to her needs on the basis of the count returned. If the count were too high, she would add another criterion to restrict the list. If the count were too low, she would expand the scope of the search. The ability to refine the search online as a self-service is of great benefit for both parties. One additional capability is a new ability to instantly get a very elementary piece of information for a small fee. The customer—either a business or a consumer—can define a simple query and be quoted a price instantly. The ultimate benefit is self-service access to information. Let us take an example in the telecommunications business.

Qualiope

In Europe, deregulation has opened the market to more than 350 different operators, who are engaged in a ruthless competition. As they face price pressure, and high customer churn rates, the telecom operators' ability to differentiate themselves comes in particular from the quality and performance of their services. However, measuring quality indicators has not been easy.

Through the Web, Qualiope, a new European Information Broker, is delivering a brand-new service named Callmetrix, which aims at measuring the quality of service provided from point to point by telecommunication operators. Thanks to a network of probes located in 50 cities across the world, they simulate calls on a three-times-a-day basis for 60 operators. Data collected through this process feeds a data warehouse, made accessible via an e-business intelligence portal to their customers. The customers are the telecom operators themselves, who use this Information Broker to obtain an independent view of the quality of their networks and as a way to manage their telecommunications costs. Qualiope implements the access exclusively through a business intelligence extranet, which provides self-service access to data and fast response to any given question.

Recently, a prospective customer in the banking sector asked Qualiope's COO about the ability to get a real-life benchmark on the telecommunications operators' performance on the major stock-exchange cities across the world (New York, Tokyo, London, Frankfurt, Paris, and so on). Qualiope had never even been exposed to such an inquiry before, but was able to give the answer immediately. One operator—unknown to the customer—had a far better performance than the most reputable ones.

Information Brokers by Circumstance

The second sort of Information Brokers—those created by ingenuity and circumstance—are being launched by companies not expressly in the business of selling data. These are companies that realized they were sitting on gilded data sets that would be of compelling interest to other parties. They have been able to learn from the business models of companies such as Lexis-Nexis and have decided to market their datastore. Let us examine three examples of companies that are leveraging their existing data assets and transforming them into new revenue streams: Peapod, an online grocery chain; Hertz Lease, the leasing arm of the well-known car rental company; and Transactional Data Sources, a joint-venture between MasterCard and Symmetrical Resources, a market research company.

Peapod

One company that has branched out from its core business into the Information Broker model is Peapod. The company, based in Skokie, Ill., runs Peapod.com, an online grocery shopping and delivery service that, like many dot coms, is struggling to find sustainable growth. Its revenues in the first quarter of 2000 were $25 million, but the company lost $12.7 million at the same time. As its executives brainstormed for differentiations and cash flow, they struck upon an idea: Peapod would become an Information Broker.

In 1999, Peapod launched a service called Consumer Directions that would provide consumer goods companies with information on consumer activities on the Internet. Consumer Directions uses the data that consumers provide in their shopping activity to give product manufacturers insights into optimal product assortments, virtual point-of-sale displays, Web advertising, and the use of personalization technology to customize products and promotions and the ideal mix of advertising by channels. Consumer Directions is offered as individual research projects using Peapod data for consumer-packaged goods subscribers, which have included Coca-Cola, Colgate-Palmolive, Kraft Foods, Sara Lee, Kimberly-Clark, Nestle, and Ralston Purina.

"The data we collect in our member profiles regarding our shoppers' purchases and behavior is extensive," said Peapod cofounder Andrew Parkinson. "When this is coupled with our ability to execute one-to-one Internet media events while a shopper is making purchase decisions, it presents a very powerful research, promotion, and advertising tool for consumer goods companies."

Hertz Lease

In Paris, Hertz Lease, which does about $100 million in business annually leasing some 17,500 vehicles to 1400 companies, is moving toward packaging the data that it gathers on vehicle performance and selling that information to car manufacturers. Hertz runs a data warehouse that tracks, among other things, maintenance required on the vehicles that it leases to customers. With a large number of vehicles leased over a number of years, the data the company collects provides an accurate view of the strengths and weaknesses of various vehicles and their components. For instance, Hertz Lease observed that a certain model of car tended to develop water pump problems at 20,000 miles. Because people tend to drive leased and rented vehicles harder than they do vehicles that they own, Hertz reasons that the results of these "stress tests" will provide early warning indicators of interest to vehicle manufacturers. Water-pump problems at 20,000 miles will likely suggest to the manufacturer that there is a problem with the vehicle's water pump. That sort of swift insight can be incredibly valuable, particularly if it spares a vehicle manufacturer a costly recall. In the process, Hertz Lease may have earned the goodwill of a manufacturer that can translate into additional leasing and other business deals.

Transactional Data Solutions

MasterCard International does not like letting its data lie fallow. MasterCard has teamed up with Symmetrical Resources, a market research company in Florida, to leverage its data on credit card transactions to merchants in a unique way to generate a new revenue stream while protecting the privacy of member banks and cardholders alike. The joint venture between MasterCard and Symmetrical, called Transactional Data Solutions, offers companies an in-depth, aggregated picture of how U.S. consumers spend money. The staff at Symmetrical work closely with the data warehouse experts at MasterCard to leverage the large data warehouse efficiently.

Transactional Data Solutions takes commercial advantage of the data that MasterCard technologists have collected in its data warehouse. That data includes details on the millions of credit card transactions that 550,000 anonymous MasterCard holders in the United States execute each year, by merchant, by product, by money spent, and so forth. Accordingly, it provides a moving picture of consumer spending. (Data that MasterCard does not have includes the name, address, and other personal information about the cardholder.) By combining MasterCard's technical savvy and its industry leadership in mining a large database with Symmetrical's statistical ingenuity, Transactional Data Solutions has delivered a unique product line.

Transactional Data Solutions has created 34 clusters of U.S. consumers by combining MasterCard's data on credit card transactions with data from Simmons Market Research, a unit of Symmetrical Resources that conducts in-depth surveys of some 33,000 adult

Americans about their buying and media habits, lifestyles, and demographics. The data that Simmons gathers cover magazines read, stores patronized, frequency of shopping, television and radio habits, leisure activities, and products purchased—nearly 8000 different brands in more than 450 product categories.

The clusters, such as "department store patrons," "heavy electronics buyers," and "cool shop-a-lots," show which consumer groups are driving sales across more than 40 retail categories, including apparel, consumer electronics, computers, and travel, and which media they turn to most frequently. For instance, the "cool shop-a-lot" cluster, which has among its favorite merchants Banana Republic, Barnes & Noble, and Circuit City, contains an above-average number of newspaper and magazine readers and Internet users and includes strong brand loyalists not inclined to impulse buying.

Through a business intelligent extranet application called Merchant Advisor, Transactional Data Solutions uses the data to provide merchants with insights into their customer base and to show a merchant how it is performing relative to the competitors in its sector, by channel, and both nationally and regionally. The data on competitors, of course, is protected: A merchant is permitted to see only how it is performing against the category as a whole. The data will answer questions as the following:

- What sort of consumers are driving sales?

- What magazines do they read, so that we know which to advertise in?

- What television programs do they watch?

- What other products do our customers buy, and where do they buy them?

- What sort of consumer buys from my competitors, but not me?

Merchant Advisor's differentiation is that it is built strictly on hard data, says Bill Engel, president and CEO of Transactional Data Solutions. The MasterCard system anonymously tracks consumer transactions in multiple purchasing mediums—drugstores, hotels, airlines, clothing outlets, restaurants, department stores, and home improvement merchants. And it tracks purchasing by channel—either in-store, by phone or mail, or, of course, over the Internet—as long as the transaction is carried out through a MasterCard credit card.

By linking transactions to consumer demographics, lifestyle, and media consumption habits, Merchant Advisor improves on traditional survey-based market research methodologies, which rely on demographic characteristics such as income, age, and geography. The transaction-based data is far more precise and enables merchants to improve on shotgun marketing by marketing to specific niches.

Summary

Becoming an Information Broker is an outstanding opportunity to generate revenue and create new relationships with different kinds of customers. Once they have identified the data as ready for consumption, companies contemplating the creation of such extranets should focus on making the solution private, secure, easy to use, and scalable.

Find the Data

Even if your organization is not a marketer of data, you may still want to be in the business of selling the information you already have. Your organization is storing information that you may be able to sell to others in your industry and other industries. You should look into your data stores with an eye for data that could be marketed to new customer constituencies.

Make It Private

While turning a data warehouse into an Information Broker can be a powerful enterprise, companies need to play close attention to privacy, security, and design issues. If your business is such that you maintain detailed records on your customers—names, addresses, phone numbers, income, marital status, and so forth—then those customers are not going to want you selling that information as is. But if the information is aggregated, with identifiers stripped out, an overall customer dataset can provide a third party with an interesting view of consumer activity.

Make It Secure

Security systems need to be implemented which ensure that a buyer of information sees only the data it is supposed to see. If your Information Broker contains information on product sales and buyer profiles from two competing companies, a subscribing company should be able to view data related only to its own transactions, not those related to any of its competitors.

Transactional Data Solutions has at its disposal credit card and demographic data that details consumer spending in thousands of stores in the United States. The company takes pains to guarantee that a retailer which has signed up for its system can view data about the retailer, but not any data of specific rival stores. Rather, Transactional Data Solutions aggregates spending data for rival stores to give the retailer a market-level view.

Make It Easy

Attention should similarly be paid to designing a system that is easy to use through a Web browser, as end users probably are not trained in the use of analytic software. They will expect to be able to run predefined reports that give them needed information without toil. As their sophistication and comfort level with your Information Broker grow, these users will be expected to seek more customized, analytic information offerings.

Make It Scalable and Accurate

An Information Broker also needs to deliver good scalability, performance, and accurate data. End users will not appreciate long delays and system unavailability when they are paying good money to access your data, particularly when an Internet search engine can deliver results in five seconds. The data, of course, should be clean and accurate. A company with a dozen disparate data stores with information that is inconsistent and unintegrated probably needs to get its own data management house in order before it is in a good position to be selling data for external parties.

13

Supply Chain Extranets

Our supply chain extranet has been an essential competitive differentiator in the medical supplies industry.

Don Stoller
Director of information management
Owens & Minor

The news sliced into Owens & Minor, a national medical supplies distributor in Virginia, like a surgical knife on its body corporate. The company's largest customer, Columbia/HCA Healthcare, decided to sever its relationship with Owens & Minor after four years of a five-year contract. The hit from the loss of business with this huge Tennessee-based hospital chain was immediate and excruciating. Some $360 million in revenue—about 12 percent of Owens & Minor's total annual revenue—disappeared in a puff of smoke.

There was more bad news to follow in this spring of 1998. Another large customer, Kaiser, also dropped Owens & Minor for $50 million in business. In a matter of weeks, the company found itself at the cusp of a $400 million black hole that threatened its very survival after 116 generally prosperous years.

"It was a big blow to us. When we lost this business, our concern was whether or not we could rebuild," recalls G. Gilmer Minor III, the chairman and CEO. Pressured by financiers and Wall Street, Owens & Minor considered massive layoffs, closing facilities, and an overall downsizing to fill the gap.

Instead, like submitting a seriously ill patient to an experimental drug, the company gambled on emerging e-business intelligence technologies that had been brewing in its IT department. The idea was to create a supply chain business intelligence extranet that would be dubbed WISDOM (WebIntelligence

Supporting Decisions from Owens & Minor). Through WISDOM, Owens & Minor's business managers envisioned that many of their 4000 customers and 1200 suppliers would find value in accessing and analyzing information on their buying and selling of products through the company.

With Owens and Minor doing some $3.2 billion in annual sales, the sums of money at stake were not small change. The company imagined that its trading partners would derive some very real bottom-line value from the information that it had, by getting a better handle on inventories, costs, shipping times, and so forth. It was right.

A pilot project rolled out several months after the devastating loss of Columbia/HCA and Kaiser. Ten customers and five suppliers, including health care heavyweights Johnson & Johnson and Kimberly Clark, rapidly embraced the pilot. Suddenly, these trading partners had access to information that they never had before. Buyers of medical supplies were able to spin reports off of Owens & Minor's data warehouse to analyze their purchase histories and negotiate better prices and terms with suppliers. Suppliers were able to better manage their production, shipping, inventory, and billings, and better target customers for deeper sales penetration.

By March 2000, Owens & Minor had 60 customers and six suppliers signed up for WISDOM. These clients pay fairly nominal access fees that enable Owens & Minor to cover its personnel and operating costs for running WISDOM. Through the extranet, Owens & Minor established a competitive advantage that its rivals could not quickly or easily match. It garnered publicity and created an electronic buzz in the old-economy health care product distribution business that drove new business and restored the ailing "patient" to financial health.

"It was very much a lifesaver," Minor says. "We felt these tools were so good and so effective, that we could rebuild the business, and in fact we have. We've put the $400 million back on the books and are now growing at a rate of 8 to 10 percent a year on top of that."

The dramatic story of Owens & Minor clearly shows the transformational power of supply chain extranets. In this chapter, we will first analyze the supply chain extranets opportunity. Then, we will review some basic supply chain concepts and discuss the idea of information supply chains that parallel an organization's physical supply chain. We will examine case studies from Penske Logistics and Ingram Micro. Finally, we will talk about the natural evolution from supply chain extranets to digital marketplaces and study how Ventro is using e-business intelligence across its family of B2B trading exchanges, including Chemdex and others.

The Supply Chain Extranet Opportunity

A supply chain extranet is a business intelligence extranet that connects an organization with its supply chain partners. The goal of supply chain extranets is to provide access to information that allows materials to flow smoothly and efficiently along an organization's business ecosystem. Thus, these extranets typically provide information both to suppliers of operating materials (e.g., paper clips and computers) and to suppliers of manufacturing inputs (e.g., raw steel, chemicals). In addition, they provide information along the distribution chain that connects an organization with its ultimate customers (e.g., distributors, resellers, agents).

In our work with customers building supply chain extranets, we have observed a number of common themes:

- Useful information is often generated as a by-product of another task

- The natural owners of information either do not have the systems necessary to analyze it or are not really the natural owners

- Supply chain extranets help procurement and logistical efficiency

- Supply chain extranets help target marketing resources and identify market opportunities

Useful Information Is Often Generated as a By-Product of Another Task

Owens & Minor's business model is based on distribution rather than resale of goods. Its principal customers are hospitals that often participate in group purchasing networks and make contracts directly with manufacturers. Owens & Minor delivers the products from distribution centers and is paid a distribution fee. The company's value proposition is that it can deliver a high fill-rate of complete orders within specified times (governed by a service-level agreement) and thereby let hospitals reduce their inventories while ensuring that there will always be enough supplies to treat patients at all times. The ability to operate with this greatly reduced inventory not only frees up working capital for the hospitals; more importantly, it lets them turn supply closets into $500-a-night rooms to care for ailing patients.

In the course of providing goods to the hospitals, though, Owens & Minor has collected a treasure trove of information on everything that each hospital is purchasing from its various suppliers. A big part of the genius of the Owens & Minor story was the simple realization that the information the company had accumulated for the purpose of streamlining its operations would be valuable to other players in the medical products supply chain. Most organizations, we believe, are sitting on such gold mines, and these organizations have not yet realized it.

The Natural Owners of Information Either Do Not Have the Systems Necessary to Analyze It or Are Not Really the Natural Owners

It seems natural that hospitals should know what they have purchased, without Owens & Minor's help. However, although hospitals have made heavy investments in the latest applications of health care technology, from CAT scanners to remote surgery techniques, their information systems are typically not fully automated. This means that the purchasing agents at the hospitals are not able to see a complete picture of what products have been bought in the course of treating patients.

Moreover, hospitals rarely purchase supplies alone. Rather, they band into a number of group-purchasing networks to get more bargaining power with suppliers. So even if a given hospital has state-of-the-art information systems, it will only be able to analyze its own purchasing history. That, of course, is not enough: What is needed to negotiate even better terms through supplier concentration, or to monitor service level agreement compliance across purchasing group, is a holistic picture of activity across all the hospitals in the network that are working with all the network's suppliers. That is, the natural owner of the information in a group purchasing scenario is not the hospital after all. It is the intermediary—the distributor—in this case, Owens & Minor.

Or take another example: business travel. The natural owner of information about a company's business travel expenses is not the company—individual flight records are rarely stored in corporate databases. It is not the airlines either that know all about the travels of individuals, except for travel on their own lines. Instead, it is the travel agent who serves as the intermediary between the two. Increasingly, we will see companies that have historically been in "intermediary" roles realize the unique value of the information they hold and start to use e-business intelligence extranets to transform themselves into "infomediaries."

Supply Chain Extranets Help Procurement and Logistical Efficiency

A hospital using the extranet is better informed to make sound procurement decisions. For instance, the purchasing agent can see at a glance if different hospitals in the group are buying the same type of surgical glove from several different suppliers. By consolidating these purchases through a single supplier, the hospital gets a better discount and directly lowers its procurement costs. This also reduces the number of trips to different suppliers that must be made to deliver the goods, which in turn helps reduce Owens & Minor's costs and allows the firm to offer its distribution services at a higher margin than that of their competitors.

Hospitals can also use the system to analyze fill rates, and detect problems with suppliers and products, and measure compliance with Owens & Minor's service-level agreements. The suppliers of medical products can analyze their inventory levels for improved manufacturing and distribution.

Supply Chain Extranets Help Target Marketing Resources and Identify Market Opportunities

The suppliers of medical products can use the extranet to get more information about the rates at which their product is consumed across different hospitals and to spot new market opportunities. For example, a bandage manufacturer can use information about purchasing trends to identify which hospitals are most likely to be interested in a new product. Then it can adapt its marketing and sales plans accordingly. Moreover, by studying the average consumption rates of products per doctor, per bed, or per hospital across a wide geographic area, the suppliers can use the Owens & Minor data warehouse to measure its relative market penetration across different territories. Again, it can then modify its sales organization and investment plans accordingly.

Supply Chain Basics

Owens & Minor's WISDOM application is an example of a supply chain extranet that ties together several links in a product supply chain. Before we explore the supply chain extranet in more detail, let us take a look at the supply chain as it reshapes itself in the Internet economy.

The term *supply chain management* is used to describe a "process umbrella" under which manufacturing and operating inputs are acquired, products are manufactured and assembled, and shipments are delivered to customers. From a structural perspective, a supply chain is a complex network of relationships that organizations maintain with trading partners to source, manufacture, and deliver products.

The Supply Chain Council, a trade organization based in Pittsburgh, boils down the supply chain into four basic processes: planning, sourcing, making, and delivering. These four processes cover managing supply and demand, sourcing raw materials and parts, manufacturing and assembly, warehousing and inventory tracking, order entry and order management, cross-channel distribution, and ultimate delivery to the customer.

In traditional supply chain management, those processes are assumed to be based on a preset quantity and growth forecast, with revenue taken as a given. As manufacturing companies move into the twenty-first century, these assumptions are being rethought to reflect emerging business trends. In particular,

- Customers expect faster, more integrated service and service solutions that do not force them to mix and match elements from different producers.

- Sales, service, and customization are no longer separate production phases. Increasingly, they are being blurred to form one overall flexible production service.

- A greater emphasis is being placed on services as high-quality production becomes commonplace. Consistent, flexible, and "easy-to-use" services, including billing, delivery, and documentation, are becoming a core part of supplying goods.

- Brands are evolving as the core competency of a "manufacturing" business. For example, companies can now be leaders in the sports shoe industry or in the Internet hardware industry, without any in-house manufacturing processes.

- "Labor" is no longer a homogenous input into the manufacturing process. People must be treated as an important and differentiated asset, something that has long been recognized in service industries.

- The dispersion of manufacturing and distribution facilities has become worldwide, meaning that any increases in the supply chain must be managed on a global basis.

Clearly, these trends require changes to the traditional model. The assumptions of preset production quantity and revenue are no longer valid. Unpredictable customer demand causes the "make to stock" model to fail, and the demand plan as a target must now be adjusted so that it moves up and down even as goods are moving through the production cycle. There is a constant challenge to ensure that production remains profitable even if demand falls, and that supply chain capability is not exceeded if demand rises.

The basic problem in the traditional model is the lack of process integration among the partners in the supply chain. The data throughout the system is inconsistent or out of date, leaving the system in a reactive, fire-fighting mode, with inadequate information and integration. Planning is not treated as an end-to-end system, and partners do not share information with others.

Optimizing the Supply Chain

In seeking to reshape themselves competitively, companies are turning to the e-supply chain—one that is enabled electronically and accessed by partners up and down the chain. It involves using new technology within the manufacturing industry to address the new dictum of ecommerce: giving customers what they want, when and how they want it, at the lowest price.

Companies such as i2 and Manugistics provide e-supply chain management products with the ability to access and share information on product demand and fulfillment with manufacturers, distributors, retailers, and any other enterprise within the extended supply chain. With these systems, manufacturers can improve how quickly they can respond to unanticipated changes in demand and supply conditions, and more reliably maintain their delivery and margin targets. By striving for a zero-inventory model, such systems help drive down inventory costs, production costs, and distribution costs, and increase the agility of the supply chain, allowing quicker reactions to competitive or market changes. As Alan Greenspan has said, "Information has become a substitute for inventory."

An e-supply chain automates and streamlines the manufacturing process through the communication of detailed "production-level" information between different steps in the process. Because of their efficiency and flexibility, e-supply chain systems allow the creation of increasingly complex supply relationships.

The deepening interdependencies and multitiered supply chains lead to complex information relationships that do not lend themselves easily to cursory reporting and analysis. However, as the overall transparency of the system rises, aggregated data from the whole "information supply chain" can be collected and stored. Then, e-business intelligence can be used to carry out more sophisticated analysis, beyond driving simple production efficiencies.

To gain competitive advantage, all parties in the supply chain—suppliers of raw materials, manufacturers, wholesalers, retailers, distributors, and purchasers—increasingly require the detailed and powerful analysis that e-business intelligence provides. There is an interesting analogy to be made with customer relationship management (CRM) here. Much as personalization engines provide real-time recommendations in CRM systems, so do supply chain packages make real-time decisions about sourcing and scheduling. But while these systems are making basic, real-time decisions, they are operational, not informational, systems by nature. That is, both CRM personalization engines and supply chain management (SCM) optimization engines are effectively "smart" operational systems. They are not business intelligence systems, because they do not provide the ability to integrate their data with data throughout the enterprise, compare it, report on it, analyze it, and share it with others. Both operational and informational systems are needed to have a fully optimized CRM or SCM environment.

Opportunities exist for both e-businesses and brick-and-mortars to gain competitive advantage by offering unique informational systems that are unavailable from other providers: systems for data analysis, financing, process management services, and other value-adds. Those who get there first stand to elevate the entry bar for their competitors, maximize revenues through agile responses to new market opportunities, and deepen supplier relationships by providing a complete view of the supply chain.

A majority of 50 companies interviewed by Forrester Research indicated that they would significantly expand the functionality of their supply chain extranets by 2002. These extranets let members of the supply chain view analytic information from other parts of the chain, even if there is no integration at the enterprise resource planning systems level. This information can be used to

- *Reduce costs.* A supply chain e-business intelligence extranet lets companies analyze their purchases to identify possible consolidation opportunities. By centralizing their purchasing and eliminating unnecessary product diversity, companies have an opportunity to increase their volume purchasing and reduce per-unit costs.

- *Improve procurement and supply decisions.* Members of the supply chain can analyze information to make intelligent choices of suppliers and chain partners, based not only on price, but on previously recorded information, including delivery delays, quality issues, and the time taken to resolve disputes.

- *Identify new market opportunities.* An e-business intelligence extranet allows information to be passed up the supply chain from the final customer, giving second-level suppliers valuable insight into how their product is being used. For example, a manufacturer of consumer electronics could be given access to an extranet operated by a high-end electronics chain. The manufacturer could use the system to analyze the penetration of its products into different geographic locations or demographic profiles. The chain store operator could provide higher order information that would otherwise be available only through industry analyst services, such as the manufacturer's market share of alarm-clock sales.

- *Increase distribution channel productivity.* An e-business intelligence extranet can be used to help distributor networks be more effective. For example, Harley-Davidson sells more than $2 billion worth of motorcycles, clothing, and accessories every year via its dealership networks. More than 340 of the company's North American distributors have online access to "HD Net," a system that provides the dealers with information about sales, inventory, and deliveries. The system lets dealers benchmark their performance against previous quarters and against other distributors and ultimately helps Harley-Davidson sell more bikes and accessories.

- *Respond quickly to product quality issues.* In today's complex, multitiered supply chain environments, product failures often need to be traced back up the supply chain in order to be corrected. For example, an information supply chain initiative is underway in the airline industry that will allow the original supplier of each element of a plane to be identified, down to the level of individual bolts and screws, for periods of over 20 years. In the event of an accident, this information will permit specific problems to be identified quickly, and changes made to other planes, as necessary.

From Road to Desktop: Penske Logistics

Penske Logistics is among the companies banking on the likelihood that supply chain extranets will soon become a checklist item as commerce continues to grow more transparent and customer expectations for easy, secure data access are elevated. The company is using the lessons learned from its construction of an internal e-business intelligence system as it rolls out an extranet that will enable customers to access and analyze information on the shipping and logistics business they do with Penske. Penske is an essential part of its customers' supply chains, making sure that deliveries run smoothly between, for example, Ford and its parts suppliers, and Kmart and the companies that provide the goods that it sells in its stores.

"Without an extranet, the door would be closed in our face," said Peter Smith, senior vice president of technology at Penske Logistics, in Beachwood, Ohio. "We would have customers throwing up their hands and being totally exasperated. For attracting new clients, if you don't have an extranet capability, many of them will simply cross you off. You are simply not equipped to their way of running their business."

Penske was preparing to roll out a pilot implementation of its extranet in mid-2000 to a select group of customers, with particular attention paid to making security bulletproof and ensuring that customers could not access information from other accounts. Through the system, customers would no longer have to rely on Penske to provide them with details on shipping movements and distribution cycles.

Customers would have access to data beamed via satellite from Penske trucks to its computing systems, substantially reducing the lag time between the occurrence of events and notification of customers. Armed with the information, customers will find it easier to reroute deliveries to respond to such circumstances as a depleted inventory or have a truck make an additional stop. That is, the system provides more flexibility and more efficiency.

The customers may use the information gleaned over the extranet to cut costs, but that does not necessarily mean that Penske's revenue will suffer. As the customer uses the information to get clearer insights into delivery delays and problems, Penske can offer the same delivery services at lower costs.

For example, a company that makes washing machines may use Penske's services to deliver its machines to retailers. Part of the information provided by Penske's satellite-linked trucks is the amount of time they have to wait at a particular drop-off location before they can actually unload. Looking at the data, the customer can determine that, for example, a particular store is in the habit of requesting that all of its suppliers deliver on the same day, but that this results in long lines to drop off goods because the loading bay is bottlenecked. With this information, the customer has a clearer idea of the total real costs associated with the sale of their goods to that store and can use the information to renegotiate prices or delivery times.

Customers also will be able to take a historical look at the data, examining it for operational weaknesses that bear improvement and correcting any errors or inconsistencies quickly. Penske officials believe that they will be first to market among shippers with such analytic capabilities, and that those capabilities will serve well as a sales tool and for customer retention. Not only does the extranet give Penske's customers powerful incentives to continue using the firm's services. It also raises the bar for competitors: They have to not only undercut Penske's prices, but also provide the same level of information service as Penske does. Thus the system discourages "experimentation" with other suppliers.

Lessons Learned

The following are among the lessons that can be learned from Penske's experience:

- Customers are becoming increasingly demanding. Start looking at possibilities today, so that you will be better prepared for the key customer who threatens to defect unless you have a supply chain extranet up and running in two weeks.

- By providing an information service wrapped around your existing product or service offering, you make it harder for your customers and suppliers to switch to other vendors.

New Windows on Business: Ingram Micro

Ingram Micro is the proverbial 800-pound gorilla of the computing and technology world. It does nearly $29 billion in business each year in more than 100 countries as a wholesale provider of high-tech goods to technology solution providers—a whopping 60 million transactions a day. Heavyweights such as IBM, Compaq, Hewlett Packard, and Microsoft distribute tremendous volumes of PCs, enterprise servers, software, and services through Ingram Micro's channels.

Ingram Micro is entering the next generation of service offering for its customers, providing the business intelligence that is critical to running a competitive business in the new economy. Despite the volume of information offered on its electronic interfaces, top suppliers cannot track exactly where their products go when they hit the channel. As the world becomes more wired, the absence of that information is becoming more critical for Ingram Micro's business partners. "These customers have an extremely high sense of urgency," says Ingram Micro CIO Guy Abramo. "It is important that we can deliver critical business information directly to them, when they need it."

Whenever you open a software package, PC, printer, or other computing device, you find collateral that insists strongly on the benefits of "registering" the product with the manufacturer or the software publisher, or an annoying box comes on the computer screen requiring you to fill out a form that is to be emailed off. All this effort is because the original manufacturer has little way of finding who bought its product and how it will be used. Ingram Micro is working to create a new-generation e-business intelligence extranet as part of its ecommerce offering, to deliver advanced information to the company's suppliers.

"Today it's incumbent on us to provide our partners with sell-through information so that they can see what happened once their PCs hit distribution," says Abramo. "That's critical for them to do inventory planning and manufacturing planning—helping them to understand what products are selling to what segments of the marketplace. Up to now we have not been doing as good a job as we could in providing them that information."

Ingram's idea is to provide customers with extranet access to information specific to the distribution of their products. It has in mind to go a step further by providing access to aggregated data that is not detailed, but that will provide strong indications of a firm's market share. Ingram Micro's objective is to provide the data in a timely fashion. Abramo envisions that an e-business intelligence extranet will provide Ingram with an advantage over its competitors, which he says do not yet have such a solution. With the information being of great value to suppliers in particular, Ingram Micro stands to tap into a significant new revenue stream.

Lessons Learned

The following are among the lessons that can be learned from Ingram Micro's experience:

- If you sell your products indirectly, through distributors or agents, a supply chain extranet can give you reliable insight into how your products are being used, without your having to rely on self-registration systems.

- Supply chain extranets can be self-financing, especially if they are selling information "up the value chain," such as market share data that would normally be available only through research services.

The Rise of Digital Marketplaces

Most of today's industries and markets are characterized by their complexity—a large number of interrelated players, with many formal relationships among the different companies. Customers purchase from several different suppliers, while each supplier sells to several different companies. Unlike simpler business-to-consumer trading, the relationships between the vendors often have formed over several years. This complex web of relationships may be depicted in a simplified way, as shown in Figure 13-1. (In reality, there will be many layers of intermediaries between the first supplier and the final buyer, the number of which will vary according to the industry.)

A supply chain extranet serves to strengthen one of the strands in the diagram; it does not disrupt the existing relationships in the industry directly (although it can do so indirectly, by promoting efficiencies and competition).

Digital marketplaces, often also known as net markets or online exchanges, take the notion of an extranet one step further, by seeking to tie together the supply chains of a large number of companies within an industry, using a common hub, like that depicted in Figure 13-2.

Digital marketplaces propose to improve the traditional supply chain with economies of scale and an array of choices that a single company cannot match. Customers can hunt for the best price and quickest delivery in one central Web location, rather than phoning suppliers with inquiries, or flipping through a catalog that was published three months ago—or for that matter, scouring scores of Web sites. Also, suppliers have another means of

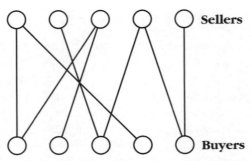

Figure 13-1   Today, Ecommerce Makes the Old System of Buying and Selling More Efficient.

moving products and a much broader audience of prospective customers, and they stand to save on sales force and customer-interaction personnel.

Hundreds of digital marketplaces cropped up and took root in virtually every industry throughout 1999 and 2000—in energy, health care, food service, chemicals, the automotive industry, and more. Some players have consolidated various vertical markets: VerticalNet, for instance, operates 56 industry-specific Web sites as business-to-business online communities for trading, information, and interaction in industries ranging from communications and manufacturing to the public sector and high technology.

Big companies have joined the fray, too. General Motors, DaimlerChrysler, and Ford Motor Co, for instance, struck a deal in early 2000 to consolidate their online purchasing exchanges into a net market called Covisint that they

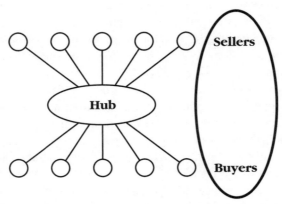

Figure 13-2   Net Markets Use the Internet as a Basis for Even More Efficient Business Models.

describe as "the world's largest Internet-based virtual marketplace." Similar exchanges are under way among leaders in other industries—consumer packaged goods, retail, health care, and convenience stores. The hundreds of digital marketplace upstarts that sprang up to fill niche applications now operate in the looming shadow of the industry giants from whom they had hoped to steal some business thunder.

The Gartner Group analyst firm estimates that by 2002 there will be between 7500 and 10,000 independent trading exchanges. How many of them survive independently and how many merge or are acquired remains to be seen.

Forrester Research has found that buyers and suppliers are about to take the plunge into the online trading exchange pool. In a study published in early 2000, the analyst firm said that its survey of 70 companies revealed apprehension about this emerging business model, but an expectation that participation will dramatically increase. The survey also found that suppliers using online trading exchanges would grow from 18 percent in early 2000 to 71 percent by 2002. Buyers using them would grow from 28 percent today to 69 percent by 2002.

Digital marketplaces, by their very nature, generate huge amounts of transaction information that can be stored and analyzed. In addition, with the intense, survival-of-the-fittest competition unfolding in the online trading exchange space, many players are looking to differentiate themselves from others through the value-added service of a supply chain extranet. They also are looking to leverage their data assets to provide trading partners with a fast, Web-based means of analyzing costs among suppliers, delivery times, inventory availability, volume discounting, and other factors. For suppliers using an e-business intelligence extranet, key questions include the following:

- Who is buying my products?

- Do I have cross-sell and upsell opportunities?

- What are my leading products and lagging products?

- How does my pricing compare with that of competitors?

- How can I use this intelligence to improve my sales, marketing, and product operations?

Buyers, meanwhile, may be interested in the following:

- How much have departments in my company spent with supplier X?

- How does X's prices compare with those of its competitors?

- What is the supplier's average delivery time?

- What's our return rate on products from competing suppliers?

Data analytics is a key component in what Forrester calls "feature function races"—mad scrambles among competing digital marketplaces to offer the latest and greatest information technology to existing and prospective customers as digital marketplaces mature to become commodities. Even the pioneers are learning every day how these digital marketplaces will shake out.

"We probably know as much about B2B economics as anyone, but we probably know only 5 percent now of what we're going to know in three years," says David Perry, CEO of Ventro, a net market company in Mountain View, California, that was created in 1997 and that provides digital marketplaces for life sciences, medical supplies, and other goods.

As it is, three models have emerged, which Forrester calls aggregators, auctions, and exchanges:

- Aggregators concentrate products for sale or concentrate buyers wanting to purchase.

- Auctions allow potential buyers to bid competitively for products or allow potential customers to "bid" for customers.

- Exchanges allow members to buy and sell products in an open marketplace.

Building an e-business intelligence extranet for a net market is complicated by the sizable quantities of fast-changing data from both customers and suppliers and the necessity of building in the requisite security systems. The many-to-many relationships found in online trading exchanges result in greater data volumes and complexity, but provide inherent opportunities for benchmarking against peer groups and best-of-class performers in a given supplier or buyer field.

A supply chain extranet is gaining recognition as a necessary value-added service for the online trading exchanges. Analysts predict that the value of an auction may go down to zero, and exchanges need to focus on additional services that lead to a complete solution and a way to show revenue.

"Extracting intelligence of how the market functions is critical," says Pierre Samec, chief technology strategist at Ventro. "A lot of our data has tremendous value—it's just critical to the suppliers and to the buyers. They're not just asking for it—they're demanding it."

Without such intelligence, of course, there are competing digital market-places that will offer it. Digital marketplaces need all the bells and whistles simply to remain viable—to maintain a critical mass of buyers and sellers that provides the site with a broad enough array of options to sustain business.

Data analytics is just one of the value-added services in the pipeline for enterprising digital marketplaces. Many also plan to arrange credit and payment options, link with distribution and logistics scheduling, integrate with financial ledgers and enterprise resource planning applications, settle and clear transactions, settle disputes among participants, and inspect goods prior to delivery, according to Forrester Research's interviews with about 50 digital marketplaces.

Leading the Exchange: Ventro

Ventro is one of the online trading exchanges designed to augment its transaction processing capabilities with e-business intelligence. The company, which began as the life sciences trading exchange Chemdex in 1997, has more than 130 customers on board and has expanded with other digital marketplaces specific to specialty medical needs, hospital supplies, process plant equipment, and food services. Ventro's quarterly revenues are up to around $30 million as of the first quarter 2000, and company officials cite estimates from financial analysts that it should turn a profit by late 2002.

Ventro is betting on e-business intelligence as a major component in enabling it to secure the first-mover advantage that its CEO, David Perry, sees as critical for online trading exchanges. The capabilities for reporting and analysis of data on transactions conducted via Ventro should provide a competitive advantage that may prompt suppliers and customers to turn to it rather than a competitor, company officials reason. Through data analysis, trading partners will be able to identify cost-savings and revenue opportunities and bring even more efficiency to the supply chain.

"The business is predicated on first-mover advantage, and being a business that can scale," Perry says. "Business intelligence is one aspect of first-mover advantage."

Ventro's data warehouse was being implemented in mid-2000, for both internal and external use. It is fed with transaction data from enterprise resource planning applications for general ledger, order entry, accounts receivable, accounts payable, and purchasing. The e-business intelligence extranet is of greatest interest to suppliers rather than buyers. "A supplier may want to see what a customer has bought in the last three months, or what's my most popular product, or what's the average order size," said Adam Lief, Ventro's senior director of ERP systems. "That can help them with pricing and inventory. Suppliers need to understand which products are doing well and which aren't—which need help, which need more promoting. If the supplier sees that a certain type of customer typically buys products A and B in combination, the supplier's marketing and sales function can do special marketing campaigns, and better position and sell to that segment." On the buyer side, a procurement manager at a pharmaceutical company could use the extranet to see that 100 of the company's employees are buying beakers in small quantities at an expensive rate and that the company could save money by consolidating the orders and buying in bulk at more favorable rates.

The idea for an e-business intelligence extranet originated from customer complaints over the data that Ventro did provide, typically in the form of paper and electronic spreadsheet invoices that consolidated data on trading activity. The problem was that some customers wanted them on paper, some wanted them electronically, and each had different requests for formatting the data.

"That caused incredible problems," Lief said. "We knew we weren't meeting customers' needs. We knew the customers need their own ability to log on and run a report the way they want. And it occurred to a lot of us that, look, this is what the data warehouse is for."

Lessons Learned

The following are among the lessons that can be learned from Ventro's experience:

- Experts predict that most manufacturing companies will join one or more digital marketplaces in the years to come. Business intelligence extranets are directly applicable to these environments; they are a key differentiating service that the net market needs to provide, as well as an important source of revenue for net market operators.

- Independently of when and whether you decide to become part of a net market, extending a supply chain extranet to your trading partners will help ensure that you have the systems in place for a smooth transition to future trading models.

Summary

Supply chain automation software helps communicate information among all of the members of a complex, multitiered supply chain, and so helps promote more flexible, efficient production and logistics.

The greater fluidity of information gives rise to an "information supply chain" that can be analyzed at an aggregate level using e-business intelligence extranets for a "big picture" view of what is happening in the industry. The key benefits of supply chain extranets include reduced costs, more efficient procurement and logistics, greater insight into new market opportunities, and more efficient distribution channels.

The natural evolution of supply chain extranets that provide point-to-point communications between suppliers and customers brings on digital marketplaces—trading hubs where supplies and customers can meet and transact. These digital marketplaces generate huge quantities of data that is valuable to all stakeholders involved: the suppliers, the customers, and the net market operator itself. Supply chain extranets can be built on top of the net market to provide those stakeholders with that information, to differentiate the net market from competition, and to provide chargeable, value-added analytic services.

Vision for Tomorrow

14

The e-Business
Intelligence Future

It's tough to make predictions, especially about the future.
Yogi Berra

The state of e-business intelligence today is strong and growing. Most large and mid-sized companies have already implemented e-business intelligence systems at the department and division level. More aggressive companies are standardizing on e-business intelligence systems, enterprisewide, in order to "information empower" everyone in their organizations and to rationalize administrative and training costs. The companies pioneering e-business intelligence extranets, which number in the hundreds today, have started to take e-business intelligence beyond the corporate walls—to their customers, suppliers, and partners.

We have already discussed scores of examples of the business benefits of e-business intelligence, and we have seen how organizations are using it to get better control over their information assets, become more agile in their decision making, gain competitive advantage, improve operational efficiency, generate new forms of revenue, and even discover new information broker opportunities. In short, we have seen organizations turn information into knowledge into profit.

So now, at some risk, we move to the dangerous ground of prediction. In our final chapter, we will discuss how we see the future of e-business intelligence evolving, how e-business intelligence will transform to touch us everyday and everywhere—at work, at home, and even in our interactions with the government. We will see not only how business intelligence will help manage our business better, but also how it will help us to manage our people, through the concept of *management by information*. We will also see how it will help eliminate the redundant storage of information. In addition, we will step back to a macroeconomic level in discussing how business intelligence can bring more predictability to business.

e-Business Intelligence Every Day

One of the first changes we will see is that people will start to use e-business intelligence systems every day, and for everyday tasks.

e-Business Intelligence at Work

At work, we will continue to use e-business intelligence to manage important processes, such as sales tracking, quality assurance, or financials. We will also start to use it for somewhat more mundane purposes—for example, to analyze the allocation of assets in our 401(k) retirement plans and to report on how much vacation we have taken during the past six months. We will be able, at a glance, to recheck the salary, bonus, bonus payment, stock option grants, and anticipated stock option value for all our employees.

In a nutshell, we are arguing that we will be able to use e-business intelligence for just about any information access that we would need in our working lives. Most of the above examples are easily implementable today using business intelligence tools. Many of the examples are things we do today, but we typically do them on paper (e.g., industry average compensation tables). These tasks are not typically implemented using e-business intelligence today because they are simply further down the corporate priority list than items such as building revenue tracking systems, sales force information systems, and customer care extranets. Nonetheless, there is clear business value in the above examples, and in the coming 3 to 5 years, organizations will start to use business intelligence, to permit the tracking of just about any information that we will need in our working life.

Lest we get overoptimistic, we should not forget that even though incredible advances have been made in software, business intelligence technologies are still not available to everyone in the workplace. Today, industry analysts estimate that only 10 to 20 percent of business managers have access to business intelligence tools. For some of us the future will bring an expansion of business intelligence to more everyday work tasks, while for others the future will simply bring business intelligence.

e-Business Intelligence at Home

We will start to see e-business intelligence touching our home lives as well. As companies realize the power of customer care extranets to differentiate their products and services, to deliver self-service customer care, and to reduce call center costs, we will see customer care extranets move from the B2B environment, in which they are largely deployed today, to B2C. Let us consider a few examples.

When you receive your telephone bill, what information do you really get from that piece of paper? To be honest, not much. It is a list of phone calls, an overall total for the invoice, and a payment due date. If you do what most people do when they receive their phone bills, you look at the amount, figure out if it looks about right (based solely on your perceived historical average), perhaps get depressed for a moment, put it aside, and then wait until the last minute to pay by sending in your check. In some cases, you may be lucky enough to get to see your phone bill in a static form over the Web. Even here, the analysis process does not change much, because you cannot manipulate a static bill, analyze it, or compare it to prior bills, or do what-if analysis determining what the bill would have been with different calling plans.

Wouldn't it be nice if you could know a few key things? Like the average cost per minute (so you could compare it with the ad for a competitive telephone carrier you just saw on TV), or the trend of your phone bill in the last 12 months. Or, if you have two lines at home, which costs more than the other, or what are the top five calls you made last month? With that information, you would suddenly gain an understanding of your telephone usage, and an understanding of your relationship with your telecom operator. To get that information, you would apply simple business intelligence techniques, the same ones, in fact, that are used in corporations and that we describe in Chapter 5. You could analyze your bill by sorting the information, graphing it, ranking the calls, slicing the information by month or line, or comparing what you spent to your budget. Telephone companies are starting to give this capability to their business customers, as it is becoming a requirement to be more competitive. In the future, they will have to provide that capability to each consumer, first as a way to differentiate their services from others, and then later as "table stakes," because over time such offerings will be seen as a standard service.

While we are talking about phone bills, wouldn't it be nice if we got just one phone bill per month—not one for the main line, one for the kids, one for mom's mobile phone, one for dad's, and one for the fax machine. Or, short of that single bill, wouldn't it be nice if we could at least consolidate our numerous phone bills for the purposes of analysis, so we could analyze how much we call Aunt Joan in England, not only on the main line but also on the mobiles? While the single bill may never come—especially if you use different providers for different services—the single point of analysis will. Just as we are seeing B2B extranets evolve to include the ability to analyze competitors' information as a strategy for competitive displacement, we will also begin to see this same phenomenon occur in the B2C environment. Companies will attempt to "steal" the analytic interface to the customer by including their competitors' data, and consumers will benefit in the process.

As another example, consider the bank statement you receive at the end of the month. What understanding of your personal finances do you get from that statement? Again, not much. However, there is so much information hidden in these pieces of paper. You should be able to determine your expenses per category, including how the distribution of expenses has changed compared with last month or the same month last year. You may want to graph this data in a pie chart or show trend lines. You would want to see exceptions, highlight all expenses above $500, for example, or highlight the top three checks you wrote last month. Or maybe you would send an alert if your account balance has gone either below $1,000 or above $25,000. Business intelligence is key in these types of requests because they are both analytic in nature and very personal.

The interactions we are describing here are analytic; they are related to your need for analysis and understanding. They have nothing to do with executing transactions. Today, most financial institutions give you the ability to do basic transactions online such as making a payment, a stock trade, or a wire transfer between accounts. Most ecommerce sites allow you to buy a product using a credit card. These types of interactions are transaction-based, meaning that they let you automate one particular process. Beyond that simple need, consumers have great needs to analyze all these transactions. Today, consumers can execute transactions. Tomorrow, consumers will want to gather insight from them.

Indeed, the interactions we are describing are also personal, in that the questions prompted by your statement relate to your personal needs. You and only you can decide what indicators and thresholds are important to you. Any system where the bank would give you a few predetermined indicators would be too limited. You will need to be able to ask questions easily and in an ad hoc way. Only business intelligence can provide these needed ad hoc analysis capabilities.

Today, virtually no telecom company or bank provides this kind of service. Most are struggling to provide a good personalized management of the basic transactions over the Internet. Tomorrow, these companies will have to use business intelligence, or let us say "consumer intelligence" to differentiate themselves from their competition.

Let us take online brokers as another example. Besides the price of a trade, what differentiates one online brokerage from another? Not much. Whether you buy stocks through E*Trade, Schwab, or DLJ Direct, the investment returns on the stocks you purchase will be the same. Using e-business intelligence, companies will move the battle for the customer from the kamikaze game of price-based differentiation to the analytic power of the information services that are offered along with an account: reports on companies, analysis of market and financial ratios, and analysis of portfolio performance itself.

e-Business Intelligence and Government

The e-business intelligence revolution will not stop with companies and consumers. It will also take over many of the interactions between the government and its constituents. Though we usually do not think of it this way, governments "manage our accounts" for many basic services, such as income taxation and tax withholding, Social Security, and, in many countries, basic medical and health insurance. Governments also run educational systems, armed services, and unemployment programs. In all of these examples, we are starting to see governmental interest in leveraging e-business intelligence to better inform its constituents, build a better relationship with them, and reduce their own operating costs.

Consider Social Security and the cost the U.S. government is undertaking to periodically mail every man, woman, and child a report that contains their historical contributions and anticipated benefits. Using e-business intelligence to make this information available on the Web, and to provide analysis of it, would not only reduce the costs of delivering the information, but would make it more useful as well. You could, for example, not only see your anticipated benefits, but do what-if modeling to predict the level of income you will need in the future and how your Social Security benefits would change as a function of retirement age.

Or, consider the thorny problem of unemployment that still plagues many countries, particularly in Europe. The government could encourage the flow of labor from low employment zones to high employment zones by providing online databases of available jobs that could be queried by applicants. Moreover, by integrating this information with a transaction system to apply for jobs, the government could verify, online, whether an unemployed person was actively seeking work and applying for jobs. Analytic calculators could be added to the site to help job seekers model the cost of moving and the cost of living in a new area to help them make educated decisions about whether they should relocate.

Intelligence Everywhere

In addition to using e-business intelligence every day, we will increasingly start to use e-business intelligence everywhere—on our personal digital assistants (PDAs), on our phones, and through our pagers.

Wireless Intelligence

Traditionally, in order for someone to use business intelligence, a person needs to be in front of a PC linked to a network. This means that the time and the place to leverage information intelligently is strictly limited to a few hours a day—i.e., when employees are on their PCs, connected to the network, and not in a meeting or on the phone. The need for intelligence is, however, permanent. There is no reason to be perfectly informed when in the office, and completely ignorant when in a meeting, in the car, or flying in a plane.

In the past few years, we have seen the rapid adoption of wireless devices as a way to link to the Internet. From a phone, we can now perform consumer operations, such as checking stock quotes, ordering a book, or checking if a flight is on time. The *wireless application protocol* (WAP) enables anybody with a WAP-enabled phone to take advantage of the Internet, without requiring a PC or network connection. PDAs, such as Palm Pilots or Pocket PCs, also enable users to surf the Web, check their appointments, and order theater tickets from just about anywhere.

The convergence of the wireless technologies, Internet access, and business intelligence will bring dramatic changes in how people understand information and make daily decisions. Today, technologies are already available to enable business intelligence access to complex information from a wireless device. Suddenly businesspeople are freed from having to sit in front of the PC at their office in order to have access to the right information. They can perform business intelligence tasks 24 hours a day, wherever they are, as long as they can get a mobile network signal.

In the future, things will get even more exciting, as third-generation (3G) services that combine high-speed mobile access with IP (Internet protocol)-

based services become available. This new packet-based IP technology will enable everyone to be online all the time, with much faster connections than are currently available using dialup, over-the-phone networks. This will give us whole new ways to communicate, access information, conduct business, and learn.

Let us imagine a simple example of how wireless intelligence might be used:

Sarah Wiles, salesperson from Super Software, is planning to visit three customers on a certain day. Early in the morning, over a cup of coffee, she logs onto the network from home, retrieves the latest customer information (e.g., billing status, service status, order history) from the corporate data warehouse, and prints it out on her local printer.

She is now ready to go on the road. On her way to the second meeting, she checks her voice mail, and her second appointment has been cancelled. She now has two hours before the third one, and because of bad traffic, going back home or to the office would be a waste of time. She takes out her cellular phone and logs into the customer warehouse over the wireless Internet using the microbrowser in her phone. She accesses her list of customers and retrieves a list of those who are active prospects and are located close to her current location. She finds one who is a five-minute drive away. Since her wireless e-business intelligence system allows ad hoc querying, she can see a full 360° view of the customer, and instantly access all of the information that she needs to be comfortable and effective in a sales situation. She is prepared to meet the customer, calls to see if she can stop by, and makes an appointment to visit. Rather than having only two meetings that day and taking a 33 percent productivity hit, she can maintain a day of full productivity. This is how wireless e-business intelligence can work in the real world.

This example is not far-fetched. To date, bandwidth limitations, spotty coverage, and the physical constraints of a small device have kept wireless e-business intelligence applications out of the mainstream. These barriers are already starting to fall down, and many companies are starting to explore the deployment of e-business intelligence over wireless Internet. In Chapter 6, we discussed how Innovex is deploying their sales and marketing data warehouse to 1200 sales representatives over the Web. The next step in their plans is to deploy it over wireless systems.

The Humble Telephone

We should not forget the humble telephone as we move into the future. With continuing technical advances in voice recognition technology (converting voice to words) and natural language processing (parsing words to get meaning), it is only a matter of time before speech becomes another interface into e-business intelligence systems. This means that at a regular land or mobile telephone, you will be able to ask questions such as "Who are the top three customers?" or "Which three of my salespeople are the furthest from plan?" simply by speaking in your preferred language.

Speech generation takes care of the rest of the solution because computers will intelligently read back the answers to questions, with features such as voice interrupt that will enable you to stop the computer if you accidentally tell it to read the names of 1000 customers to you.

These *voice portals* will provide other functions as well. You will be able to generate reports on demand ("Please run the compensation report right now and mail it to me"), or on a scheduled basis ("...and also run it every Sunday night for the next six weeks"). You'll also be able to get the resolutions of more complex problems, such as "compare the top three salespeople this quarter and the last with respect to the number of cold calls made, leads processed, and quota attained." This is a pretty complex question, but one whose answer is a manageable six data points, which can easily be read back by the computer over the phone.

Root Cause Analysis to Handle an Overabundance of Alerts

One mixed blessing the future will bring is an abundance of business intelligence alerts. Earlier in this book, we explained the concepts of broadcasting and narrowcasting, where the e-business intelligence system automatically sends alert messages to pagers or cellular phones when certain conditions occur. Broadcasting sends the message to a broad population based on an event of broad interest. Narrowcasting sends messages to individuals based on their subscription to specific events. Both basic business intelligence broadcasting and narrowcasting functionalities are available today. In the future, we will see an ability to sign up for increasingly complex events—for example, today we can say "notify me if we are 10 percent below plan," while tomorrow we will be able to easily sign up for the much more meaningful, "notify me if we are 10 percent below plan relative to where we usually are with an equal number of days remaining in the quarter."

Regarding the number of events about which we are going to be alerted, early experience is giving us a taste of what the future will likely bring. While everyone likes the concept of "management by exception," and the ability alerts provide to hear about things only when there is a problem, experience has shown that users consistently tend to oversubscribe to alerts. That is, they tend to sign up for notification of a large number of different events, and then are subsequently inundated with alerts. As they become overwhelmed by the number of alerts they receive, they become numb to the information packaged within them. Simply put, alerts provide an easy opportunity to have too much of a good thing.

The solution to this future problem is for business intelligence to borrow ideas from network management systems, which are constantly managing and reporting on a flow of network events. In fact, in a communications network, when a construction worker saws through a fiber-optic cable, the system will generate literally thousands of alarms as various computers, hubs, routers, and switches indicate that they have lost contact with the other side of the link. Network management systems deal with this situation by using sophisticated artificial intelligence (AI) technology to perform "root cause analysis"—which filters through the various alarms and dependencies among them until it determines the underlying cause. In the not too distant future, we will see similar technologies used in business intelligence to automatically determine that the root reason for the drop of the forecast, a 90-day-old receivable, two critical customer support escalations, and the western region's profitability plan dropping below target, is because a major customer is experiencing a severe service problem, has not paid its bills, and is canceling a current order.

Intelligence for All

As we start to be touched by e-business intelligence on a more frequent basis and through new mechanisms—such as Web, voice, and wireless interfaces—more and more people will be exposed to e-business intelligence technologies. Deriving intelligence from these technologies will require two key actions: one technical, one societal.

On the technical side, vendors of e-business intelligence systems will need to continue to make e-business intelligence easier and easier to use. While today's e-business intelligence systems are more than easy enough for the professional audience that they address, as we move into the future, more steps need to be taken to ensure that business intelligence is easy enough for everyone to use. Vendors will need to resist the inexorable tendency toward "bloatware" where incremental functionality is continually added to meet the needs of power users, loading the software with functionality, making it large, cumbersome, and difficult for new or basic users.

On the societal side, the public education systems and/or corporate education programs will need to provide more training on how to perform the analytic process. Information is subject to selective filtering and misinterpretation, and once the proper information infrastructure is in place, the next barrier will be people's ability to understand and analyze data themselves.

Interestingly, the education problem does not end there. There is a small, but growing, branch of academia that we believe will become much more mainstream in the years to come. This branch consists of a combination of psychology and business professors who study the actual process of making decisions, and teach people how to make them better. The ultimate goal of all e-business intelligence systems is not simply to provide information, but in the end to enable people to make better decisions. By handing off to the person who makes those decisions, we risk dropping the ball, unless he or she has been properly trained in how to make an intelligent decision.

Paradoxically, while most managers agree with the statement "my job is to make decisions," there are few MBA or other educational programs that actually teach this process. Worse yet, most people do not believe they need training in decision-making, and the very idea strikes some as bizarre. In the future this will change. Ultimately, if an organization wishes to be both agile and successful, it must not simply make decisions quickly; it must make the right decisions quickly.[1] Smart, winning organizations will be those which invest in a combination of information systems infrastructure and their own human resources.

Management by Information

Companies have always used e-business intelligence to report on the execution status of business processes. In the future, we will see organizations start to transform other management processes by exploiting the power of e-business intelligence in creative ways.

A Fresh Look at Policies

In the hurry-up culture of the Internet age, corporations cannot afford the time to execute the "checkers checking checkers" policy enforcement model of past eras. As we move into the future, we will see companies start to give employees more latitude to make more basic decisions than ever before. Why? Because the power of information can provide policy enforcement mechanisms that are superior to the traditional approaches used today.

---

[1] For more information on the interesting topic of improving decision-making ability, read *Decision Traps* by Jay Russo, Ph.D.

Traditionally, companies often create extremely detailed policies (e.g., purchasing, travel, compensation) in an attempt to anticipate every single exception possible, resulting in policy manuals that are thicker than the U.S. Constitution. Because of the complexity of these policies, only a few can fully interpret them, and valuable management time goes to resolve mundane questions like:

- Can Bob spend $50 more than the lowest airfare so he can get home in time for his brother's wedding rehearsal dinner?

- Can we give Sara $2000 more per year than the average E18 who achieved OP+ performance because she is a superstar and is being ruthlessly pursued by headhunters?

Companies will replace the 100-page policy manual with a set of more general guidelines (e.g., the average raise should be 6 percent; employees should take the cheapest flight wherever possible) and use the power of information and peer pressure to enforce the guidelines. Companies will provide open access to aggregated information, so that a group of managers, for example, will be able to see and discuss each other's average travel costs, and a system alert will automatically highlight when one department is spending 15 percent more per day or mile traveled than the average.

As a result, people will be more empowered than ever to exercise their judgment. They will spend less time filling out paperwork and griping to their officemates about bureaucracy. People will exercise their judgment knowing full well that their behaviors will be disclosed. People will be able to move faster, resulting in an overall increase in corporate agility.

MBOs Revisited

Another change the future will bring is a fresh look at implementing management by objective (MBO). MBOs are one of the most popular management techniques in use today. Literally tens of millions of people are measured and incented by quarterly performance objectives. Yet, when we look at how most MBO systems are implemented, we find that MBOs are written into Word or Excel documents where they are difficult to share or consolidate. Also, we find that, for the most part, MBOs are written down at the start of the quarter, largely ignored during the quarter, and then reviewed at the end.

The result is a fairly large management blind spot because managers are not able to accurately track progress on the single most important tool they are using to manage their departments. Nor are they able to quickly locate individuals with performance problems ("who is more than 20 percent behind quarter-to-date?") or projects that may be in trouble ("across a set of people working on different objectives on one project, are there any cases where the project is more than 20 percent behind quarter-to-date?").

The future will bring MBOs to the world of databases and e-business intelligence. Rather than storing MBOs as a set of nonintegrated Word documents, they will be stored in databases. Managers will automatically receive weekly update reports that slice and dice the objectives by project and by person, so they can instantly get status on how their department is doing. Senior managers will be able to see a consolidated view that shows MBO status by department or by major project.

In several departments at Business Objects, today, this technique is already in use. For the first time in their management careers, our managers are able to get up-to-date information related to their most important day-to-day management tool. No one who has made the change would ever go back to the document-based way MBOs were handled before. In the not too distant future, all of us will be able to manage MBOs in this way.

A "Normalized" World

If we take a step back and look at the current state of the "information age," there is a lot that has been accomplished, but our level of inefficiency remains, to some degree, quite laughable. Information is supposed to flow at the speed of light, and everyone, from the mountains in Nepal to the suburbs of Paris, can now communicate instantly. However, networks around the world are often clogged, sometimes paralyzed, and much of the information whizzing around is inaccurate. The same information is duplicated thousands or even millions of times. Information flow, and overall intelligence, will be massively improved when we are able to eliminate this tremendous redundancy.

In technical terms, normalizing data means successively finding and eliminating redundancy. Why is this important? Because redundancy can breed inconsistency, and inconsistency is not acceptable in an information system. By definition, the same question cannot have two different answers.

Well, if you think about the sum total of your company's databases, or an even bigger picture, if you think of the whole Internet as one giant database, it is clear that a huge amount of redundancy and inconsistency exists. Moving into the future, we will begin to see slow, but inexorable, movement toward cleaning up, making it consistent, and effectively normalizing data across companies and across the Internet itself.

The Massive Duplication of Information

Duplicating information creates multiple versions of that information. Let us take an interesting metaphor, time. Consider that billions of people on the planet have a watch, and each of these watches duplicates the same information—the current time. This little piece of information is re-created, in a slightly inaccurate way (the time you have on your watch is never perfect), billions of times. Also, when we change to daylight savings time, hundreds of millions of people need to change their watches. When we travel and we change time zones, we all have to reset watches, computers, alarm clocks, PDAs, and telephones. What a waste! Would it not be simpler if all these devices were linked to one system that was perfectly accurate? Based on where you are, the hypothetical system would adjust your watch to daylight saving time and adjust it according to the appropriate time zones. Hopefully, the Internet or its future incarnation (being infinitely fast, always available, and anywhere in the world) will take care of that. You might ask, do we really need this? Is it so complicated to change the time on your watch and other devices? Should our life depend on one centralized system with all the risk of failure. Do we care? Not really. That is why nobody is worrying about it, the current process will not change, and why we should look at it as just an interesting metaphor. However, other kinds of examples of information duplication exist in the real world, in particular the business world. They create real pain points that should be addressed.

For instance, how many times and in how many systems do you think the address of your company headquarters is being duplicated? It exists in the computer systems of all your suppliers and all your customers (and is probably duplicated many times since each of them has it in his or her database for sales, customer support, finance, order entry, supply chain, marketing references, and more). It also exists in telephone directories, in databases of companies that sell addresses, and in government and public legal databases.

So, every time your company changes headquarters, then, thousands and thousands of systems are instantly wrong and inaccurate. Since there is no automatic link between their static information and yours, it will take months, if not years, to get your company's address information up to date. So how should we cope with this problem? We should do what the Internet has taught us—we should use hyperlinks more and duplicate less. The headquarters information should be maintained by the natural owner of that information, the company itself. Every single organization, supplier, customer, government agency, or employee needing that information should be able to refer, with a link, to that reference data. The data would no longer be duplicated, and it would always be accurate. It is stored in one location, once and only once. When your company changes headquarters, that information for all its business partners is immediately accurate. By using links to the natural owner of a piece of data, we normalize our databases, eliminate inconsistency, and save massive amounts of storage space.

Let us take another example. How many times and in how many systems do you think currency exchange rates are being duplicated? Probably millions. Every time a financial analyst or a controller needs to get a price in euros from a price in dollars, he or she needs to look up the current exchange rate and key it in the computer he or she works on. The next day, the information is obsolete. The solution? All these systems should be linked to a trusted source of data on currency exchange rates. That source would be public and its quality would be certified by clear standards. Its access methods would be standardized. Of course, the system needs to provide both real-time information (the so-called spot rate), as well as historical information. That way, currencies obtained from international transactions could be easily converted, using the exchange rate on the date of the transaction, even if it were weeks or months ago. Here, we have used links not to the natural owner of a piece of data—because there is no clear natural owner—but to a trusted infomediary, as the way of normalizing the data, eliminating redundant storage, inconsistency, and wasted space.

The Corporation Virtual Information Universe

Perhaps this is beginning to sound a bit theoretical, but when you think about it, there are many places in your business where you can derive real business benefit from this simple concept of normalization, or information reduction.

- Take a look at the data that is repeated many times in your company's databases, from one system to another.

- Eliminate the redundancies by linking these systems together.

- In a second step, take a look at the data you duplicate in your systems whose source is outside your organization.

- Investigate how you could link to this external data source automatically, as opposed to re-creating that information in your company's databases.

By performing these steps you could have more current and accurate information, and save storage space as well. So far, companies have duplicated information for a number of good reasons:

- There were no trusted data sources to connect to; before the Internet, a lot of these ideas were not possible.

- Even today, the Internet is not yet available on a 24x7x365 basis; it can be too slow and too unreliable. For the most part, today, you cannot access it unless you are connected through a PC.

- It is fairly inexpensive to duplicate some information locally and to have control over it.

Today, there is no such thing as an ubiquitous and instantaneous network. These ideas become a lot more feasible tomorrow when network connections not only exist, but go faster over the air than they go over the physical lines many of us use today.

At Business Objects, the manufacturing and shipping department created an innovative application using this concept back in late 1997. As a company with customers located all over the world, Business Objects was using United Parcel Service (UPS) as its primary partner for shipping its software products around the planet. As soon as an order was recorded in the company's order entry system, then a request to ship the product was sent to UPS and UPS took control of the delivery process. That worked great, but Philippe Baumann, the head of our manufacturing and shipping department, was confronted with another problem: How could he answer a customer or distributor in, say, Japan, who inquired about the delivery status of a package?

The desired information was held by UPS. Duplicating that information at Business Objects would have been impossible as the information was highly dynamic—it changed everyday, as the package moved through the delivery system. Calling UPS each time was cumbersome and slow. Also, communicating with the Japanese customers was not easy either, because both parties would be communicating in their second language. By working with UPS, he and his team built a customer care application that linked reports on customer orders with the UPS shipping database through the Internet. Suddenly, when a customer called, by looking up the order in question in a report, he could click a button and on the UPS screen would show all the details of where the package was at the time. The team was now able to answer all questions in a matter of seconds, the customers were delighted with the instantaneous response time, and no duplication of data was necessary. The obvious next step is to develop this application into a customer care extranet where the customers can get the same information without the phone call, and that deployment is in procress.

This application is not a *technical* miracle—it is quite easy to do, in fact—but for our Japanese customers, it certainly was a *business* miracle. It represents the kind of quick-hit, big-win applications you can build when you link with the natural owner of a piece of data in your information systems. Also, as is often the case with e-business intelligence systems, the ultimate benefit for Business Objects did not come from the reduced costs of answering phone calls. It came from the elimination of this opportunity cost. Instead of spending his time sending faxes back and forth to Japan, Baumann could focus his time on higher value-added work, such as strategizing to wring out other costs in the delivery cycle. His high value-added work eventually resulted in a productivity increase of two percentage points, increasing our software gross margins from 95 to 97 percent, and saving us about $5 million in 1999, and about $7 million in 2000.

The Big Hits and Misses

You can also use e-business intelligence to help solve a billion-dollar problem: how to bring predictability to business. Each quarter we see horror stories of major corporations missing Wall Street expectation on revenue and earnings, and losing one-third to one-half of their market value as a result. The question is, can e-business intelligence help here? In other words, can e-business intelligence be used to bring predictability to business, which, after all, is inherently unpredictable?

I believe the answer is yes. While e-business intelligence will never be able to eliminate these surprises, as we continue to see organizations use e-business intelligence to get better information faster, not only from their own subsidiaries but also from their distribution channels, I believe that organizations will be able to see problems develop faster, react to them faster, and change course to correct them faster. A quarter is not a long time period in which to make major course corrections to a business and most worldwide information systems have latencies of at least a month. Thus, most businesses get maybe one or two chances per quarter to make corrections that could prevent these surprises.

By increasing what Forrester research calls the *velocity* of information through these systems, and by improving the agility of organizations, I believe, in the next 3 to 5 years we will start to see e-business intelligence have a material impact on helping to bring predictability to business. Simply by providing everyone in an organization with the ability to access, analyze, and share nearly real-time information—accompanied by some basic training in the analytic and decision-making processes—organizations will be able to detect problems as they develop, to fix them before they spin out of control, and hopefully to help them avoid the shock and cost of earnings surprises that cost them billions in their market value. Using e-business intelligence, one day companies may be able to make surprises in business a thing of the past.

Summary

In the years to come, information will be better used and will radically change the enterprise and the home. At work, as radical transformations occur in the way data is stored and distributed throughout the organization, information and therefore intelligence will become ubiquitous. It will not be the privilege of the few, but the standard expectation of all. This new and collective intelligence will reinvigorate the workplace in ways we cannot yet imagine, resulting in drastic changes to the management and employee cultures. Companies will encourage intelligence in all their processes, including their management techniques. Finally, intelligence will reach into the home, enabling consumers to gain insights into how they interact with many different institutions—their banks, their phone companies, or their government.

Final Note to the Reader

If you have not done so already, you should start planning your e-business intelligence strategy now. It is only a matter of time before your competitors do—if they have not started already. If you implement e-business intelligence better and faster, you will operate more efficiently, get insights into your business, and service your customers better. In the end, you will gain crucial competitive advantage.

The word *strategy* is important. One of the points we have already made is that e-business intelligence warrants a strategic approach. Using e-business intelligence in 24 different departments, with seven different architectures and five different tools is an ad hoc approach. Using whatever e-business intelligence tool or data mart that "came in the box" with an operational application is an ad hoc approach. To get the true benefits of e-business intelligence, however, you must approach the problem strategically and use business intelligence not to mirror the fragmentation found in a company's operational systems, but to use business intelligence as the great integrator.

You have a tremendous opportunity to use business intelligence to create a single platform for information. You can integrate data from your disparate operational systems and create a single way of accessing that information for anyone in your organization. It does not matter if there is still work to be done in the underlying architecture of your operational systems, or if your employees are spread throughout the globe. It is up to you to use e-business intelligence today to turn information into knowledge and profit, and win in the marketplace.

A

Popular Misconceptions about an e-Business Intelligence Implementation

Implementing an enterprise business intelligence system can be a significant departure from traditional business methods. As a result, it requires strong internal communication to change conventional mindsets and encourage people to embrace this type of change. It is important that IT and business managers alike be aware of common misconceptions and be committed to address them in order to take advantage of the business value of enterprise business intelligence. Common misconceptions include the following:

- Sharing information means losing control.
- Self-service is a waste of time for the users.
- IT cannot understand the business.
- We do not need all that data anyway.

Misconception No. 1: Sharing Information Means Losing Control

Many people believe that owning a certain piece of information is the key to power. They accumulate lots of information and tend to share very little. They may share what everybody already knows, but real insights, especially ones that contradict conventional business practices, are usually not disclosed. Many managers will therefore worry that deploying an enterprise business intelligence system means they will lose control over their information. They will be hesitant about allowing employees or other departments to access their data. This is typically true for companies in which the corporate culture is fairly closed and centralized.

On the contrary, sharing information and revealing insights will allow the whole organization, and therefore the people who participate proactively, to benefit greatly. The trend to share data is inexorable and those who resist will eventually be left behind. They will be remembered as the managers of the past who were resistant to change. As competition intensifies in a new and ever-changing economic environment, businesses are forced to reduce costs, improve quality, and move faster. In an effort to make their companies more reactive to change, companies need to decentralize their organization and empower workers to make faster decisions. They need to open up and to flatten their hierarchy. Resistance to the proposition of enterprise business intelligence is fortunately starting to wane, even among traditionally conservative companies.

Misconception No. 2: Self-Service Is a Waste of Time for the Users

Managers may be concerned that enterprise business intelligence shifts costs from IT to end users. "My staff shouldn't be doing IT's work" is one way of framing the concern. "I do not pay them to sit and play with data all day" is another common way. Enterprise business intelligence indeed frees up valuable IT time, and the more advanced ad hoc querying and reporting may take up some business managers' time. However, this is time well spent. When managers use enterprise business intelligence themselves, they get far more out of their queries and reports than when they have to request them from IT. Reports from IT can take up to several days to arrive. And when they do, they are often not exactly what the user has in mind or the information is out of date. Self-service means that users

- Get exactly what they want

- Get it exactly when they want it

For example: A manager is in the process of preparing a presentation, either to persuade upper management to invest in a project or to convince a client that the company's products deliver better value than the competition's. Suppose the manager has a notion, for example, that sales of product X do better in regions covered by a direct mail piece or that average support call resolution time has dropped over the last six months.

Getting information immediately, in the form needed, is of immense value to the manager. Given the urgency of most tasks, a manager who has to go through the IT department might not go to the trouble of getting the information, thereby losing an opportunity to make a convincing argument.

If a manager prioritizes data analysis over another activity, it means that, by definition, the manager has decided the most important action for the success of an activity is to better understand what is happening in a particular situation.

Business intelligence relies on a very fundamental assumption: The number of potential questions a business user has about its business is almost infinite and is not predictable. Therefore, the IT staff will never be able to respond to all the questions the users will have over time.

However, the fact that users have self-service does not mean it is the only data access mechanism. Virtually all companies that use business intelligence provide a set of IT-developed and -maintained standard reports as well, and these standard reports are often the launch point for more in-depth analysis.

Misconception No. 3: IT Cannot Understand the Business

In many organizations, the IT group and the business operations are at odds with each other. IT argues that business users have unrealistic demands and have no understanding of the technical difficulties of implementation or of the need to have standards in the organization. The business users argue that IT cannot help them as they have no understanding of the business and its requirements.

However, pressures of the accelerated e-business economy are driving the sometimes adversarial camps of business and IT closer together. Implementing an e-business strategy requires total cooperation between users who understand the requirements of the business and IT people who can drive the implementation of new technology platforms. One without the other cannot achieve the goals of building an intelligent e-business.

IT can help the implementation of the enterprise strategy by advocating enterprisewide business intelligence to managers who are looking at just solving their departmental information issue. As an example, the manager of the shipping and distribution department may be under the misconception that a deployment of PC desktop databases would solve the pain of his entity. To this, the savvy IT manager points out that an enterprisewide business intelligence system would enable data access and analysis of not only shipping and distribution, but the closely related business areas of manufacturing and inventory as well.

In the most advanced organizations, the ones that have implemented a successful e-business strategy, IT and business operations are cross-pollinating ideas and objectives like never before. According to a survey run by *Information Week* in 1999 of 375 business and IT executives, e-business initiatives are being driven by IT management.

More and more, CIOs are being viewed as business leaders. And in the process, they are changing the IT department from a cost center to a profit center. At Cisco, CIO Peter Solvik has been responsible not only for Cisco's Internet-based customer service tools, wide and local area networks, business applications, and telecommunications, but also for leading Cisco's Internet business organization. Under his leadership, the Cisco Connection Online site has surpassed a $4 billion annual run rate. At Schwab, CIO Dawn Lepore led the company's online efforts by demonstrating how they could move stock trading online. Schwab is now the leader in online trading and Lepore has been promoted to vice chairman.

And these changes are not taking place just at the CIO level. They can occur at all levels of the IT organization. Don Stoller, a senior director in the IT department of the medical distributor Owens & Minor (discussed in several chapters of the book), was recently called an "IT hero" in the June 14, 1999 *ComputerWorld* article on "What Makes IT 'Stars' Shine" and was recognized in early 2000 by the same publication as one of the Top 100 Executives in IT.

As Owens & Minor's extranet took off and started to deliver real business value to the company and its customers, Don Stoller's career rose with it. He was promoted several times, and regularly flies on the corporate jet to demonstrate the company's supply chain extranet to its most important customers and prospects.

Misconception No. 4: We Do Not Need All That Data Anyway

A further concern regarding enterprise business intelligence systems is that they may not be used efficiently. The fear is that introducing a new reporting tool may simply add to a manager's pile of reports waiting in his or her inbox, or that users will get carried away with analysis for analysis' sake.

Guy Abramo, the CIO at Ingram Micro, is sensitive to that issue: "One of the downsides to a good business intelligence tool is that the 'gee whiz' factor can kill you," Abramo says. "It's the 'what's interesting' versus 'what's relevant' discussion. What can happen is you get your staff wanting to build these 'interesting' reports, but not reports that are necessarily going to change the business. It's really incumbent upon me to have very, very clearly defined needs for analysis, otherwise we'll be in analysis-paralysis and all we'll be doing is looking at streams and streams of data."

A disciplined, well-defined system that governs the use of enterprise business intelligence tools is important to help companies maximize their rewards. The stack of reports will not grow, as only the most pertinent, summarized information is published.

In many cases, the "gee whiz" factor tends to be transient and progressively goes away as the user gets used to being information empowered. The system regulates itself after a while as the desire to "play" with information is balanced by the need to spend time on making decisions and taking actions. The new information empowerment enthusiasm must nevertheless be channeled properly: first, toward understanding how to use the tool, which typically takes one-half to one day, and second, toward understanding the meaning of the data that has been made available, which typically takes one to two days. The value of enterprise business intelligence systems is that they can provide "the right information" to answer the business users' questions.

As a conclusion, business intelligence is an opportunity to introduce a positive cultural change in an organization. Access to information will make users more autonomous. This Information Democracy can lead to decentralization, flatter hierarchies, and a more entrepreneurial culture. However, for it to generate the greatest benefits, its implementation must not be left to the IT department alone. Business managers must drive it, as a part of the organization's operational strategy.

B

The Search for Return: Justifying the Investment

Like any project, implementing a business intelligence strategy throughout the enterprise has a cost, and that cost needs to be justified with quantified value gains. Information technology has come of age, and it is expected to make a significant contribution to the bottom line. Management is no longer prepared to sink large sums in IT projects simply because they are the latest and greatest technology.

In addition, enterprise business intelligence is only one piece in a company's computing infrastructure. Competition for dollars can be intense, particularly with e-business initiatives commanding hefty spending for hardware, software, and qualified personnel.

When business intelligence is acquired at a department level, the business users will typically be the ones driving the purchase. However, when central IT sees that business intelligence is being successfully deployed at a department level, and that various departments have chosen different business intelligence solutions and architectures, they will logically wish to step in and rationalize the acquisition of the technology through the creation of corporate standards. So although the business case may be self-evident for a department or a line of business investing in business intelligence, central IT will often have to prove the business benefits of such rationalization. These benefits include

- *Reduced administration and setup fees* achieved by eliminating the creation of redundant infrastructure

- *Reduced licensing fees* due to the volumes associated with enterprise-level purchasing

- *Reduced training costs* because users and administrators need to be trained on only one tool

- *Easier migration of staff between departments and businesses* because if there is a common infrastructure and information environment, it is relatively easy for an IT person or a business user to switch business areas

- *Simpler IT acquisition strategy.* In this merger-and-acquisition-crazed environment, IT must be prepared for the effects of sudden or unanticipated acquisitions. Standardizing the environment internally makes it obvious what the business intelligence strategy should be in any acquisition. In addition, the company will have built experience in migration through the internal standardization process.

The Challenges of Quantifying Business Intelligence Benefits

Despite a clear list of qualitative business benefits, organizations, either on the IT or the business user side (and often both), are often asked to provide detailed return on investment (ROI) analyses for their business intelligence investments.

Attempting to calculate precise ROI on enterprise business intelligence systems may not be the best approach to demonstrating their value. Exact ROI calculations are difficult, primarily because of the nonquantifiable nature of most enterprise business intelligence benefits. Nonetheless, here is some advice based on our experience working with organizations that have done ROI studies.

Some Benefits Are Quantifiable.   Quantifiable benefits include worker-hours saved in producing reports, information sold to external parties, and cost savings realized by analyzing procurement and negotiating more advantageous contracts. Chase Manhattan Bank, for instance, implemented an enterprise business intelligence system that cut report development time from months to days and hours. And champagne producer Moët et Chandon cut its IT costs per bottle in half, down to about 14 cents.

Some Benefits Are Indirectly Quantifiable.   Indirectly quantifiable benefits can be evaluated through indirect evidence: Improved customer service means repeat business from a customer, and differentiated service brings new customers. A customer of Owens & Minor, a large distributor of medical and surgical supplies, cited Owens & Minor's Web-based WISDOM enterprise business intelligence extranet as the primary reason for giving the company an additional $44 million in business. At Allegiance Healthcare, the business intelligence system allows the production of daily income statements. This paperless accounting not only produces quantifiable benefits, such as the time-value-of-money saved by catching errors in 24 hours or less, but also indirect benefits, such as enabling management to keep abreast of the state of the business and change course more quickly. One example of an indirectly quantifiable benefit was the catching of the application of a discount at a wrong unit of measure. The product's cost was supposed to be $10/item; it accidentally was billed as $10/pallet (a pallet contains 1000 items). This error was caught by seeing a depressed gross margin in the daily income statement the next day.

Some Benefits Are Unquantifiable. Unquantifiable benefits include improved communication throughout the enterprise, improved job satisfaction of empowered users, and improved knowledge sharing. Just because they are unquantifiable, however, does not mean that these benefits are not very real. So, in ROI justifications, you should provide the business case using a combination of direct and indirect quantifiable benefits, and then drive your point home with the additional advantage of unquantifiable benefits.

Some Benefits Are Completely Unpredictable. Some benefits come from the result of discoveries made by creative users, and can result in great savings. As an example, Nat West, the large U.K.-based financial institution, invested in a business intelligence system to improve decision making and speed financial processing. After only one month of usage, it discovered a wire fraud in the foreign exchange department. The bank took immediate action, which resulted in bringing down a multimillion dollar international wire fraud ring, thus saving the bank over 3 million pounds on a 100,000 pound investment after only two months.

A Model for Return on Investment

When looking at the financial ramifications of implementing an enterprise business intelligence solution, one needs to carefully look at the total cost of ownership (TCO) of such a solution. The TCO includes hardware, software, consulting fees, personnel costs to set up and maintain the system, and other future ongoing costs. It is important to bear in mind that the architecture of the environment can have a great impact on total costs (e.g., environments that are less well integrated will generate labor costs that typically far exceed any savings in software license).

However, in many cases, people examining the financial implications of implementing an enterprise business intelligence solution focus solely on TCO. A business intelligence system should be viewed as an investment, and as such, the point is not so much to minimize cost, but to maximize return.

Although it is usually illusory to attempt to offer precise numbers for total enterprise business intelligence ROI, a somewhat simplified way to determine if the ROI will be positive is to follow the steps below:

- Quantify the expected measurable benefits.

- Describe the anticipated intangible benefits qualitatively, as precisely as possible.

- Estimate the TCO.

- Apply the following decision rule (see Figures B-1 and B-2 below):

If TCO < total measurable benefits ($A + B$), then the system is clearly worth the expenditure.

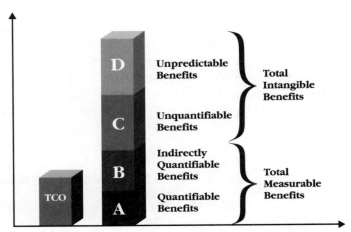

Figure B-1   If measurable benefits outweigh TCO, then the enterprise business intelligence solution will yield a positive return.

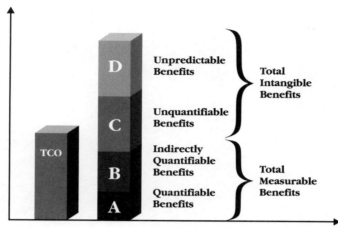

Figure B-2   Intangible benefits must also be considered if TCO exceeds measurable benefits.

If TCO $> A + B$, then you must evaluate the intangible benefits to make your decision. This decision is a judgment call. However, bear in mind that owners of existing enterprise business intelligence systems often consider that the intangible benefits far outweigh the measurable ones.

This model is obviously highly simplified and does not intend to provide a real financial analysis. A more complete analysis would involve calculating the net present value of the investment over time using discounted cash flows and weighted cost of capital. The opportunity cost would also need to be taken into account.

Eventually, once a company understands the value of making better decisions at all levels of the organization and of giving employees greater access to information to empower them, it needs only to focus on implementing the systems in the best and most efficient way.

Bibliography

Chapter 1

Survey.com. "Database Solutions III" (December 1999).

Chapter 5

Inmon, William H. *Building the Data Warehouse.* New York: John Wiley & Sons, 1996.

Kimball, Ralph, Reeves, Laura, Ross, Margy, and Thornthwaite, Warren. *The Data Warehouse Lifecycle Toolkit: Expert Methods for Designing, Developing, and Deploying Data Warehouses.* New York: John Wiley & Sons, 1998.

Mokyr, Joel. *Lever of Riches: Technological Creativity and Economic Progress.* Oxford: Oxford University Press, 1992.

Russo, J. Edward, and J. H. Schoemaker. *Decision Traps: Ten Barriers to Brilliant Decision-Making and How to Overcome Them.* Fireside, 1990.

Chapter 6

Survey.com. "ERP, BI, and e-Commerce: Where Are the winners?" (May 2000).

Davenport, Thomas H. "Putting the Enterprise into the Enterprise System," *Harvard Business Review* (July–August 1998).

Chapter 7

Meta Group survey. *Information Week* (May 2000).

Chapter 8

Forrester Research. "Measuring Web Success" (November 1999).

Kimball, Ralph. "The Special Dimensions of the Clickstream," *Intelligent Enterprise* (January 2000).

Mowrey, Mark A., "Thank You, Please Come Again," *Industry Standard* (March 2000).

Chapter 9
Camp, L. Jean. *Trust and Risk in Internet Commerce*. Cambridge: MIT Press, 2000.

Chapter 13
Forrester Research. "eMarketplaces Boost B2B Trade" (February 2000).

Forrester Research. "Net Marketplaces Grow Up" (December 1999).

Chapter 14
Russo, J. Edward, and J. H. Schoemaker. *Decision Traps: Ten Barriers to Brilliant Decision-Making and How to Overcome Them*. Fireside, 1990.

Glossary

Analytic applications Software solutions designed to address a specific data analysis need, e.g., financial analysis or customer intelligence. These applications are presented as "turnkey" solutions, ready to be deployed to address a business department's specific data analysis needs. In practice, as with all packaged applications, the software needs to be customized to mirror the processes in place within the specific organization. Business intelligence software is a key component of analytic applications.

ASP Application Service Provider. Term used to describe third-party vendors that host and administer all or part of a company's software applications. While the concept of outsourcing computer services is as old as the computer industry itself, the acronym ASP is a relatively recent one. Note: The computer industry also uses the acronym ASP to describe Active Server Pages, a Microsoft programming environment related to the Internet.

Balanced scorecard A management process introduced by Robert Kaplan and David Norton. Companies use the balanced scorecard method to measure and refine current performance as well as to formulate future strategy. The method consists of measuring business performance in four categories to align individual, organizational, and cross-departmental initiatives. The four categories of indicators measured are financial performance, customer knowledge, internal business processes, and learning and growth.

B2B Abbreviation for "business to business," often used to describe software aimed at facilitating the interaction between business partners. *See also* B2C.

B2C Abbreviation for "business to consumer," often used to describe software aimed at facilitating the interaction between a corporate entity and individual consumers. *See also* B2B.

Canned reports The modern equivalent of old paper reports. Just as paper reports with business information can be useful but are restricted to a "frozen set" of data that ages as the paper sits on a desk, canned reports reflect collections of online data that are not tied to the company's database system and can therefore not be refreshed.

Clickstream analysis   Analysis of logged data which captures step by step the activity of visitors on a Web site. In the context of a Web browser, when visiting a Web site, a user clicks the mouse to navigate from one part of the Web site to the other. Just as brick-and-mortar retail stores study the movement of customers within the building, by analyzing the trail or "stream" of each user's clicks, analysts can gain insight into users' preferences and into the appeal of each part of their Web site.

CRM   Customer Relationship Management. Term used to describe both a business process and an associated software application family. The process relates to a company leveraging its customer information to better serve its customers. A flurry of related software has surfaced in recent years aiming to facilitate this business process. e-Business intelligence is a key component of CRM software solutions.

Data broadcasting   One-way distribution of data from one central location to multiple remote recipients. The recipients may be viewing the data on a PC, a Web browser, or a wireless device such as a cellular phone or a personal digital assistant.

Database query   Term that describes a request for data from a database. While historically a detailed understanding of the technical nature and design of a database and knowledge of a database access language such as SQL was required before a user could formulate a request for data, modern query tools allow users to make such requests using familiar business terms. *See also* Semantic layer; SQL.

Data mart   A form of data storage geared at business intelligence or decision support. The term was introduced as an alternative to data warehouses. Unlike data warehouses, which are more ambitious in scope (and cost) and aim to serve multiple divisions of a company, data marts are more limited in scope and typically aim to address the needs of a single division or group of corporate users.

Data mining   A component of business intelligence. Data mining relates to discovering previously unknown patterns within a data set, typically by testing the validity of different ways of describing the data. In technical texts, data mining is often described in the context of machine learning and knowledge discovery in databases (KDD). The two primary goals of data mining are *prediction* and *description*. Prediction consists of using existing data within the database to predict unknown future values for the data. Description focuses on finding patterns that describe the data. Note: Some nontechnical texts use the term *data mining* in a much broader sense to describe the entire process of extracting and interpreting data out of databases.

Data warehouse　A form of data storage geared at business intelligence or decision support. A data warehouse integrates operational data from various parts of the company. Data is typically loaded into the data warehouse en masse on regular intervals. Unlike operational data, which typically includes only current data, a data warehouse incorporates historical information, enabling the analysis of business performance over time. *See also* Data marts; ETL.

Decision support system (DSS)　Term used in the 1970s, 1980s, and early 1990s to describe a business intelligence system.

Drill down/up　A component of OLAP analysis. The term *drill down*, in the context of data analysis, refers to the process of navigating from less detailed aggregated information to more granular data. For example, one drills down to move from a view of business information by country to view the same information by city. Moving in the opposite direction, from city- to country-level data, is referred to as *drill up*. *See also* OLAP.

EIS　Executive Information System. A precursor to business intelligence systems. Before the democratization of information, customized views of business data was accessible by only a limited elite of senior executives via EIS systems. EIS systems were typically expensive to build and difficult to modify, hence slow to adapt to the rapidly changing needs of modern corporations.

Enterprise deployment　Term commonly used in the computer industry to describe hardware and software configurations that aim to address the needs of an entire corporation as opposed to a single department or business function.

ERP　Enterprise Resource Planning system. Popular abbreviation for a broader category of enterprise software systems (a.k.a. enterprise business applications). An enterprise system enables a company to integrate data used throughout the organization in functions such as finance, operations and logistics, human resources, and sales and marketing. Central to an ERP system is a database that integrates all the software applications which support the company's various business functions. The proliferation of ERP systems in the 1990s has dramatically extended the pool of information available for business intelligence.

ETL   Extraction, Transformation, and Loading (of data). Term used to describe the process of extracting data out of a production system, then transforming and cleansing it before loading it into a database dedicated to business intelligence. The term is also used to describe a software industry segment and set of software products designed to manage the data extraction, transformation, and loading process.

Extranet   Variation of the word *internet* used to refer to Web-based applications where a company shares information with external customers, suppliers, or partners. *See also* intranet.

Information brokers   Companies who sell information for profit. Traditionally reserved to companies who focused exclusively on selling information, this segment has recently seen many new and previously unexpected entrants. The new entrants are companies that focus primarily on other businesses, but that now realize that the data they collect in their warehouses can be marketed and sold to other organizations.

Intranet   Variation of the word *internet* used to refer to Web-based applications where a company shares information internally with employees. *See also* Extranet.

Knowledge management   The challenge of capturing the collective experience, core values, and expertise of an organization. Organizational knowledge is embedded not only in data and documents, but also in organizational practices and processes. Business intelligence-related texts often refer to the transition from raw data to information to knowledge. By facilitating the extraction of useful information out of corporate data, business intelligence is a key component of knowledge management systems.

Metadata   Literally "data about data." Refers to the information used to describe a particular set of data. For example, the statement, "the previous paragraph consisted of XX words," is a simple form of metadata on the contents of the previous paragraph.

Multidimensional analysis   Also known as *dimensional analysis*. The analysis of business indicators by examining them from different points of view. For example one can examine revenue by product, or revenue by geography, or revenue by time period. In this example, revenue is the business indicator under examination, while product, geography, and time period are the points of view or dimensions. *See also* OLAP; drill down; slice and dice.

Net markets   Also known as *eHubs, B2B marketplaces, digital exchanges, online trading exchanges.* These exchanges aim to leverage the Internet to bring together huge numbers of buyers and sellers, automate transactions, expand the choices available to buyers, give sellers access to new customers, and reduce transaction costs for all players.[1] The business model for these exchanges is still being defined.

OLAP   Online Analytical Processing. Popular term used to describe the multidimensional analysis of data. The term *OLAP* itself is somewhat confusing and was popularized simply to highlight the difference between databases designed for analysis (OLAP) and databases designed for updates and transaction processing (OLTP). *See also* Multidimensional analysis; drill down; slice and dice.

OLTP database   Online transaction processing database. Refers to databases designed to handle a large volume of concurrent updates from a large number of users. The performance of OLTP databases is often measured in terms of transactions per second or TPS.

Portals   Literally, entry point. Describes the entry point for users to information available via the Worldwide Web. Examples of portals include enterprise information portals (EIP) and business intelligence portals (BIP). Unlike enterprise information portals, which aim to create an entry point for users to all corporate and external information necessary for their job, business intelligence portals provide an entry point to business intelligence information such as online reports, spreadsheets, and other related documents. A BIP can be part of the broader EIP user interface.

RDBMS   Relational database management systems. A popular architecture for database systems. *See also* SQL.

Semantic layer   A software "layer" which insulates business users from the technical intricacies of a database (e.g., esoteric table or column names, and relations between tables). With the semantic layer in place, available data is presented to users as familiar business terms. The semantic layer is technology patented by Business Objects and is essential to e-business intelligence.

---

[1] For more information on B2B marketplaces, see the May-June 2000 issue of the *Harvard Business Review*.

Set-based analysis   A relatively recent data analysis method (in the context of the business intelligence software industry) which incorporates the use of groups or sets. Set-based analysis (based on the homonymous branch of mathematics) facilitates the examination and comparison of the properties of groups of data, e.g., the characteristics of groups (or segments) of customers, or lines of products.

SFA   Sales Force Automation. A category of software applications which enable sales teams to coordinate activities. SFA software facilitates the management and communication of sales forecasts, the creation of customized proposals and quotes, and the communication with prospects and customers. Business intelligence software complements and is often bundled with sales force automation software.

Slice and dice   Term used in the context of OLAP to describe the examination of business indicators from different perspectives. An imaginary multidimensional "hypercube" which encompasses the business data is sliced to reveal a view of the business indicators from a specific point of view (see the detailed illustration in Chapter 5).

SQL   Structured Query Language. Industry standard database access protocol introduced by researchers at IBM in the 1970s in the context of relational database management systems. *See also* RDBMS.

Supply chain   From a business process perspective, a supply chain is a complex network of relationships that organizations maintain with trading partners to source, manufacture, and deliver products. Associated with this supply chain of products or resources is a flow of information between the business partners. The Internet and e-business intelligence offer businesses new opportunities to improve supply chain efficiencies.

WAP   Wireless Application Protocol. Industry standard which allows the projection of Internet data onto a small screen on a wireless device such as a cellular phone or a personal digital assistance. The convergence of wireless devices and the Internet introduces a new and rapidly proliferating medium for the use of e-business intelligence by mobile users.

XML   Extensible Markup Language. An industry standard for the design and formatting of Web documents. More powerful and flexible than HTML (though less forgiving for programmers), XML is becoming increasingly popular for the presentation, exchange, and distribution of Web-based information.

Zero administration client A key business driver for the adoption of Internet-based business solutions and in particular of e-business intelligence. True Web-based software solutions require nothing other than a Web browser to be installed on the user's desktop. This simplifies significantly the administrative burden of making a software application available to business users.

Index

About the Authors

Bernard Liautaud is president and CEO of Business Objects, the world's leading provider of e-business intelligence solutions. Liautaud co-founded Business Objects in 1990, and in 1996 he was named one of the "Hottest Entrepreneurs of the Year" by *Business Week*. In just under 10 years he has built Business Objects into a global corporation with over 10,000 customers and more than $240M in annual revenue. Business Objects was the first European software company to go public on Nasdaq (ticker symbol BOBJ). It is also included, along with Microsoft, Oracle, Siebel Systems, and SAP, in *Intelligent Enterprise*'s January 2000 "12 Most Influential Companies in the Information Technology Industry."

Mark Hammond is a freelance writer based in San Francisco. A lifelong journalist, Hammond covered the business intelligence, data warehousing, and database industries from the San Francisco bureau of *PC Week* magazine after a dozen years as an award-winning reporter for daily newspapers in New York's Capital Region.